G. A. (George Albert) Wentworth

A Text-Book of Geometry

G. A. (George Albert) Wentworth

A Text-Book of Geometry

ISBN/EAN: 9783743305267

Manufactured in Europe, USA, Canada, Australia, Japa

Cover: Foto ©Paul-Georg Meister /pixelio.de

Manufactured and distributed by brebook publishing software (www.brebook.com)

G. A. (George Albert) Wentworth

A Text-Book of Geometry

MATHEMATICAL TEXT-BOOKS

By G. A. WENTWORTH, A.M.

Mental Arithmetic.
Elementary Arithmetic.
Practical Arithmetic.
Primary Arithmetic.
Grammar School Arithmetic.
High School Arithmetic.
High School Arithmetic (Abridged).
First Steps in Algebra.
School Algebra.
College Algebra.
Elements of Algebra.
Complete Algebra.
Shorter Course in Algebra.
Higher Algebra.
New Plane Geometry.
New Plane and Solid Geometry.
Syllabus of Geometry.
Geometrical Exercises.
Plane and Solid Geometry and Plane Trigonometry.
New Plane Trigonometry.
New Plane Trigonometry, with Tables.
New Plane and Spherical Trigonometry.
New Plane and Spherical Trig., with Tables.
New Plane and Spherical Trig., Surv., and Nav.
New Plane Trig. and Surv., with Tables.
New Plane and Spherical Trig., Surv., with Tables.
Analytic Geometry.

A

TEXT-BOOK

OF

GEOMETRY.

REVISED EDITION.

BY

G. A. WENTWORTH, A.M.,
AUTHOR OF A SERIES OF TEXT-BOOKS IN MATHEMATICS.

———oo·ɢ·oo———

BOSTON, U.S.A.:
PUBLISHED BY GINN & COMPANY.
1898

Entered, according to Act of Congress, in the year 1888, by
G. A. WENTWORTH,
in the Office of the Librarian of Congress, at Washington.

ALL RIGHTS RESERVED.

TYPOGRAPHY BY J. S. CUSHING & CO., BOSTON, U.S.A.
PRESSWORK BY GINN & CO., BOSTON, U.S.A.

PREFACE.

MOST persons do not possess, and do not easily acquire, the power of abstraction requisite for apprehending geometrical conceptions, and for keeping in mind the successive steps of a continuous argument. Hence, with a very large proportion of beginners in Geometry, it depends mainly upon the *form* in which the subject is presented whether they pursue the study with indifference, not to say aversion, or with increasing interest and pleasure.

In compiling the present treatise, the author has kept this fact constantly in view. All unnecessary discussions and scholia have been avoided; and such methods have been adopted as experience and attentive observation, combined with repeated trials, have shown to be most readily comprehended. No attempt has been made to render more intelligible the simple notions of position, magnitude, and direction, which every child derives from observation; but it is believed that these notions have been limited and defined with mathematical precision.

A few symbols, which stand for words and not for operations, have been used, but these are of so great utility in giving *style* and *perspicuity* to the demonstrations that no apology seems necessary for their introduction.

Great pains have been taken to make the page attractive. The figures are large and distinct, and are placed in the middle of the page, so that they fall directly under the eye in immediate connection with the corresponding text. The *given* lines of the figures are full lines, the lines employed as *aids* in the demonstrations are short-dotted, and the *resulting* lines are long-dotted.

In each proposition a concise statement of what is given is printed in one kind of type, of what is required in another, and the demonstration in still another. The reason for each step is indicated in small type between that step and the one following, thus preventing the necessity of interrupting the process of the argument by referring to a previous section. The number of the section, however, on which the reason depends is placed at the side of the page. The constituent parts of the propositions are carefully marked. *Moreover, each distinct assertion in the demonstrations and each particular direction in the construction of the figures, begins a new line; and in no case is it necessary to turn the page in reading a demonstration.*

This arrangement presents obvious advantages. The pupil perceives at once what is given and what is required, readily refers to the figure at every step, becomes perfectly familiar with the language of Geometry, acquires facility in simple and accurate expression, rapidly *learns to reason*, and lays a foundation for completely establishing the science.

Original exercises have been given, not so difficult as to discourage the beginner, but well adapted to afford an effectual test of the degree in which he is *mastering* the subjects of his reading. Some of these exercises have been placed in the early part of the work in order that the student may discover, at the outset, that to commit to memory a number of theorems and to reproduce them in an examination is a useless and pernicious labor; but to learn their uses and applications, and to acquire a readiness in exemplifying their utility is to derive the full benefit of that mathematical training which looks not so much to the *attainment of information* as to the *discipline of the mental faculties.*

G. A. WENTWORTH.

Exeter, N.H.
1878.

TO THE TEACHER.

WHEN the pupil is reading each Book for the first time, it will be well to let him write his proofs on the blackboard in his own language; care being taken that his language be the simplest possible, that the arrangement of work be vertical (without side work), and that the figures be accurately constructed.

This method will furnish a valuable exercise as a language lesson, will cultivate the habit of neat and orderly arrangement of work, and will allow a brief interval for deliberating on each step.

After a Book has been read in this way, the pupil should review the Book, and should be required to draw the figures free-hand. He should state and prove the propositions orally, using a pointer to indicate on the figure every line and angle named. He should be encouraged, in reviewing each Book, to do the original exercises; to state the converse of propositions; to determine from the statement, if possible, whether the converse be true or false, and if the converse be true to demonstrate it; and also to give well-considered answers to questions which may be asked him on many propositions.

The Teacher is strongly advised to illustrate, geometrically and arithmetically, the principles of limits. Thus a rectangle with a constant base b, and a variable altitude x, will afford an obvious illustration of the axiomatic truth that the product of a constant and a variable is also a variable; and that the limit of the product of a constant and a variable is the product of the constant by the limit of the variable. If x increases and approaches the altitude a as a limit, the area of the rectangle increases and approaches the area of the rectangle ab as a limit; if, however, x decreases and approaches zero as a limit, the area of the rectangle decreases and approaches zero for a limit. An arithmetical illustration of this truth may be given by multiplying a constant into the approximate values of any repetend. If, for example, we take the constant 60 and the repetend 0.3333, etc., the approximate values of the repetend will be $\frac{3}{10}$, $\frac{33}{100}$,

$\frac{333}{1000}$, $\frac{3333}{10000}$, etc., and these values multiplied by 60 give the series 18, 19.8, 19.98, 19.998, etc., which evidently approaches 20 as a limit; but the product of 60 into $\frac{1}{3}$ (the limit of the repetend 0.333, etc.) is also 20.

Again, if we multiply 60 into the different values of the decreasing series $\frac{1}{30}$, $\frac{1}{300}$, $\frac{1}{3000}$, $\frac{1}{30000}$, etc., which approaches zero as a limit, we shall get the decreasing series 2, $\frac{1}{5}$, $\frac{1}{50}$, $\frac{1}{500}$, etc.; and this series evidently approaches zero as a limit.

In this way the pupil may easily be led to a complete comprehension of the subject of limits.

The Teacher is likewise advised to give frequent written examinations. These should not be too difficult, and sufficient time should be allowed for accurately constructing the figures, for choosing the best language, and for determining the best arrangement.

The time necessary for the reading of examination-books will be diminished by more than one-half, if the use of the symbols employed in this book be allowed.

G. A. W.

EXETER, N.H.
1879.

NOTE TO REVISED EDITION.

THE first edition of this Geometry was issued about nine years ago. The book was received with such general favor that it has been necessary to print very large editions every year since, so that the plates are practically worn out. Taking advantage of the necessity for new plates, the author has re-written the whole work; but has retained all the distinguishing characteristics of the former edition. A few changes in the order of the subject-matter have been made, some of the demonstrations have been given in a more concise and simple form than before, and the treatment of Limits and of Loci has been made as easy of comprehension as possible.

More than seven hundred exercises have been introduced into this edition. These exercises consist of theorems, loci, problems of construction, and problems of computation, *carefully graded and specially adapted to beginners.* No geometry can now receive favor unless it provides exercises for independent investigation, which must be of such a kind as to interest the student as soon as he becomes acquainted with the methods and the spirit of geometrical reasoning. The author has observed with the greatest satisfaction the rapid growth of the demand for original exercises, and he invites particular attention to the systematic and progressive series of exercises in this edition.

The part on Solid Geometry has been treated with much greater freedom than before, and the formal statement of the reasons for the separate steps has been in general omitted, for the purpose of giving a more elegant form to the demonstrations.

A brief treatise on Conic Sections (Book IX) has been prepared, and is issued in pamphlet form, at a very low price. It will also be bound with the Geometry if that arrangement is found to be generally desired.

PREFACE.

The author takes this opportunity to express his grateful appreciation of the generous reception given to the Geometry heretofore by the great body of teachers throughout the country, and he confidently anticipates the same generous judgment of his efforts to bring the work up to the standard required by the great advance of late in the science and method of teaching.

The author is indebted to many correspondents for valuable suggestions; and a special acknowledgment is due, for criticisms and careful reading of proofs, to Messrs. C. H. Judson, of Greenville, S.C.; Samuel Hart, of Hartford, Conn.; J. M. Taylor, of Hamilton, N.Y.; W. Le Conte Stevens, of Brooklyn, N.Y.; E. R. Offutt, of St. Louis, Mo.; J. L. Patterson, of Lawrenceville, N. J.; G. A. Hill, of Cambridge, Mass.; T. M. Blakslee, of Des Moines, Ia.; G. W. Sawin, of Cambridge, Mass.; Ira M. De Long, of Boulder, Col.; and W. J. Lloyd, of New York, N.Y.

Corrections or suggestions will be thankfully received.

G. A. WENTWORTH.

EXETER, N.H.,
1888.

CONTENTS.

GEOMETRY.

	PAGE
DEFINITIONS	1
STRAIGHT LINES	5
PLANE ANGLES	7
MAGNITUDE OF ANGLES	9
ANGULAR UNITS	10
METHOD OF SUPERPOSITION	11
SYMMETRY	13
MATHEMATICAL TERMS	14
POSTULATES	15
AXIOMS	16
SYMBOLS	16

PLANE GEOMETRY.

BOOK I. THE STRAIGHT LINE.

THE STRAIGHT LINE	17
PARALLEL LINES	22
PERPENDICULAR AND OBLIQUE LINES	33
TRIANGLES	40
QUADRILATERALS	56
POLYGONS IN GENERAL	66
EXERCISES	72

BOOK II. THE CIRCLE.

	PAGE
DEFINITIONS	75
ARCS AND CHORDS	77
TANGENTS	89
MEASUREMENT	92
THEORY OF LIMITS	94
MEASURE OF ANGLES	98
PROBLEMS OF CONSTRUCTION	106
EXERCISES	126

BOOK III. PROPORTIONAL LINES AND SIMILAR POLYGONS.

THEORY OF PROPORTION	131
PROPORTIONAL LINES	138
SIMILAR TRIANGLES	145
SIMILAR POLYGONS	153
NUMERICAL PROPERTIES OF FIGURES	156
PROBLEMS OF CONSTRUCTION	167
PROBLEMS OF COMPUTATION	173
EXERCISES	175

BOOK IV. AREAS OF POLYGONS.

AREAS OF POLYGONS	180
COMPARISON OF POLYGONS	188
PROBLEMS OF CONSTRUCTION	192
PROBLEMS OF COMPUTATION	204
EXERCISES	205

BOOK V. REGULAR POLYGONS AND CIRCLES.

REGULAR POLYGONS AND CIRCLES	209
PROBLEMS OF CONSTRUCTION	222
MAXIMA AND MINIMA	230
EXERCISES	237
MISCELLANEOUS EXERCISES	240

GEOMETRY.

DEFINITIONS.

1. If a block of wood or stone be cut in the shape represented in Fig. 1, it will have *six flat faces*.

Each face of the block is called a *surface;* and if these faces are made smooth by polishing, so that, when a straight-edge is applied to any one of them, the straight edge in every part will touch the surface, the faces are called *plane surfaces*, or *planes*.

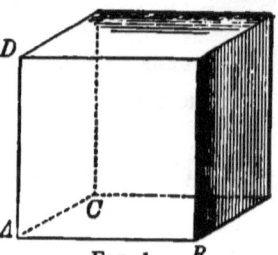

Fig. 1.

2. The *edge* in which any two of these surfaces meet is called a *line*.

3. The *corner* at which any three of these lines meet is called a *point*.

4. For computing its volume, the block is measured in *three* principal directions:

> From left to right, A to B.
> From front to back, A to C.
> From bottom to top, A to D.

These three measurements are called the *dimensions* of the block, and are named *length*, *breadth* (or *width*), *thickness* (*height* or *depth*).

A solid, therefore, has three dimensions, length, breadth, and thickness.

5. The surface of a solid is no part of the solid. It is simply the boundary or limit of the solid. *A surface, therefore, has only two dimensions, length and breadth.* So that, if any number of flat surfaces be put together, they will coincide and form one surface.

6. A line is no part of a surface. It is simply a boundary or limit of the surface. *A line, therefore, has only one dimension, length.* So that, if any number of straight lines be put together, they will coincide and form one line.

7. A point is no part of a line. It is simply the limit of the line. *A point, therefore, has no dimension, but denotes position simply.* So that, if any number of points be put together, they will coincide and form a single point.

8. A *solid*, in common language, is a limited portion of space *filled with matter;* but in Geometry we have nothing to do with the matter of which a body is composed; we study simply its *shape* and *size;* that is, we regard a solid as a limited portion of space which may be occupied by a physical body, or marked out in some other way. Hence,

A geometrical solid is a limited portion of space.

9. It must be distinctly understood at the outset that the points, lines, surfaces, and solids of Geometry are *purely ideal*, though they can be represented to the eye in only a material way. Lines, for example, drawn on paper or on the blackboard, will have some width and some thickness, and will so far fail of being *true lines;* yet, when they are used to help the mind in reasoning, it is assumed that they represent perfect lines, without breadth and without thickness.

DEFINITIONS. 3

10. A point is *represented* to the eye by a fine dot, and named by a letter, as *A* (Fig. 2); a line is named by two letters, placed one at each end, as *BF*; a surface is represented and named by the lines which bound it, as *BCDF*; a solid is represented by the faces which bound it.

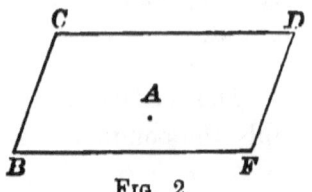

Fig. 2.

11. By supposing a solid to diminish gradually until it vanishes we may consider the vanishing point, a *point* in space, independent of a line, having *position* but *no extent*.

12. If a point moves continuously in space, its path is a line. This line may be supposed to be of *unlimited extent*, and may be considered independent of the idea of a surface.

13. A surface may be conceived as generated by a line moving in space, and as of *unlimited extent*. A surface can then be considered independent of the idea of a solid.

14. A solid may be conceived as generated by a surface in motion.

Thus, in the diagram, let the upright surface *ABCD* move to the right to the position *EFGH*. The points *A*, *B*, *C*, and *D* will generate the lines *AE*, *BF*, *CG*, and *DH*, respectively. The lines *AB*, *BC*, *CD*, and *AD* will generate the surfaces *AF*, *BG*, *CH*, and *AH*, respectively. The surface *ABCD* will generate the solid *AG*.

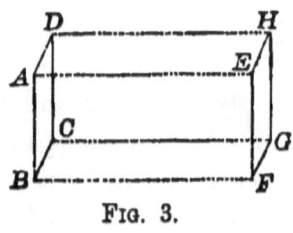

Fig. 3.

15. *Geometry* is the science which treats of *position, form,* and *magnitude*.

16. Points, lines, surfaces, and solids, with their relations, constitute the subject-matter of Geometry.

17. A *straight line*, or *right line*, is a line which has the same direction throughout its whole extent, as the line AB.

18. A *curved line* is a line no part of which is straight, as the line CD.

19. A *broken line* is a series of different successive straight lines, as the line EF.

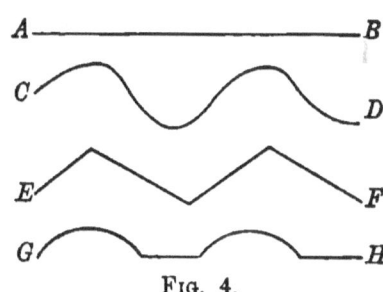

Fig. 4.

20. A *mixed line* is a line composed of straight and curved lines, as the line GH.

A straight line is often called simply a *line*, and a curved line, a *curve*.

21. A *plane surface*, or a *plane*, is a surface in which, if any two points be taken, the straight line joining these points will lie wholly in the surface.

22. A *curved surface* is a surface no part of which is plane.

23. *Figure* or *form* depends upon the relative position of points. Thus, the figure or form of a line (straight or curved) depends upon the relative position of the points in that line; the figure or form of a surface depends upon the relative position of the points in that surface.

24. With reference to *form* or *shape*, lines, surfaces, and solids are called *figures*.

With reference to *extent*, lines, surfaces, and solids are called *magnitudes*.

25. A *plane figure* is a figure all points of which are in the same plane.

26. Plane figures formed by straight lines are called *rectilinear* figures; those formed by curved lines are called *curvilinear* figures; and those formed by straight and curved lines are called *mixtilinear* figures.

DEFINITIONS.

27. Figures which have the same *shape* are called *similar* figures. Figures which have the same *size* are called *equivalent* figures. Figures which have the same *shape and size* are called *equal* or *congruent* figures.

28. Geometry is divided into two parts, Plane Geometry and Solid Geometry. Plane Geometry treats of figures all points of which are in the same plane. Solid Geometry treats of figures all points of which are not in the same plane.

Straight Lines.

29. Through a point an indefinite number of straight lines may be drawn. These lines will have different directions.

30. If the direction of a straight line and a point in the line are known, the position of the line is known; in other words, a straight line is *determined* if its direction and one of its points are known. Hence,

All straight lines which pass through the same point in the same direction coincide, and form but one line.

31. Between two points one, and only one, straight line can be drawn; in other words, a straight line is determined if two of the points are known. Hence,

Two straight lines which have two points in common coincide throughout their whole extent, and form but one line.

32. Two straight lines can *intersect* (cut each other) in only one point; for if they had two points common, they would coincide and not intersect.

33. Of all lines joining two points the *shortest* is the straight line, and the length of the straight line is called the *distance* between the two points.

6   GEOMETRY.

34. A straight line determined by two points is considered as prolonged indefinitely both ways. Such a line is called an *indefinite straight line*.

35. Often only the part of the line between two fixed points is considered. This part is then called a *segment* of the line.

For brevity, we say "the line AB" to designate a segment of a line limited by the points A and B.

36. Sometimes, also, a line is considered as proceeding from a fixed point and extending in only one direction. This fixed point is then called the *origin* of the line.

37. If any point C be taken in a given straight line AB, the two parts CA and CB are said to have *opposite directions* from the point C.

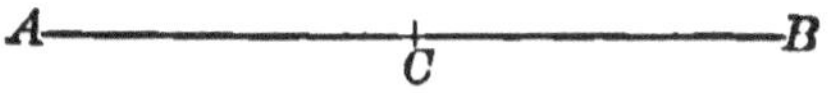

Fig. 5.

38. Every straight line, as AB, may be considered as having opposite directions, namely, from A towards B, which is expressed by saying "line AB"; and from B towards A, which is expressed by saying "line BA."

39. If the magnitude of a given line is changed, it becomes longer or shorter.

Thus (Fig. 5), by prolonging AC to B we add CB to AC, and $AB = AC + CB$. By diminishing AB to C, we subtract CB from AB, and $AC = AB - CB$.

If a given line increases so that it is prolonged by its own magnitude several times in succession, the line is *multiplied*, and the resulting line is called a *multiple* of the given line. Thus (Fig. 6), if $AB = BC = CD = DE$, then $AC = 2AB$, $AD = 3AB$, and $AE = 4AB$. Also, $AB = \frac{1}{2}AC$, $AB = \frac{1}{3}AD$, and $AB = \frac{1}{4}AE$. Hence,

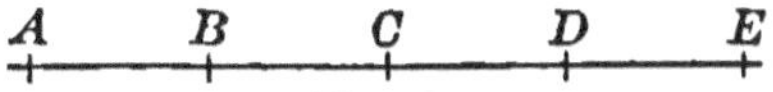

Fig. 6.

DEFINITIONS. 7

Lines of given length may be added and subtracted; they may also be multiplied and divided by a number.

Plane Angles.

40. The *opening* between two straight lines which meet is called a *plane angle*. The two lines are called the *sides*, and the point of meeting, the *vertex*, of the angle.

41. If there is but one angle at a given vertex, it is designated by a capital letter placed at the vertex, and is read by simply naming the letter; as, angle A (Fig. 7).

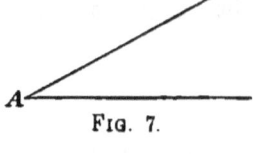

Fig. 7.

But when two or more angles have the same vertex, each angle is designated by three letters, as shown in Fig. 8, and is read by naming the three letters, the one at the vertex between the others. Thus, the angle DAC means the angle formed by the sides AD and AC.

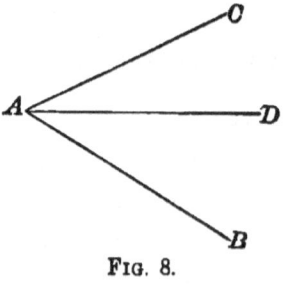

Fig. 8.

It is often convenient to designate an angle by placing a small *italic* letter between the sides and near the vertex, as in Fig. 9.

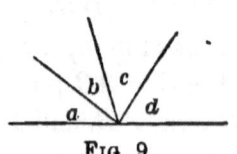

Fig. 9.

42. Two angles are *equal* if they can be made to coincide.

43. If the line AD (Fig. 8) is drawn so as to divide the angle BAC into two equal parts, BAD and CAD, AD is called the *bisector* of the angle BAC. In general, a line that divides a geometrical magnitude into two equal parts is called a bisector of it.

44. Two angles are called *adjacent* when they have the same vertex and a common side between them; as, the angles *BOD* and *AOD* (Fig. 10).

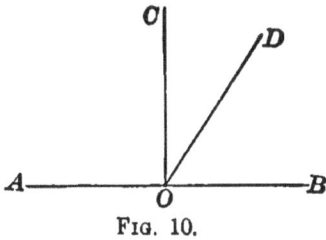

Fig. 10.

45. When one straight line stands upon another straight line and makes the *adjacent angles equal*, each of these angles is called a *right angle*. Thus, the equal angles *DCA* and *DCB* (Fig. 11) are each a right angle.

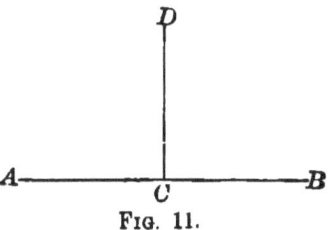

Fig. 11.

46. When the sides of an angle extend in opposite directions, so as to be in the same straight line, the angle is called a *straight angle*. Thus, the angle formed at *C* (Fig. 11) with its sides *CA* and *CB* extending in opposite directions from *C*, is a straight angle. Hence a *right angle* may be defined as *half a straight angle*.

47. A *perpendicular* to a straight line is a straight line that makes a right angle with it. Thus, if the angle *DCA* (Fig. 11) is a right angle, *DC* is perpendicular to *AB*, and *AB* is perpendicular to *DC*.

48. The point (as *C*, Fig. 11) where a perpendicular meets another line is called the *foot* of the perpendicular.

49. Every angle less than a right angle is called an *acute angle*; as, angle *A*.

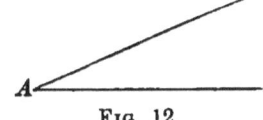

Fig. 12.

50. Every angle greater than a right angle and less than a straight angle is called an *obtuse angle*; as, angle *C* (Fig. 13).

DEFINITIONS. 9

51. Every angle greater than a straight angle and less than two straight angles is called a *reflex angle;* as, angle O (Fig. 14).

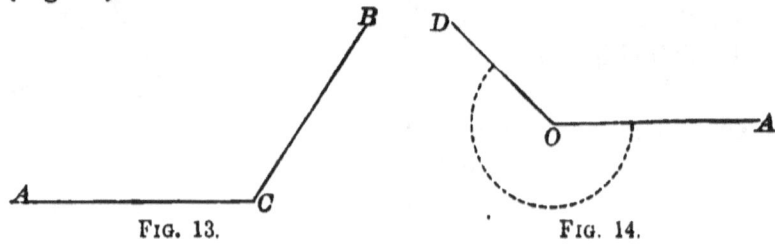

FIG. 13. FIG. 14.

52. Acute, obtuse, and reflex angles, in distinction from right and straight angles, are called *oblique* angles; and intersecting lines that are not perpendicular to each other are called *oblique lines.*

53. When two angles have the same vertex, and the sides of the one are prolongations of the sides of the other, they are called *vertical angles.* Thus, a and b (Fig. 15) are vertical angles.

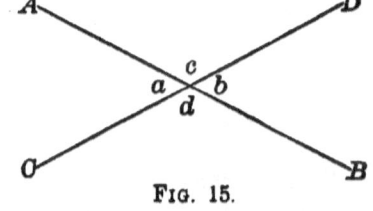

FIG. 15.

54. Two angles are called *complementary* when their sum is equal to a right angle; and each is called the *complement* of the other; as, angles DOB and DOC (Fig. 10).

55. Two angles are called *supplementary* when their sum is equal to a straight angle; and each is called the *supplement* of the other; as, angles DOB and DOA (Fig. 10).

MAGNITUDE OF ANGLES.

56. The *size* of an angle depends upon the *extent of opening* of its sides, and not upon their length. Suppose the straight line *OC* to move in the plane of the paper from coincidence with *OA*, about the point *O* as a pivot, to the position *OC*; then the line *OC* describes or generates *the angle AOC*, and the magnitude of the angle *AOC* depends upon the *amount of rotation* of the line from the position *OA* to the position *OC*.

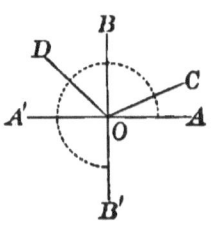

Fig. 16.

If the rotating line moves from the position *OA* to the position *OB*, perpendicular to *OA*, it generates the right angle *AOB*; if it moves to the position *OD*, it generates the obtuse angle *AOD*; if it moves to the position *OA'*, it generates the straight angle *AOA'*; if it moves to the position *OB'*, it generates the reflex angle *AOB'*, indicated by the dotted line; and if it continues its rotation to the position *OA*, whence it started, it generates two straight angles.

Hence the whole angular magnitude about a point in a plane is equal to two straight angles, or four right angles; and the angular magnitude about a point on one side of a straight line drawn through that point is equal to one straight angle, or two right angles.

Angles are magnitudes that can be added and subtracted; they may also be multiplied and divided by a number.

Angular Units.

57. If we suppose *OC* (Fig. 17) to turn about *O* from a position coincident with *OA* until it makes a complete revolution and comes again into coincidence with *OA*, it will describe *the whole angular magnitude about the point O*, while its end point *C* will describe a curve called a *circumference*.

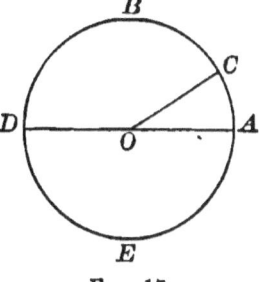

Fig. 17.

DEFINITIONS.

58. By adopting a suitable unit of angles we are able to express the magnitudes of angles in numbers.

If we suppose OC (Fig. 17) to turn about O from coincidence with OA until it makes *one three hundred and sixtieth* of a revolution, it generates an angle at O, which is taken as the unit for measuring angles. This unit is called a *degree*.

The degree is subdivided into sixty equal parts called *minutes*, and the minute into sixty equal parts, called *seconds*.

Degrees, minutes, and seconds are denoted by symbols. Thus, 5 degrees 13 minutes 12 seconds is written, 5° 13′ 12″.

A right angle is generated when OC has made *one-fourth* of a revolution and is an angle of 90°; a straight angle is generated when OC has made *one-half* of a revolution and is an angle of 180°; and the whole angular magnitude about O is generated when OC has made a complete revolution, and contains 360°.

The natural angular unit is one complete revolution. But the adoption of this unit would require us to express the values of all angles by fractions. The advantage of using the degree as the unit consists in its convenient size, and in the fact that 360 is divisible by so many different integral numbers.

Method of Superposition.

59. The test of the equality of two geometrical magnitudes is that they coincide throughout their whole extent.

Thus, two straight lines are equal, if they can be so placed that the points at their extremities coincide. Two angles are equal, if they can be so placed that they coincide.

In applying this test of equality, we assume that a line may be moved from one place to another without altering its length; that an angle may be taken up, turned over, and put down, without altering the difference in direction of its sides.

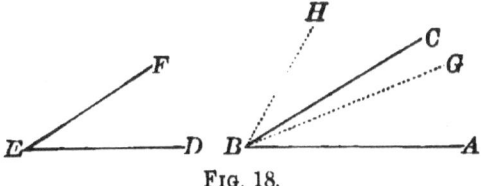

Fig. 18.

This method enables us to compare magnitudes of the same kind. Suppose we have two angles, *ABC* and *DEF*. Let the side *ED* be placed on the side *BA*, so that the vertex *E* shall fall on *B*; then, if the side *EF* falls on *BC*, the angle *DEF* equals the angle *ABC*; if the side *EF* falls between *BC* and *BA* in the direction *BG*, the angle *DEF* is less than *ABC*; but if the side *EF* falls in the direction *BH*, the angle *DEF* is greater than *ABC*.

This method enables us to add magnitudes of the same kind. Thus, if we have two straight lines *AB* and *CD*, by placing the point *C* on *B*, and keeping *CD* in the same direction with *AB*, we shall have one continuous straight line *AD* equal to the sum of the lines *AB* and *CD*.

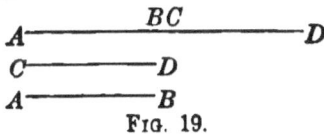

Fig. 19.

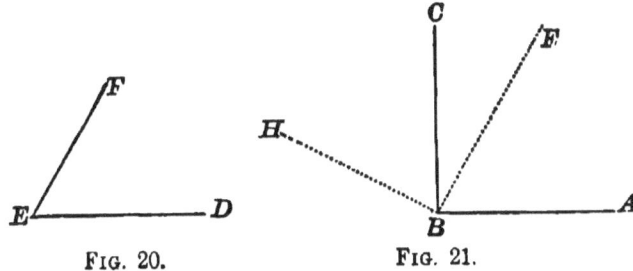

Fig. 20.   Fig. 21.

Again : if we have the angles *ABC* and *DEF*, and place the vertex *E* on *B* and the side *ED* in the direction of *BC*, the angle *DEF* will take the position *CBH*, and the angles *DEF* and *ABC* will together equal the angle *ABH*.

If the vertex *E* is placed on *B*, and the side *ED* on *BA*, the angle *DEF* will take the position *ABF*, and the angle *FBC* will be the difference between the angles *ABC* and *DEF*.

DEFINITIONS.

SYMMETRY.

60. Two points are said to be *symmetrical* with respect to a third point, called the *centre of symmetry*, if this third point bisects the straight line which joins them. Thus, P and P' are symmetrical with respect to C as a centre, if C bisects the straight line PP'.

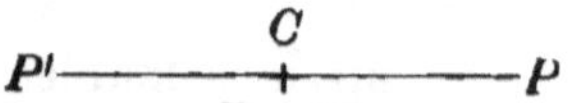

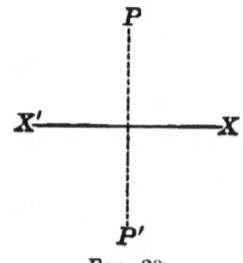

FIG. 22.

61. Two points are said to be *symmetrical* with respect to a straight line, called the *axis of symmetry*, if this straight line bisects at right angles the straight line which joins them. Thus, P and P' are symmetrical with respect to XX' as an axis, if XX' bisects PP' at right angles.

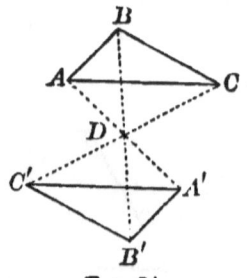

FIG. 23.

62. Two figures are said to be symmetrical with respect to a centre or an axis if every point of one has a corresponding symmetrical point in the other. Thus, if every point in the figure $A'B'C'$ has a symmetrical point in ABC, with respect to D as a centre, the figure $A'B'C'$ is symmetrical to ABC with respect to D as a centre.

FIG. 24.

63. If every point in the figure $A'B'C'$ has a symmetrical point in ABC, with respect to XX' as an axis, the figure $A'B'C'$ is symmetrical to ABC with respect to XX' as an axis.

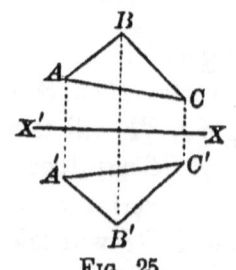

FIG. 25.

64. A figure is symmetrical with respect to a point, if the point bisects every straight line drawn through it and terminated by the boundary of the figure.

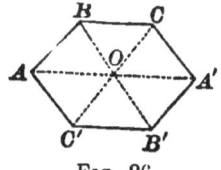

Fig. 26.

65. A plane figure is symmetrical with respect to a straight line, if the line divides it into two parts, which are symmetrical with respect to this straight line.

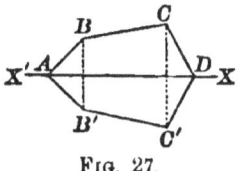

Fig. 27.

MATHEMATICAL TERMS.

66. A *proof* or *demonstration* is a course of reasoning by which the truth or falsity of any statement is logically established.

67. A *theorem* is a statement to be proved.

68. A theorem consists of two parts: the hypothesis, or that which is assumed; and the conclusion, or that which is asserted to follow from the hypothesis.

69. An *axiom* is a statement the truth of which is admitted without proof.

70. A *construction* is a graphical representation of a geometrical figure.

71. A *problem* is a question to be solved.

72. The solution of a problem consists of four parts:

(1) The *analysis*, or course of thought by which the construction of the required figure is discovered;

(2) The *construction* of the figure with the aid of ruler and compasses;

(3) The *proof* that the figure satisfies all the given conditions;

DEFINITIONS. 15

(4) The *discussion* of the limitations, which often exist, within which the solution is possible.

73. A *postulate* is a construction admitted to be possible.

74. A *proposition* is a general term for either a theorem or a problem.

75. A *corollary* is a truth easily deduced from the proposition to which it is attached.

76. A *scholium* is a remark upon some particular feature of a proposition.

77. The *converse* of a theorem is formed by interchanging its hypothesis and conclusion. Thus,

If A is equal to B, C is equal to D. (Direct.)
If C is equal to D, A is equal to B. (Converse.)

78. The *opposite* of a proposition is formed by stating the negative of its hypothesis and its conclusion. Thus,

If A is equal to B, C is equal to D. (Direct.)
If A is not equal to B, C is not equal to D. (Opposite.)

79. The converse of a truth is not *necessarily* true. Thus, Every horse is a quadruped is a true proposition, but the converse, Every quadruped is a horse, is not true.

80. *If a direct proposition and its converse are true, the opposite proposition is true; and if a direct proposition and its opposite are true, the converse proposition is true.*

81.   POSTULATES.

Let it be granted —

1. That a straight line can be drawn from any one point to any other point.

2. That a straight line can be produced to any distance, or can be terminated at any point.

3. That a circumference may be described about any point as a centre with a radius of given length.

82. AXIOMS.

1. Things which are equal to the same thing are equal to each other.
2. If equals are added to equals the sums are equal.
3. If equals are taken from equals the remainders are equal.
4. If equals are added to unequals the sums are unequal, and the greater sum is obtained from the greater magnitude.
5. If equals are taken from unequals the remainders are unequal, and the greater remainder is obtained from the greater magnitude.
6. Things which are double the same thing, or equal things, are equal to each other.
7. Things which are halves of the same thing, or of equal things, are equal to each other.
8. The whole is greater than any of its parts.
9. The whole is equal to all its parts taken together.

83. SYMBOLS AND ABBREVIATIONS.

+ increased by.
− diminished by.
× multiplied by.
÷ divided by.
= is (or are) equal to.
⇌ is (or are) equivalent to.
> is (or are) greater than.
< is (or are) less than.
∴ therefore.
∠ angle.
⦞ angles.
⊥ perpendicular.
⊥s perpendiculars.
∥ parallel.
∥s parallels.
△ triangle.
△s triangles.
▱ parallelogram.
▱s parallelograms.

⊙ circle. ⊙ circles.
Def. . . . definition.
Ax. . . . axiom.
Hyp. . . hypothesis.
Cor. . . . corollary.
Adj. . . . adjacent.
Iden. . . identical.
Cons. . . construction.
Sup. . . . supplementary.
Sup.-adj. supplementary.
Ext.-int. exterior-interior.
Alt.-int. alternate-interior.
Ex. . . . exercise.
rt. . . . . right.
st. . . . . straight.
Q.E.D. . . quod erat demonstrandum, *which was to be proved.*
Q.E.F. . . quod erat faciendum, *which was to be done.*

PLANE GEOMETRY.

BOOK I.

THE STRAIGHT LINE.

PROPOSITION I. THEOREM.

84. *All straight angles are equal.*

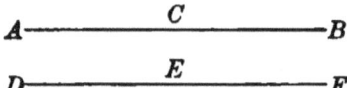

Let ∠ BCA and ∠ FED be any two straight angles.

To prove ∠ BCA = ∠ FED.

Proof. Apply the ∠ BCA to the ∠ FED, so that the vertex C shall fall on the vertex E, and the side CB on the side EF.

Then CA will coincide with ED,

(*because BCA and FED are straight lines and have two points common*).

Therefore the ∠ BCA is equal to the ∠ FED.   § 59

Q. E. D.

85. COR. 1. *All right angles are equal.*   Ax. 7.

86. COR. 2. *The angular units have constant values.*

87. COR. 3. *The complements of equal angles are equal.* Ax. 3.

88. COR. 4. *The supplements of equal angles are equal.* Ax. 3.

89. COR. 5. *At a given point in a given straight line one perpendicular, and only one, can be erected.*

HINT. Consider the given point as the vertex of a straight angle, and draw the bisector of the angle.

Proposition II. Theorem.

90. *If two adjacent angles have their exterior sides in a straight line, these angles are supplements of each other.*

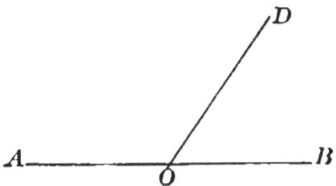

Let the exterior sides OA and OB of the adjacent ∠ AOD and BOD be in the straight line AB.

To prove ∠ AOD and BOD supplementary.

Proof. AOB is a straight line.   Hyp.

∴ the ∠ AOB is a st. ∠.   § 46

But   the ∠ AOD + ∠ BOD = the st. ∠ AOB.   Ax. 9

∴ the ∠ AOD and BOD are supplementary.   § 55

Q. E. D.

91. Scholium. Adjacent angles that are supplements of each other are called *supplementary-adjacent angles*.

92. Cor. Since the angular magnitude about a point is neither increased nor diminished by the number of lines which radiate from the point, it follows that,

The sum of all the angles about a point in a plane is equal to two straight angles, or four right angles.

The sum of all the angles about a point on the same side of a straight line passing through the point is equal to a straight angle, or two right angles.

Proposition III. Theorem.

93. Conversely: *If two adjacent angles are supplements of each other, their exterior sides lie in the same straight line.*

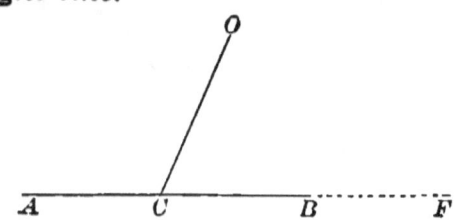

Let the adjacent $\angle OCA + \angle OCB = 2$ rt. $\angle$.

To prove AC and CB in the same straight line.

Proof. Suppose CF to be in the same line with AC. § 81

Then $\qquad \angle OCA + \angle OCF = 2$ rt. $\angle$, § 90
$\qquad\qquad$ (*being sup.-adj. $\angle$*).

But $\qquad \angle OCA + \angle OCB = 2$ rt. $\angle$. Hyp.

$\therefore \angle OCA + \angle OCF = \angle OCA + \angle OCB$. Ax. 1

Take away from each of these equals the common $\angle OCA$.

Then $\qquad \angle OCF = \angle OCB$. Ax. 3

$\therefore CB$ and CF coincide.

$\therefore AC$ and CB are in the same straight line. Q.E.D.

94. Scholium. Since Propositions II. and III. are true, their opposites are true; namely, § 80

If the exterior sides of two adjacent angles are not in a straight line, these angles are not supplements of each other.

If two adjacent angles are not supplements of each other, their exterior sides are not in the same straight line.

Proposition IV. Theorem.

95. *If one straight line intersects another straight line, the vertical angles are equal.*

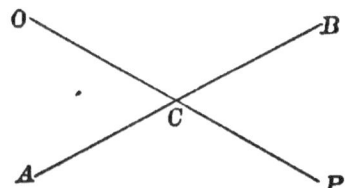

Let line OP **cut** AB **at** C.

To prove $\angle OCB = \angle ACP$.

Proof. $\angle OCA + \angle OCB = 2$ rt. $\angle$, § 90

(*being sup.-adj.* $\angle$).

$\angle OCA + \angle ACP = 2$ rt. $\angle$, § 90

(*being sup.-adj.* $\angle$).

$\therefore \angle OCA + \angle OCB = \angle OCA + \angle ACP$. Ax. 1

Take away from each of these equals the common $\angle OCA$.

Then $\angle OCB = \angle ACP$. Ax. 3

In like manner we may prove

$\angle ACO = \angle PCB$. Q. E. D.

96. Cor. *If one of the four angles formed by the intersection of two straight lines is a right angle, the other three angles are right angles.*

Proposition V. Theorem.

97. *From a point without a straight line one perpendicular, and only one, can be drawn to this line.*

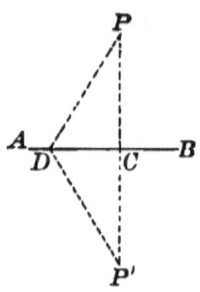

Let P be the point and AB the line.

To prove that one perpendicular, and only one, can be drawn from P to AB.

Proof. Turn the part of the plane above AB about AB as an axis until it falls upon the part below AB, and denote by P' the position that P takes.

Turn the revolved plane about AB to its original position, and draw the straight line PP', cutting AB at C.

Take any other point D in AB, and draw PD and $P'D$.

Since PCP' is a straight line, PDP' is not a straight line.
(*Between two points only one straight line can be drawn.*)

$\therefore \angle PCP'$ is a st. $\angle$, and $\angle PDP'$ is not a st. $\angle$.

Turn the figure PCD about AB until P falls upon P'.

Then CP will coincide with CP', and DP with DP'.

$\therefore \angle PCD = \angle P'CD$, and $\angle PDC = \angle P'DC$. § 59

$\therefore \angle PCD$, the half of st. $\angle PCP'$, is a rt. $\angle$; and $\angle PDC$, the half of $\angle PDP'$, is not a rt. $\angle$.

$\therefore PC$ is $\perp$ to AB, and PD is not $\perp$ to AB. § 47

$\therefore$ one $\perp$, and only one, can be drawn from P to AB.

Q. E. D.

Parallel Lines.

98. Def. *Parallel lines* are lines which lie in the same plane and do not meet however far they are prolonged in both directions.

99. Parallel lines are said to lie in the same direction when they are on the same side of the straight line joining their origins, and in opposite directions when they are on opposite sides of the straight line joining their origins.

Proposition VI.

100. *Two straight lines in the same plane perpendicular to the same straight line are parallel.*

Let AB and CD be perpendicular to AC.
To prove   *AB and CD parallel.*

Proof. If AB and CD are not parallel, they will meet if sufficiently prolonged, and we shall have two perpendicular lines from their point of meeting to the same straight line; but this is impossible.   § 97
(*From a given point without a straight line, one perpendicular, and only one, can be drawn to the straight line.*)
∴ AB and CD are parallel.   Q.E.D.

Remark. Here the supposition that AB and CD are *not* parallel leads to the conclusion that two perpendiculars can be drawn from a given point to a straight line. The conclusion is *false*, therefore the supposition is *false;* but if it is false that AB and CD are not parallel, it is true that they are parallel. This method of proof is called the *indirect method.*

101. Cor. *Through a given point, one straight line, and only one, can be drawn parallel to a given straight line.*

Proposition VII. Theorem.

102. *If a straight line is perpendicular to one of two parallel lines, it is perpendicular to the other.*

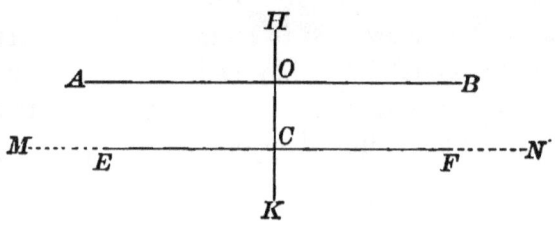

Let AB and EF be two parallel lines, and let HK be perpendicular to AB, and cut EF at C.

To prove $\qquad HK \perp EF$.

Proof. Suppose MN drawn through $C \perp$ to HK.
Then $\qquad MN$ is $\parallel$ to AB, $\qquad$ § 100
$\quad$ (*two lines in the same plane $\perp$ to a given line are parallel*).
But $\qquad EF$ is $\parallel$ to AB. $\qquad$ Hyp.
$\quad \therefore EF$ coincides with MN, $\qquad$ § 101
(*through the same point only one line can be drawn $\parallel$ to a given line*).
$\qquad \therefore EF$ is $\perp$ to HK,
that is, $\qquad HK$ is $\perp$ to EF. $\qquad$ Q.E.D.

103. If two straight lines AB and CD are cut by a third line EF, called a *transversal*, the eight angles formed are named as follows:

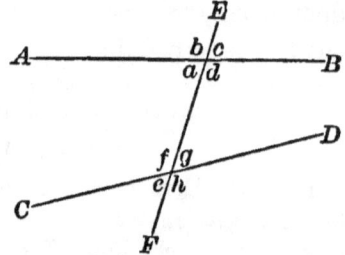

The angles a, d, f, g are called *interior*; b, c, e, h are called *exterior* angles.

The angles d and f, or a and g, are called *alt.-int.* angles.
The angles b and h, or c and e, are called *alt.-ext.* angles.
The angles b and f, c and g, a and e, or d and h, are called *ext.-int.* angles.

Proposition VIII. Theorem.

104. *If two parallel straight lines are cut by a third straight line, the alternate-interior angles are equal.*

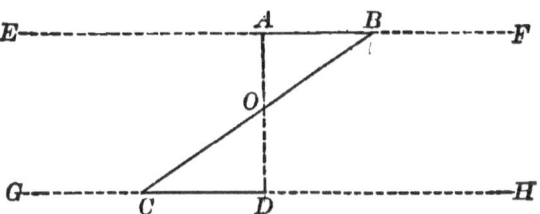

Let EF and GH be two parallel straight lines cut by the line BC.

To prove $\angle B = \angle C$.

Proof. Through O, the middle point of BC, suppose AD drawn $\perp$ to GH.

Then AD is likewise $\perp$ to EF,   § 102

(*a straight line $\perp$ to one of two ‖s is $\perp$ to the other*),

that is, CD and BA are both $\perp$ to AD.

Apply figure COD to figure BOA, so that OD shall fall on OA.

Then OC will fall on OB,   § 95

(*since $\angle COD = \angle BOA$, being vertical ∠s*);

and   the point C will fall upon B,

(*since $OC = OB$ by construction*).

Then the $\perp CD$ will coincide with the $\perp BA$,   § 97

(*from a point without a straight line only one $\perp$ to that line can be drawn*).

∴ $\angle OCD$ coincides with $\angle OBA$, and is equal to it. §59

Q. E. D.

Ex. 1. Find the value of an angle if it is double its complement; if it is one-fourth of its complement.

Ex. 2. Find the value of an angle if it is double its supplement; if it is one-third of its supplement.

PROPOSITION IX. THEOREM.

105. CONVERSELY: *When two straight lines are cut by a third straight line, if the alternate-interior angles are equal, the two straight lines are parallel.*

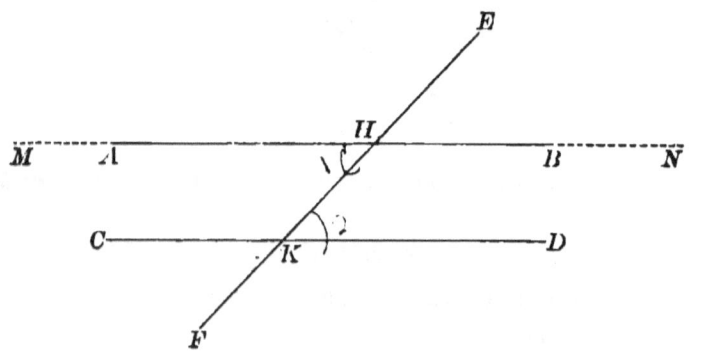

Let EF cut the straight lines AB and CD in the points H and K, and let the ∠AHK = ∠HKD.

To prove   AB ∥ to CD.

Proof. Suppose MN drawn through H ∥ to CD;   § 101
then   ∠MHK = ∠HKD,   § 104
             (being alt.-int. ⦞ of ∥ lines).
But   ∠AHK = ∠HKD.   Hyp.
∴ ∠MHK = ∠AHK.   Ax. 1
∴ the lines MN and AB coincide.
But   MN is ∥ to CD.   Cons.
∴ AB, which coincides with MN, is ∥ to CD.
                                                    Q. E. D.

Ex. 3. How many degrees in the angle formed by the hands of a clock at 2 o'clock? 3 o'clock? 4 o'clock? 6 o'clock?

Proposition X. Theorem.

106. *If two parallel lines are cut by a third straight line, the exterior-interior angles are equal.*

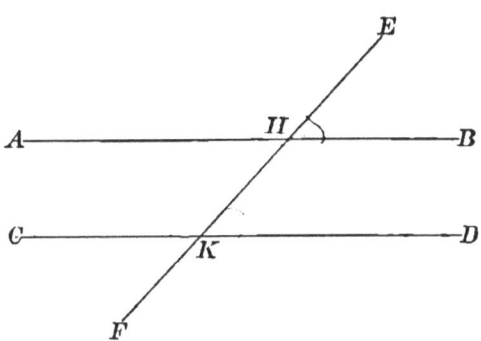

Let *AB* and *CD* be two parallel lines cut by the straight line *EF*, in the points *H* and *K*.

To prove $\angle EHB = \angle HKD$.

Proof. $\angle EHB = \angle AHK$, § 95
(*being vertical* △).

But $\angle AHK = \angle HKD$, § 104
(*being alt.-int.* △ *of* ∥ *lines*).

∴ $\angle EHB = \angle HKD$. Ax. 1

In like manner we may prove

$\angle EHA = \angle HKC.$

Q. E. D.

107. Cor. *The alternate-exterior angles EHB and CKF, and also AHE and DKF, are equal.*

Ex. 4. If an angle is bisected, and if a line is drawn through the vertex perpendicular to the bisector, this line forms equal angles with the sides of the given angle.

Ex. 5. If the bisectors of two adjacent angles are perpendicular to each other, the adjacent angles are supplementary.

Proposition XI. Theorem.

108. Conversely: *When two straight lines are cut by a third straight line, if the exterior-interior angles are equal, these two straight lines are parallel.*

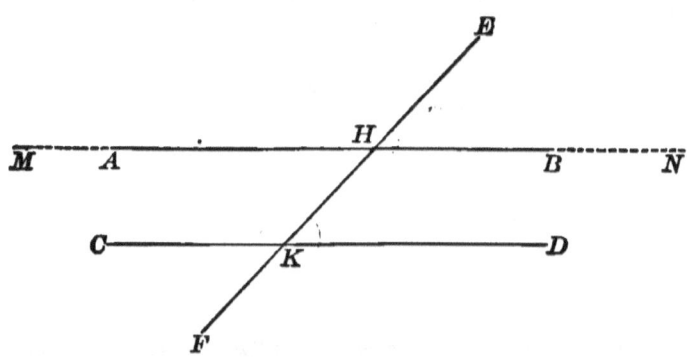

Let EF **cut the straight lines** AB **and** CD **in the points** H **and** K**, and let the** $\angle EHB = \angle HKD$**.**

To prove $\qquad AB \parallel$ to CD.

Proof. Suppose MN drawn through $H \parallel$ to CD. § 101

Then $\qquad \angle EHN = \angle HKD$, § 106
(being ext.-int. $\angle$ of $\parallel$ lines).

But $\qquad \angle EHB = \angle HKD$. Hyp.

$\therefore \angle EHB = \angle EHN$. Ax. 1

$\therefore$ the lines MN and AB coincide.

But $\qquad MN$ is $\parallel$ to CD. Cons.

$\therefore AB$, which coincides with MN, is $\parallel$ to CD.

Q. E. D.

Ex. 6. The bisector of one of two vertical angles bisects the other.

Ex. 7. The bisectors of the two pairs of vertical angles formed by two intersecting lines are perpendicular to each other.

Proposition XII. Theorem.

109. *If two parallel lines are cut by a third straight line, the sum of the two interior angles on the same side of the transversal is equal to two right angles.*

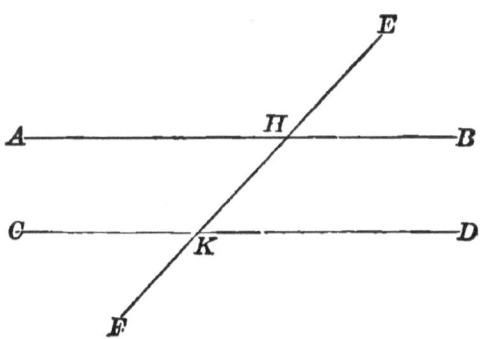

Let AB and CD be two parallel lines cut by the straight line EF in the points H and K.

To prove $\angle BHK + \angle HKD = 2$ rt. $\angle$s.

Proof. $\angle EHB + \angle BHK = 2$ rt. $\angle$s, § 90

(*being sup.-adj. $\angle$s*).

But $\angle EHB = \angle HKD$, § 106

(*being ext.-int. $\angle$s of ∥ lines*).

Substitute $\angle HKD$ for $\angle EHB$ in the first equality;

then $\angle BHK + \angle HKD = 2$ rt. $\angle$s.

Q. E. D.

Ex. 8. If the angle AHE is an angle of 135°, find the number of degrees in each of the other angles formed at the points H and K.

Ex. 9. Find the angle between the bisectors of adjacent complementary angles.

Proposition XIII. Theorem.

110. Conversely: *When two straight lines are cut by a third straight line, if the two interior angles on the same side of the transversal are together equal to two right angles, then the two straight lines are parallel.*

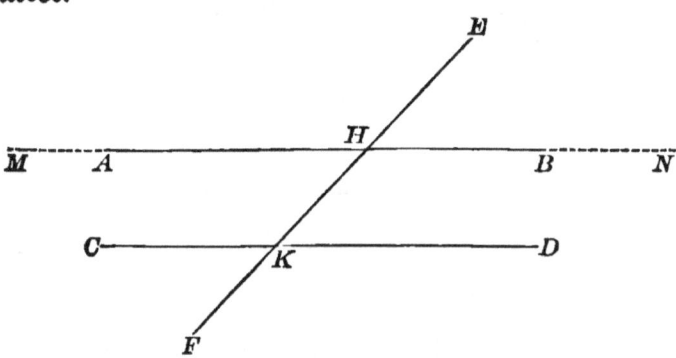

Let EF cut the straight lines AB and CD in the points H and K, and let the $\angle BHK + \angle HKD$ equal two right angles.

To prove $\quad\quad\quad AB \parallel$ to CD.

Proof. Suppose MN drawn through $H \parallel$ to CD.

Then $\quad\quad \angle NHK + \angle HKD = 2$ rt. $\angle$, $\quad\quad$ § 109

(*being two interior $\angle$ of $\parallel$s on the same side of the transversal*).

But $\quad\quad \angle BHK + \angle HKD = 2$ rt. $\angle$. $\quad\quad$ Hyp.

$\therefore \angle NHK + \angle HKD = \angle BHK + \angle HKD.$ $\quad$ Ax. 1

Take away from each of these equals the common $\angle HKD$;

then $\quad\quad\quad \angle NHK = \angle BHK.$ $\quad\quad\quad\quad$ Ax. 3

$\therefore$ the lines AB and MN coincide.

But $\quad\quad\quad MN$ is $\parallel$ to CD. $\quad\quad\quad\quad$ Cons.

$\therefore AB$, which coincides with MN, is $\parallel$ to CD.

Q. E. D.

Proposition XIV. Theorem.

111. *Two straight lines which are parallel to a third straight line are parallel to each other.*

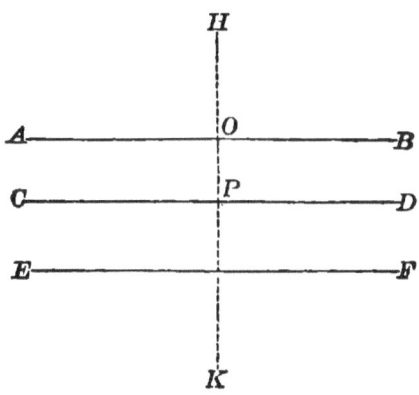

Let AB and CD be parallel to EF.

To prove $AB \parallel$ to CD.

Proof. Suppose HK drawn $\perp$ to EF. § 97

Since CD and EF are $\parallel$, HK is $\perp$ to CD, § 102

(*if a straight line is $\perp$ to one of two $\parallel$s, it is $\perp$ to the other also*).

Since AB and EF are $\parallel$, HK is also $\perp$ to AB. § 102

$$\therefore \angle HOB = \angle HPD,$$

(*each being a rt. $\angle$*).

$$\therefore AB \text{ is } \parallel \text{ to } CD, \qquad \S 108$$

(*when two straight lines are cut by a third straight line, if the ext.-int. $\angle$s are equal, the two lines are parallel*).

Q. E. D.

Ex. 10. It has been shown that if two parallels are cut by a transversal, the alternate-interior angles are equal, the exterior-interior angles are equal, the two interior angles on the same side of the transversal are supplementary. State the opposite theorems. State the converse theorems.

PARALLEL LINES.   31

Proposition XV. Theorem.

112. *Two angles whose sides are parallel, each to each, are either equal or supplementary.*

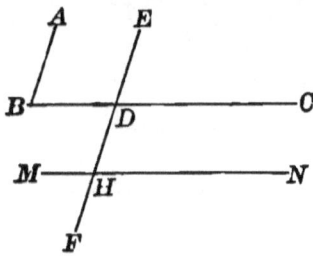

Let AB be parallel to EF, and BC to MN.

To prove $\angle ABC$ equal to $\angle EHN$, and to $\angle MHF$, and supplementary to $\angle EHM$ and to $\angle NHF$.

Proof. Prolong (if necessary) BC and FE until they intersect at D. § 81 (2)

Then $\qquad\qquad \angle B = \angle EDC,$ § 106

and $\qquad\qquad \angle DHN = \angle EDC.$ § 106

(*being ext.-int. $\angle$ of* ‖ *lines*),

$\qquad\qquad \therefore \angle B = \angle DHN;$ Ax. 1

and $\quad \angle B = \angle MHF$ (the vert. $\angle$ of DHN).

Now $\angle DHN$ is the supplement of $\angle EHM$ and $\angle NHF$.

$\therefore \angle B$, which is equal to $\angle DHN$,

is the supplement of $\angle EHM$ and of $\angle NHF$.

Q. E. D.

Remark. The angles are *equal* when both pairs of parallel sides extend in the same direction, or in opposite directions, from their vertices; the angles are *supplementary* when two of the parallel sides extend in the same direction, and the other two in opposite directions, from their vertices.

Proposition XVI. Theorem.

113. *Two angles whose sides are perpendicular, each to each, are either equal or supplementary.*

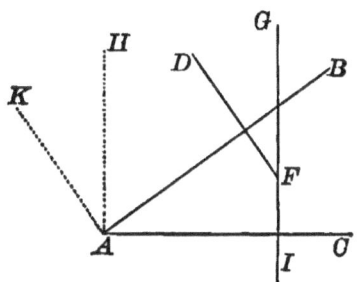

Let AB be perpendicular to FD, and AC to GI.

To prove ∠ BAC equal to ∠ DFG, and supplementary to ∠ DFI.

Proof. Suppose AK drawn ⊥ to AB, and AH ⊥ to AC.

Then AK is ∥ to FD, and AH to IG, § 100
(*two lines ⊥ to the same line are parallel*).

∴ ∠ DFG = ∠ KAH, § 112

(*two angles are equal whose sides are ∥ and extend in the same direction from their vertices*).

The ∠ BAK is a right angle by construction.

∴ ∠ BAH is the complement of ∠ KAH.

The ∠ CAH is a right angle by construction.

∴ ∠ BAH is the complement of ∠ BAC.

∴ ∠ BAC = ∠ KAH, § 87

(*complements of equal angles are equal*).

∴ ∠ DFG = ∠ BAC. Ax. 1

∴ ∠ DFI, the supplement of ∠ DFG, is also the supplement of ∠ BAC.   Q. E. D.

Remark. The angles are *equal* if both are acute or both obtuse; they are *supplementary* if one is acute and the other obtuse.

PERPENDICULAR AND OBLIQUE LINES.

Proposition XVII. Theorem.

114. *The perpendicular is the shortest line that can be drawn from a point to a straight line.*

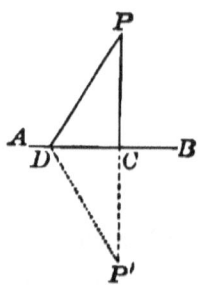

Let AB be the given straight line, P the given point, PC the perpendicular, and PD any other line drawn from P to AB.

To prove $PC < PD$.

Proof. Produce PC to P', making $CP' = PC$; and draw DP'.

On AB as an axis, fold over CPD until it comes into the plane of $CP'D$.

The line CP will take the direction of CP',

(*since $\angle PCD = \angle P'CD$, each being a rt. $\angle$ by hyp.*).

The point P will fall upon the point P',

(*since $PC = P'C$ by cons.*).

$\therefore$ line $PD = $ line $P'D$,

$\therefore PD + P'D = 2\, PD$,

and $PC + CP' = 2\, PC$.   Cons.

But $PC + CP' < PD + DP'$,

(*a straight line is the shortest distance between two points*).

$\therefore 2\, PC < 2\, PD$, or $PC < PD$.   Q.E.D.

115. Scholium. The *distance* of a point from a line is understood to mean the length of the perpendicular from the point to the line.

Proposition XVIII. Theorem.

116. *Two oblique lines drawn from a point in a perpendicular to a given line, cutting off equal distances from the foot of the perpendicular, are equal.*

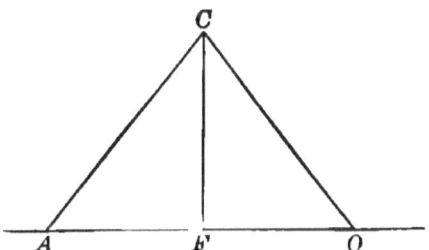

Let *FC* be the perpendicular, and *CA* and *CO* two oblique lines cutting off equal distances from *F*.

To prove $CA = CO$.

Proof. Fold over *CFA*, on *CF* as an axis, until it comes into the plane of *CFO*.

FA will take the direction of *FO*,

(*since* ∠ *CFA* = ∠ *CFO*, *each being a rt.* ∠ *by hyp.*).

Point *A* will fall upon point *O*,

(*since FA = FO by hyp.*).

∴ line $CA = $ line *CO*,

(*their extremities being the same points*). Q. E. D.

117. Cor. *Two oblique lines drawn from a point in a perpendicular to a given line, cutting off equal distances from the foot of the perpendicular, make equal angles with the given line, and also with the perpendicular.*

Proposition XIX. Theorem.

118. *The sum of two lines drawn from a point to the extremities of a straight line is greater than the sum of two other lines similarly drawn, but included by them.*

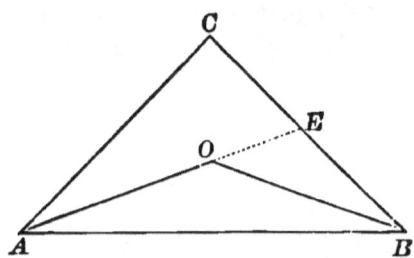

Let CA and CB be two lines drawn from the point C to the extremities of the straight line AB. Let OA and OB be two lines similarly drawn, but included by CA and CB.

To prove $\qquad CA + CB > OA + OB$.

Proof. Produce AO to meet the line CB at E.

Then $\qquad AC + CE > OA + OE$,

(*a straight line is the shortest distance between two points*),

and $\qquad BE + OE > BO$.

Add these inequalities, and we have

$$CA + CE + BE + OE > OA + OE + OB.$$

Substitute for $CE + BE$ its equal CB,

and take away OE from each side of the inequality.

We have $\qquad CA + CB > OA + OB$. $\qquad$ Ax. 5 Q.E.D.

Proposition XX. Theorem.

119. *Of two oblique lines drawn from the same point in a perpendicular, cutting off unequal distances from the foot of the perpendicular, the more remote is the greater.*

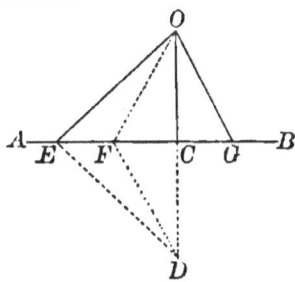

Let OC be perpendicular to AB, OG and OE two oblique lines to AB, and CE greater than CG.

To prove $\qquad OE > OG$.

Proof. Take CF equal to CG, and draw OF.

Then $\qquad OF = OG$, $\qquad$ § 116

(*two oblique lines drawn from a point in a* ⊥, *cutting off equal distances from the foot of the* ⊥, *are equal*).

Prolong OC to D, making $CD = OC$.

Draw ED and FD.

Since AB is ⊥ to OD at its middle point,

$\qquad FO = FD$, and $EO = ED$, $\qquad$ § 116

But $\qquad OE + ED > OF + FD$, $\qquad$ § 118

(*the sum of two oblique lines drawn from a point to the extremities of a straight line is greater than the sum of two other lines similarly drawn, but included by them*).

$\therefore 2OE > 2OF$, or $OE > OF$.

But $OF = OG$. Hence $OE > OG$. $\qquad$ Q.E.D.

120. Cor. *Only two equal straight lines can be drawn from a point to a straight line; and of two unequal lines, the greater cuts off the greater distance from the foot of the perpendicular.*

Proposition XXI. Theorem.

121. *Two equal oblique lines, drawn from the same point in a perpendicular, cut off equal distances from the foot of the perpendicular.*

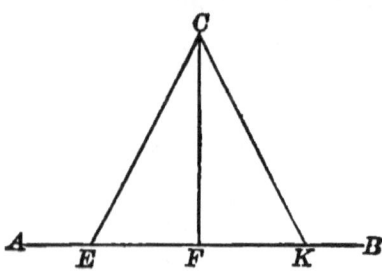

Let CF be the perpendicular, and CE and CK be two equal oblique lines drawn from the point C to AB.

To prove $\qquad FE = FK$.

Proof. Fold over CFA on CF as an axis, until it comes into the plane of CFB.

The line FE will take the direction FK,

(*since* $\angle CFE = \angle CFK$, *each being a rt.* $\angle$ *by hyp.*).

Then the point E must fall upon the point K,

and $FE = FK$.

Otherwise one of these oblique lines must be more remote from the perpendicular, and therefore greater than the other; which is contrary to the hypothesis that they are equal. § 119

Q. E. D.

Ex. 11. Show that the bisectors of two supplementary-adjacent angles are perpendicular to each other.

Ex. 12. Show that the bisectors of two vertical angles form one straight line.

Ex. 13. Find the complement of an angle containing 26° 52′ 37″. Find the supplement of the same angle.

PROPOSITION XXII. THEOREM.

122. *Every point in the perpendicular, erected at the middle of a given straight line, is equidistant from the extremities of the line, and every point not in the perpendicular is unequally distant from the extremities of the line.*

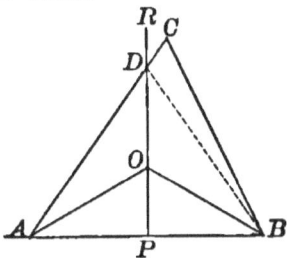

Let PR be a perpendicular erected at the middle of the straight line AB, O any point in PR, and C any point without PR.

Draw OA and OB, CA and CB.

To prove OA and OB equal, CA and CB unequal.

Proof. $\qquad PA = PB.$ \hfill Hyp.

$\qquad\qquad \therefore OA = OB,$ \hfill § 116

(*two oblique lines drawn from the same point in a $\perp$, cutting off equal distances from the foot of the $\perp$, are equal*).

Since C is without the perpendicular, one of the lines, CA or CB, will cut the perpendicular.

Let CA cut the $\perp$ at D, and draw DB.

$\qquad\qquad$ Then $DB = DA,$ \hfill § 116

(*two oblique lines drawn from the same point in a $\perp$, cutting off equal distances from the foot of the $\perp$, are equal*).

But $\qquad\qquad CB < CD + DB,$

(*a straight line is the shortest distance between two points*).

Substitute in this inequality DA for DB, and we have

$\qquad\qquad CB < CD + DA.$

That is, $\qquad\qquad CB < CA.$ \hfill Q.E.D.

123. Since two points determine the position of a straight line, *two points equidistant from the extremities of a line determine the perpendicular at the middle of that line.*

The Locus of a Point.

124. If it is required to find a point which shall fulfil a *single* geometric condition, the point will have an unlimited number of positions, but will be confined to a *particular line*, or *group of lines*.

Thus, if it is required to find a point equidistant from the extremities of a given straight line, it is obvious from the last proposition that *any* point in the perpendicular to the given line at its middle point does fulfil the condition, and that *no other* point does; that is, the required point is confined to this perpendicular. Again, if it is required to find a point at a given distance from a fixed straight line of indefinite length, it is evident that the point must lie in one of two straight lines, so drawn as to be everywhere at the given distance from the fixed line, one on one side of the fixed line, and the other on the other side.

The *locus of a point* under a given condition is the line, or group of lines, which contains all the points that fulfil the given condition, and no other points.

125. Scholium. In order to prove *completely* that a certain line is the locus of a point under a given condition, it is necessary to prove that *every point in the line satisfies the given condition;* and secondly, that *every point which satisfies the given condition lies in the line* (the converse proposition), or that *every point not in the line does not satisfy the given condition* (the opposite proposition).

126. Cor. *The locus of a point equidistant from the extremities of a straight line is the perpendicular bisector of that line.*

§§ 122, 123

Triangles.

127. A *triangle* is a portion of a plane bounded by three straight lines; as, *ABC*.

The bounding lines are called the *sides* of the triangle, and their sum is called its *perimeter;* the angles formed by the sides are called the *angles* of the triangle, and the vertices of these angles, the *vertices* of the triangle.

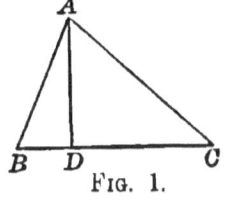
Fig. 1.

128. An *exterior angle* of a triangle is an angle formed between a side and the prolongation of another side; as, *ACD*. The interior angle *ACB* is adjacent to the exterior angle; the other two interior angles, *A* and *B*, are called *opposite-interior angles*.

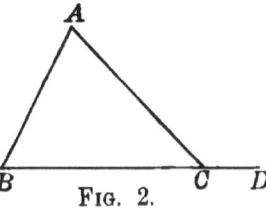
Fig. 2.

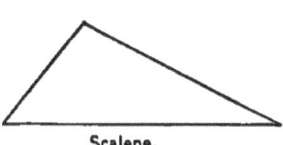
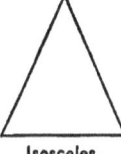
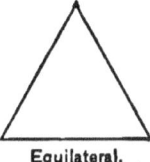

Scalene. Isosceles. Equilateral.

129. A triangle is called, with reference to its sides, a *scalene triangle* when no two of its sides are equal; an *isosceles triangle*, when two of its sides are equal; an *equilateral triangle*, when its three sides are equal.

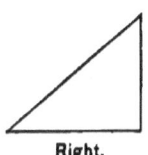
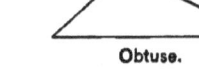
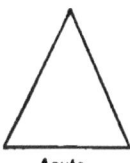

Right. Obtuse. Acute. Equiangular.

130. A triangle is called, with reference to its angles, a *right triangle*, when one of its angles is a right angle; an *obtuse* *triangle*, when one of its angles is an obtuse angle; an *acute triangle*, when all three of its angles are acute angles; an *equiangular triangle*, when its three angles are equal.

131. In a right triangle, the side opposite the right angle is called the *hypotenuse*, and the other two sides the *legs*, of the triangle.

132. The side on which a triangle is supposed to stand is called the *base* of the triangle. Any one of the sides may be taken as the base. In the isosceles triangle, the equal sides are generally called the legs, and the other side, the base.

133. The angle opposite the base of a triangle is called the *vertical angle*, and its vertex the *vertex* of the triangle.

134. The *altitude* of a triangle is the perpendicular distance from the vertex to the base, or to the base produced; as, AD.

135. The three perpendiculars from the vertices of a triangle to the opposite sides (produced if necessary) are called the *altitudes;* the three bisectors of the angles are called the *bisectors;* and the three lines from the vertices to the middle points of the opposite sides are called the *medians* of the triangle.

136. If two triangles have the angles of the one equal respectively to the angles of the other, the equal angles are called *homologous angles*, and the sides opposite the equal angles are called *homologous sides*.

In general, points, lines, and angles, similarly situated in equal or similar figures, are called *homologous*.

137. THEOREM. *The sum of two sides of a triangle is greater than the third side, and their difference is less than the third side.*

In the $\triangle ABC$ (Fig. 1), $AB+BC>AC$, for a straight line is the shortest distance between two points; and by taking away BC from both sides, $AB>AC-BC$, or $AC-BC<AB$.

Proposition XXIII. Theorem.

138. *The sum of the three angles of a triangle is equal to two right angles.*

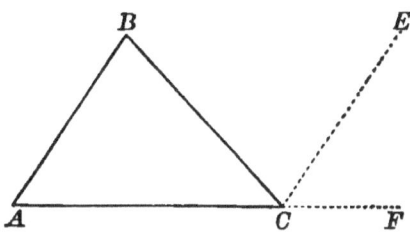

Let ABC be a triangle.

To prove $\angle B + \angle BCA + \angle A = 2$ rt. $\angle$.

Proof. Suppose CE drawn ∥ to AB, and prolong AC to F.

Then $\angle ECF + \angle ECB + \angle BCA = 2$ rt. $\angle$, § 92

(*the sum of all the $\angle$ about a point on the same side of a straight line* = 2 rt. $\angle$).

But $\angle A = \angle ECF$, § 106

(*being ext.-int. $\angle$ of ∥ lines*).

and $\angle B = \angle BCE$, § 104

(*being alt.-int. $\angle$ of ∥ lines*).

Substitute for $\angle ECF$ and $\angle BCE$ the equal $\angle$ A and B.

Then $\angle A + \angle B + \angle BCA = 2$ rt. $\angle$.

Q. E. D.

139. Cor. 1. *If the sum of two angles of a triangle is subtracted from two right angles, the remainder is equal to the third angle.*

140. Cor. 2. *If two triangles have two angles of the one equal to two angles of the other, the third angles are equal.*

141. Cor. 3. *If two right triangles have an acute angle of the one equal to an acute angle of the other, the other acute angles are equal.*

142. Cor. 4. *In a triangle there can be but one right angle, or one obtuse angle.*

143. Cor. 5. *In a right triangle the two acute angles are complements of each other.*

144. Cor. 6. *In an equiangular triangle, each angle is one-third of two right angles, or two-thirds of one right angle.*

PROPOSITION XXIV. THEOREM.

145. *The exterior angle of a triangle is equal to the sum of the two opposite interior angles.*

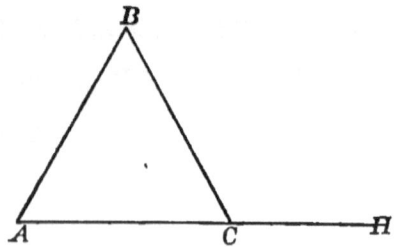

Let BCH be an exterior angle of the triangle ABC.

To prove $\quad \angle BCH = \angle A + \angle B.$

Proof. $\quad \angle BCH + \angle ACB = 2 \text{ rt. } \angle\text{s},$
(being sup.-adj. ∠s).

$\angle A + \angle B + \angle ACB = 2 \text{ rt. } \angle\text{s},$ § 138
(the sum of the three ∠s of a △ = 2 rt. ∠s).

∴ $\angle BCH + \angle ACB = \angle A + \angle B + \angle ACB.$ Ax. 1

Take away from each of these equals the common $\angle ACB$;

then $\quad \angle BCH = \angle A + \angle B.$ Ax. 3

Q. E. D.

146. Cor. *The exterior angle of a triangle is greater than either of the opposite interior angles.*

Proposition XXV. Theorem.

147. *Two triangles are equal if a side and two adjacent angles of the one are equal respectively to a side and two adjacent angles of the other.*

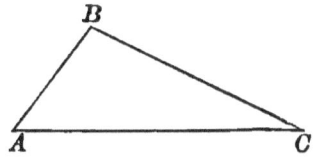 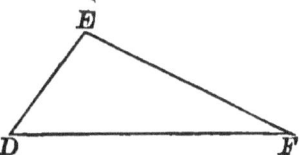

In the triangles ABC and DEF, let $AB = DE$, $\angle A = \angle D$, $\angle B = \angle E$.

To prove $\triangle ABC = \triangle DEF$.

Proof. Apply the $\triangle ABC$ to the $\triangle DEF$ so that AB shall coincide with DE.

AC will take the direction of DF,
 (for $\angle A = \angle D$, by hyp.);

the extremity C of AC will fall upon DF or DF produced.

BC will take the direction of EF,
 (for $\angle B = \angle E$, by hyp.);

the extremity C of BC will fall upon EF or EF produced.

∴ the point C, falling upon both the lines DF and EF, must fall upon the point common to the two lines, namely, F.

∴ the two $\triangle$ coincide, and are equal.   Q.E.D.

148. Cor. 1. *Two right triangles are equal if the hypotenuse and an acute angle of the one are equal respectively to the hypotenuse and an acute angle of the other.*

149. Cor. 2. *Two right triangles are equal if a side and an acute angle of the one are equal respectively to a side and homologous acute angle of the other.*

Proposition XXVI. Theorem.

150. *Two triangles are equal if two sides and the included angle of the one are equal respectively to two sides and the included angle of the other.*

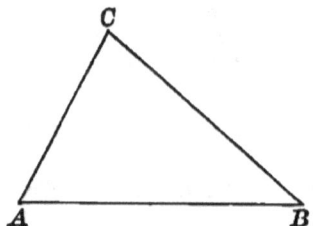 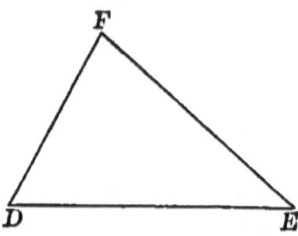

In the triangles ABC and DEF, let $AB = DE$, $AC = DF$, $\angle A = \angle D$.

To prove $\triangle ABC = \triangle DEF$.

Proof. Apply the $\triangle ABC$ to the $\triangle DEF$ so that AB shall coincide with DE.

Then AC will take the direction of DF,

(for $\angle A = \angle D$, by hyp.);

the point C will fall upon the point F,

(for $AC = DF$, by hyp.).

$\therefore CB = FE$,

(*their extremities being the same points*).

$\therefore$ the two $\triangle$ coincide, and are equal.

Q. E. D.

151. Cor. *Two right triangles are equal if their legs are equal, each to each.*

46   PLANE GEOMETRY. — BOOK I.

PROPOSITION XXVII. THEOREM.

152. *If two triangles have two sides of the one equal respectively to two sides of the other, but the included angle of the first greater than the included angle of the second, then the third side of the first will be greater than the third side of the second.*

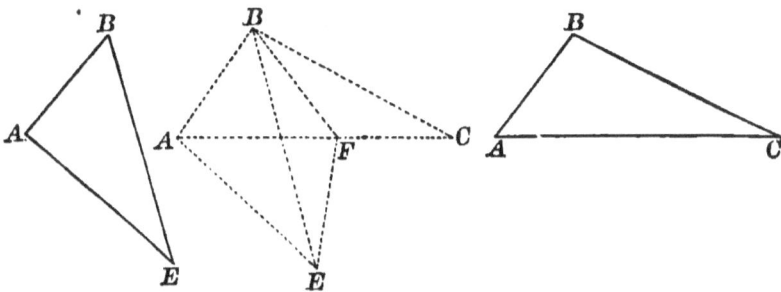

In the triangles ABC and ABE, let $AB = AB$, $BC = BE$; but ∠ ABC **greater than** ∠ ABE.

To prove $AC > AE$.

Proof. Place the △ so that AB of the one shall coincide with AB of the other.

Suppose BF drawn so as to bisect ∠ EBC.
Draw EF.

In the △ EBF and CBF

$EB = BC$,	Hyp.
$BF = BF$,	Iden.
∠ $EBF =$ ∠ CBF.	Cons.

∴ the △ EBF and CBF are equal,   § 150

(*having two sides and the included* ∠ *of one equal respectively to two sides and the included* ∠ *of the other*).

∴ $EF = FC$, ·

(*being homologous sides of equal* △).

Now $AF + FE > AE$,   § 137

(*the sum of two sides of a* △ *is greater than the third side*).

∴ $AF + FC > AE$;
or, $AC > AE$.   Q. E. D.

Proposition XXVIII. Theorem.

153. Conversely. *If two sides of a triangle are equal respectively to two sides of another, but the third side of the first triangle is greater than the third side of the second, then the angle opposite the third side of the first triangle is greater than the angle opposite the third side of the second.*

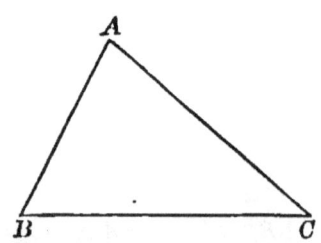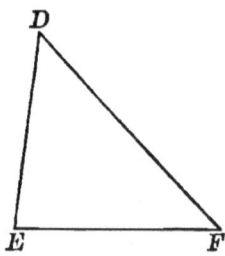

In the triangles ABC and DEF, let $AB = DE$, $AC = DF$; but let BC be greater than EF.

To prove $\angle A$ greater than $\angle D$.

Proof. Now $\angle A$ is equal to $\angle D$, or less than $\angle D$, or greater than $\angle D$.

But $\angle A$ is not equal to $\angle D$, for then $\triangle ABC$ would be equal to $\triangle DEF$, § 150

(*having two sides and the included $\angle$ of the one respectively equal to two sides and the included $\angle$ of the other*),

and BC would be equal to EF.

And $\angle A$ is not less than $\angle D$, for then BC would be less than EF. § 152

∴ $\angle A$ is greater than $\angle D$.

Q. E. D.

PROPOSITION XXIX. THEOREM.

154. *In an isosceles triangle the angles opposite the equal sides are equal.*

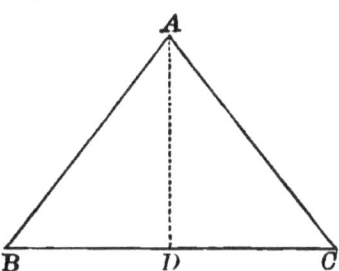

Let *ABC* be an isosceles triangle, having the sides *AB* and *AC* equal.

To prove $\angle B = \angle C$.

Proof. Suppose *AD* drawn so as to bisect the $\angle BAC$.

In the $\triangle$ *ADB* and *ADC*,

$AB = AC.$	Hyp.
$AD = AD,$	Iden.
$\angle BAD = \angle CAD.$	Cons.
$\therefore \triangle ADB = \triangle ADC,$	§ 150

(*two $\triangle$ are equal if two sides and the included $\angle$ of the one are equal respectively to two sides and the included $\angle$ of the other*).

$\therefore \angle B = \angle C.$ Q. E. D.

155. COR. *An equilateral triangle is equiangular, and each angle contains* 60°.

Ex. 14. The bisector of the vertical angle of an isosceles triangle bisects the base, and is perpendicular to the base.

Ex. 15. The perpendicular bisector of the base of an isosceles triangle passes through the vertex and bisects the angle at the vertex.

Proposition XXX. Theorem.

156. *If two angles of a triangle are equal, the sides opposite the equal angles are equal, and the triangle is isosceles.*

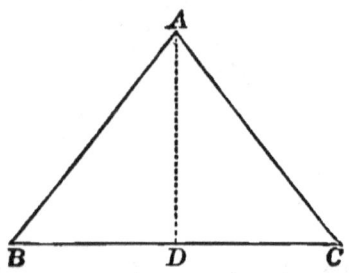

In the triangle ABC, let the $\angle B = \angle C$.

To prove $AB = AC.$

Proof.   Suppose AD drawn $\perp$ to $BC.$

In the rt. $\triangle$ ADB and ADC,

$$AD = AD, \qquad \text{Iden.}$$

$$\angle B = \angle C. \qquad \text{Hyp.}$$

$$\therefore \text{rt.} \triangle ADB = \text{rt.} \triangle ADC, \qquad \S\ 149$$

(*having a side and an acute $\angle$ of the one equal respectively to a side and an homologous acute $\angle$ of the other*).

$$\therefore AB = AC,$$

(*being homologous sides of equal $\triangle$*).

Q. E. D.

157. Cor. *An equiangular triangle is also equilateral.*

Ex. 16. The perpendicular from the vertex to the base of an isosceles triangle is an axis of symmetry.

PROPOSITION XXXI. THEOREM.

158. *If two sides of a triangle are unequal, the angles opposite are unequal, and the greater angle is opposite the greater side.*

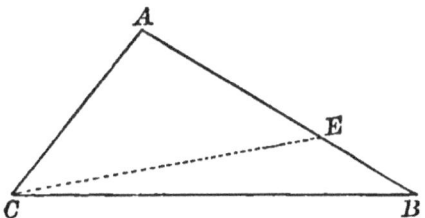

In the triangle ACB let AB be greater than AC.

To prove $\angle ACB$ greater than $\angle B$.

Proof. Take AE equal to AC.

Draw EC.

$$\angle AEC = \angle ACE, \qquad §\,154$$

(*being* $\angle$ *opposite equal sides*).

But $\angle AEC$ is greater than $\angle B$, §\,146

(*an exterior* $\angle$ *of a* $\triangle$ *is greater than either opposite interior* $\angle$).

and $\angle ACB$ is greater than $\angle ACE$. Ax. 8

Substitute for $\angle ACE$ its equal $\angle AEC$,

then $\angle ACB$ is greater than $\angle AEC$.

Much more, then, is the $\angle ACB$ greater than $\angle B$.
Q. E. D.

Ex. 17. If the angles ABC and ACB, at the base of an isosceles triangle, be bisected by the straight lines BD, CD, show that DBC will be an isosceles triangle.

Proposition XXXII. Theorem.

159. Conversely: *If two angles of a triangle are unequal, the sides opposite are unequal, and the greater side is opposite the greater angle.*

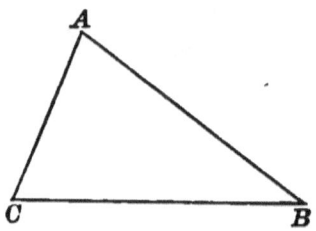

In the triangle ACB, **let angle** ACB **be greater than angle** B.

To prove $\qquad AB > AC.$

Proof. Now AB is equal to AC, or less than AC, or greater than AC.

But AB is not equal to AC, for then the $\angle C$ would be equal to the $\angle B$, § 154

(*being ∡ opposite equal sides*).

And AB is not less than AC, for then the $\angle C$ would be less than the $\angle B$, § 158

(*if two sides of a △ are unequal, the ∡ opposite are unequal, and the greater ∠ is opposite the greater side*).

$\therefore AB$ is greater than AC.

Q. E. D.

Ex. 18. ABC and ABD are two triangles on the same base AB, and on the same side of it, the vertex of each triangle being without the other. If AC equal AD, show that BC cannot equal BD.

Ex. 19. The sum of the lines which join a point within a triangle to the three vertices is less than the perimeter, but greater than half the perimeter.

PROPOSITION XXXIII. THEOREM.

160. *Two triangles are equal if the three sides of the one are equal respectively to the three sides of the other.*

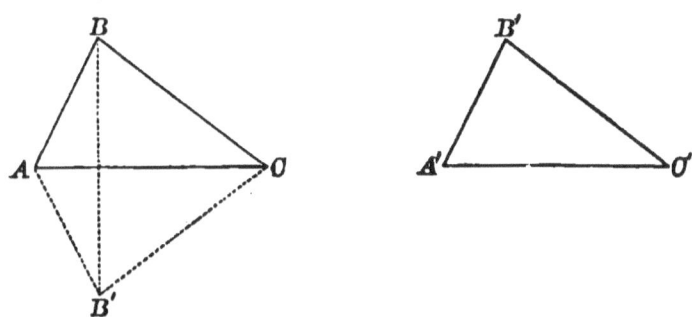

In the triangles ABC and $A'B'C'$, let $AB = A'B'$, $AC = A'C'$, $BC = B'C'$.

To prove $\triangle ABC = \triangle A'B'C'$.

Proof. Place $\triangle A'B'C'$ in the position $AB'C$, having its greatest side $A'C'$ in coincidence with its equal AC, and its vertex at B', opposite B; and draw BB'.

Since $AB = AB'$,		Hyp.
$\angle ABB' = \angle AB'B$,		§ 154

(*in an isosceles $\triangle$ the $\triangle$ opposite the equal sides are equal*).

Since $CB = CB'$,		Hyp.
$\angle CBB' = \angle CB'B$.		§ 154
Hence, $\angle ABC = \angle AB'C$,		Ax. 2
$\therefore \triangle ABC = \triangle AB'C = \triangle A'B'C'$		§ 150

(*two $\triangle$ are equal if two sides and included $\angle$ of one are equal to two sides and included $\angle$ of the other*).

Q. E. D.

Proposition XXXIV. Theorem.

161. *Two right triangles are equal if a side and the hypotenuse of the one are equal respectively to a side and the hypotenuse of the other.*

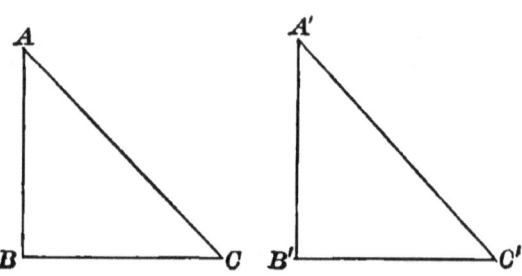

In the right triangles ABC **and** $A'B'C'$, **let** $AB = A'B'$, **and** $AC = A'C'$.

To prove $\triangle ABC = \triangle A'B'C'$.

Proof. Apply the $\triangle ABC$ to the $\triangle A'B'C'$, so that AB shall coincide with $A'B'$, A falling upon A', B upon B', and C and C' upon the same side of $A'B'$.

Then BC will take the direction of $B'C'$,

(for $\angle ABC = \angle A'B'C'$, each being a rt. $\angle$).

Since $AC = A'C'$,

the point C will fall upon C', §121

(*two equal oblique lines from a point in a* $\perp$ *cut off equal distances from the foot of the* $\perp$).

∴ the two △ coincide, and are equal.

Q. E. D.

PROPOSITION XXXV. THEOREM.

162. *Every point in the bisector of an angle is equidistant from the sides of the angle.*

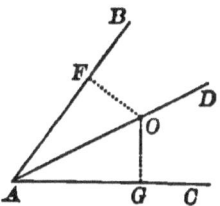

Let AD be the bisector of the angle BAC, and let O be any point in AD.

To prove that O is equidistant from AB and AC.

Proof. Draw OF and $OG \perp$ to AB and AC respectively.

In the rt. △ AOF and AOG

$$AO = AO, \qquad \text{Iden.}$$

$$\angle BAO = \angle CAO. \qquad \text{Hyp.}$$

$$\therefore \triangle AOF = \triangle AOG, \qquad \S\ 148$$

(*two rt. △ are equal if the hypotenuse and an acute ∠ of the one are equal respectively to the hypotenuse and an acute ∠ of the other*).

$$\therefore OF = OG,$$

(*homologous sides of equal △*).

$\therefore O$ is equidistant from AB and AC.

Q. E. D.

What is the locus of a point:

Ex. 20. At a given distance from a fixed point? § 57.

Ex. 21. Equidistant from two fixed points? § 119.

Ex. 22. At a given distance from a fixed straight line of indefinite length?

Ex. 23. Equidistant from two given parallel lines?

Ex. 24. Equidistant from the extremities of a given line?

TRIANGLES. 55

PROPOSITION XXXVI. THEOREM.

163. *Every point within an angle, and equidistant from its sides, is in the bisector of the angle.*

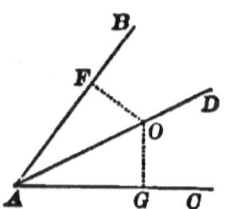

Let O be equidistant from the sides of the angle BAC, and let AO join the vertex A and the point O.

To prove that AO is the bisector of $\angle BAC$.

Proof. Suppose OF and OG drawn $\perp$ to AB and AC, respectively.

In the rt. $\triangle$ AOF and AOG

$$OF = OG, \qquad \text{Hyp.}$$

$$AO = AO. \qquad \text{Iden.}$$

$$\therefore \triangle AOF = \triangle AOG, \qquad \S\,161$$

(*two rt. $\triangle$ are equal if the hypotenuse and a side of the one are equal to the hypotenuse and a side of the other*).

$$\therefore \angle FAO = \angle GAO,$$

(*homologous $\angle$ of equal $\triangle$*).

$$\therefore AO \text{ is the bisector of } \angle BAC.$$

Q. E. D.

164. COR. *The locus of a point within an angle, and equidistant from its sides, is the bisector of the angle.*

QUADRILATERALS.

165. A *quadrilateral* is a portion of a plane bounded by four straight lines.

The bounding lines are the *sides*, the angles formed by these sides are the *angles*, and the vertices of these angles are the *vertices*, of the quadrilateral.

166. A *trapezium* is a quadrilateral which has no two sides parallel.

167. A *trapezoid* is a quadrilateral which has two sides, and only two sides, parallel.

168. A *parallelogram* is a quadrilateral which has its opposite sides parallel.

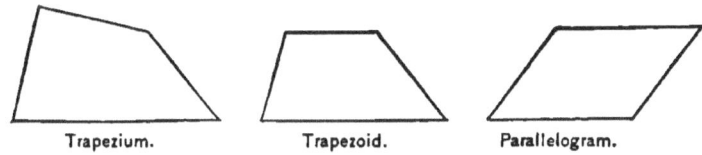

Trapezium.   Trapezoid.   Parallelogram.

169. A *rectangle* is a parallelogram which has its angles right angles.

170. A *rhomboid* is a parallelogram which has its angles oblique angles.

171. A *square* is a rectangle which has its sides equal.

172. A *rhombus* is a rhomboid which has its sides equal.

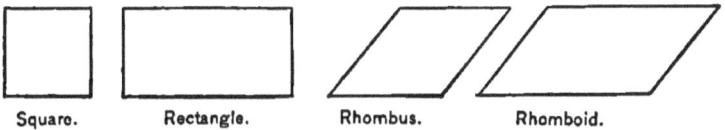

Square.   Rectangle.   Rhombus.   Rhomboid.

173. The side upon which a parallelogram stands, and the opposite side, are called its lower and upper *bases*.

QUADRILATERALS. 57

174. The parallel sides of a trapezoid are called its *bases*, the other two sides its *legs*, and the line joining the middle points of the legs is called the *median*.

175. A trapezoid is called an *isosceles trapezoid* when its legs are equal.

176. The *altitude* of a parallelogram or trapezoid is the perpendicular distance between its bases.

177. The *diagonal* of a quadrilateral is a straight line joining two opposite vertices.

PROPOSITION XXXVII.   THEOREM.

178. *The diagonal of a parallelogram divides the figure into two equal triangles.*

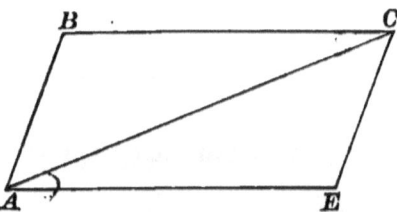

Let ABCE be a parallelogram and AC its diagonal.
To prove $\triangle ABC = \triangle AEC$.
In the $\triangle$ ABC and AEC,

$$AC = AC, \qquad \text{Iden.}$$
$$\angle ACB = \angle CAE, \qquad \S\,104$$
and $\qquad \angle CAB = \angle ACE,$
(being alt.-int. $\triangle$ of ∥ lines).

$$\therefore \triangle ABC = \triangle AEC, \qquad \S\,147$$
(having a side and two adj. $\triangle$ of the one equal respectively to a side and two adj. $\triangle$ of the other).

Q. E. D.

PLANE GEOMETRY. — BOOK I.

PROPOSITION XXXVIII. THEOREM.

179. *In a parallelogram the opposite sides are equal, and the opposite angles are equal.*

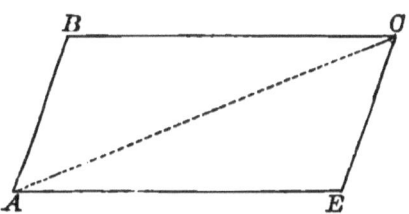

Let the figure ABCE be a parallelogram.

To prove $\quad BC = AE$, and $AB = EC$,

also, $\quad \angle B = \angle E$, and $\angle BAE = \angle BCE$.

Proof. $\qquad$ Draw AC.

$$\triangle ABC = \triangle AEC, \qquad \S\ 178$$

(*the diagonal of a ▱ divides the figure into two equal ▲*).

$$\therefore BC = AE, \text{ and } AB = CE,$$

(*being homologous sides of equal ▲*).

Also, $\quad \angle B = \angle E$, and $\angle BAE = \angle BCE,\qquad \S\ 112$

(*having their sides ∥ and extending in opposite directions from their vertices*).

Q. E. D.

180. Cor. 1. *Parallel lines comprehended between parallel lines are equal.*

181. Cor. 2. *Two parallel lines are everywhere equally distant.* For if AB and DC are parallel, ⊥s dropped from *any* points in AB to DC, measure the distances of these points from DC. But these ⊥s are equal, by § 180; hence, *all* points in AB are equidistant from DC.

QUADRILATERALS.

PROPOSITION XXXIX. THEOREM.

182. *If two sides of a quadrilateral are equal and parallel, then the other two sides are equal and parallel, and the figure is a parallelogram.*

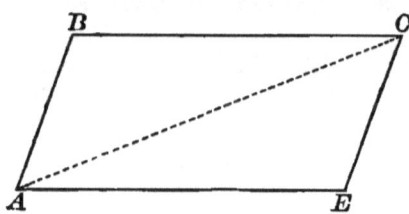

Let the figure ABCE be a quadrilateral, having the side AE equal and parallel to BC.

To prove AB equal and $\parallel$ to EC.

Proof.   Draw AC.

In the $\triangle$ ABC and AEC

$$BC = AE, \qquad \text{Hyp.}$$
$$AC = AC, \qquad \text{Iden.}$$
$$\angle BCA = \angle CAE, \qquad \S\,104$$
(being alt.-int. $\triangle$ of $\parallel$ lines).

$$\therefore \triangle ABC = \triangle ACE, \qquad \S\,150$$
(having two sides and the included $\angle$ of the one equal respectively to two sides and the included $\angle$ of the other).

$$\therefore AB = EC,$$
(being homologous sides of equal $\triangle$).

Also, $\angle BAC = \angle ACE,$
(being homologous $\triangle$ of equal $\triangle$).

$$\therefore AB \text{ is } \parallel \text{ to } EC, \qquad \S\,105$$
(when two straight lines are cut by a third straight line, if the alt.-int. $\triangle$ are equal, the lines are parallel).

$$\therefore \text{ the figure } ABCE \text{ is a } \square, \qquad \S\,168$$
(the opposite sides being parallel).

                                                         Q. E. D.

PROPOSITION XL. THEOREM.

183. *If the opposite sides of a quadrilateral are equal, the figure is a parallelogram.*

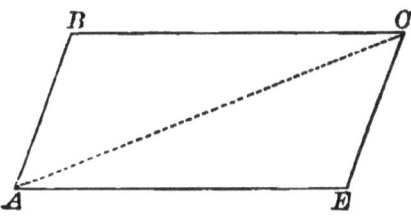

Let the figure $ABCE$ be a quadrilateral having $BC = AE$ and $AB = EC$.

To prove figure $ABCE$ a $\square$.

Proof. Draw AC.

In the $\triangle ABC$ and AEC

$$BC = AE, \qquad \text{Hyp.}$$
$$AB = CE, \qquad \text{Hyp.}$$
$$AC = AC. \qquad \text{Iden.}$$
$$\therefore \triangle ABC = \triangle AEC, \qquad \S\ 160$$

(*having three sides of the one equal respectively to three sides of the other*).

$$\therefore \angle ACB = \angle CAE,$$
and $$\angle BAC = \angle ACE,$$
(*being homologous $\angle$ of equal $\triangle$*).

$$\therefore BC \text{ is } \| \text{ to } AE,$$
and $$AB \text{ is } \| \text{ to } EC, \qquad \S\ 105$$

(*when two straight lines lying in the same plane are cut by a third straight line, if the alt.-int. $\angle$ are equal, the lines are parallel*).

$$\therefore \text{ the figure } ABCE \text{ is a } \square, \qquad \S\ 168$$

(*having its opposite sides parallel*).

Q. E. D.

Proposition XLI. Theorem.

184. The diagonals of a parallelogram bisect each other.

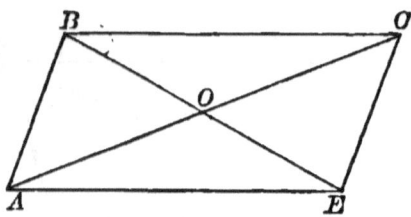

Let the figure $ABCE$ be a parallelogram, and let the diagonals AC and BE cut each other at O.

To prove $AO = OC$, and $BO = OE$.

In the $\triangle\ AOE$ and BOC

$$AE = BC, \qquad \S\ 179$$
(*being opposite sides of a ▱*).

$$\angle OAE = \angle OCB, \qquad \S\ 104$$

and $\qquad \angle OEA = \angle OBC,$
(*being alt.-int. ∠s of ∥ lines*).

$$\therefore \triangle AOE = \triangle BOC, \qquad \S\ 147$$
(*having a side and two adj. ∠s of the one equal respectively to a side and two adj. ∠s of the other*).

$$\therefore AO = OC, \text{ and } BO = OE,$$
(*being homologous sides of equal △s*).

Q. E. D.

Ex. 25. If the diagonals of a quadrilateral bisect each other, the figure is a parallelogram.

Ex. 26. The diagonals of a rectangle are equal.

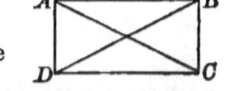

Ex. 27. If the diagonals of a parallelogram are equal, the figure is a rectangle.

Ex. 28. The diagonals of a rhombus are perpendicular to each other, and bisect the angles of the rhombus.

Ex. 29. The diagonals of a square are perpendicular to each other, and bisect the angles of the square.

PROPOSITION XLII. THEOREM.

185. *Two parallelograms, having two sides and the included angle of the one equal respectively to two sides and the included angle of the other, are equal.*

In the parallelograms $ABCD$ and $A'B'C'D'$, let $AB = A'B'$, $AD = A'D'$, and $\angle A = \angle A'$.

To prove that the ▱ are equal.

Apply ▱ $ABCD$ to ▱ $A'B'C'D'$, so that AD will fall on and coincide with $A'D'$.

Then AB will fall on $A'B'$,
(for $\angle A = \angle A'$, by hyp.),
and the point B will fall on B',
(for $AB = A'B'$, by hyp.).

Now, BC and $B'C'$ are both ∥ to $A'D'$ and are drawn through point B'.

∴ the lines BC and $B'C'$ coincide, § 101
and C falls on $B'C'$ or $B'C'$ produced.

In like manner, DC and $D'C'$ are ∥ to $A'B'$ and are drawn through the point D'.

∴ DC and $D'C'$ coincide. § 101

∴ the point C falls on $D'C'$, or $D'C'$ produced.

∴ C falls on both $B'C'$ and $D'C'$.

∴ C must fall on the point common to both, namely, C'.

∴ the two ▱ coincide, and are equal.

Q. E. D.

186. COR. *Two rectangles having equal bases and equal altitudes are equal.*

QUADRILATERALS. 63

Proposition XLIII. Theorem.

187. *If three or more parallels intercept equal parts on any transversal, they intercept equal parts on every transversal.*

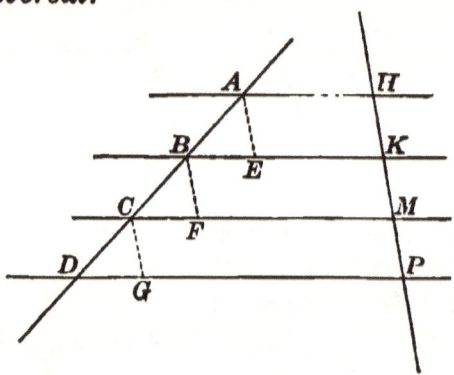

Let the parallels AH, BK, CM, DP intercept equal parts HK, KM, MP on the transversal HP.

To prove that they intercept equal parts AB, BC, CD on the transversal AD.

Proof. From A, B, and C suppose AE, BF, and CG drawn ∥ to HP.

Then $AE = HK$, $BF = KM$, $CG = MP$, § 180
(*parallels comprehended between parallels are equal*).

∴ $AE = BF = CG$. Ax. 1

Also $\angle A = \angle B = \angle C$, § 106
(*being ext.-int. ∠ of ∥ lines*);

and $\angle E = \angle F = \angle G$, § 112
(*having their sides ∥ and directed the same way from the vertices*).

∴ $\triangle ABE = \triangle BCF = \triangle CDG$, § 147
(*each having a side and two adj. ∠ respectively equal to a side and two adj. ∠ of the others*).

∴ $AB = BC = CD$,
(*homologous sides of equal △*). Q.E.D.

188. Cor. 1. *The line parallel to the base of a triangle and bisecting one side bisects the other side also.*

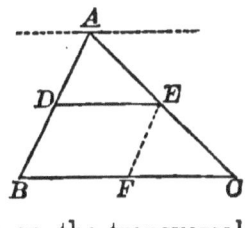

For, let DE be ∥ to BC and bisect AB. Draw through A a line ∥ to BC. Then this line is ∥ to DE, by § 111. The three parallels by hypothesis intercept equal parts on the transversal AB, and therefore, by § 187, they intercept equal parts on the transversal AC; that is, the line DE bisects AC.

189. Cor. 2. *The line which joins the middle points of two sides of a triangle is parallel to the third side, and is equal to half the third side.* For, a line drawn through D, the middle point of AB, ∥ to BC, passes through E, the middle point of AC, by § 188. Therefore, the line joining D and E coincides with this parallel and is ∥ to BC. Also, since EF drawn ∥ to AB bisects AC, it bisects BC, by § 188; that is, $BF = FC = \frac{1}{2} BC$. But $BDEF$ is a ▱ by construction, and therefore $DE = BF = \frac{1}{2} BC$.

190. Cor. 3. *The line which is parallel to the bases of a trapezoid and bisects one leg of the trapezoid bisects the other leg also.* For if parallels intercept equal parts on any transversal, they intercept equal parts on every transversal by § 187.

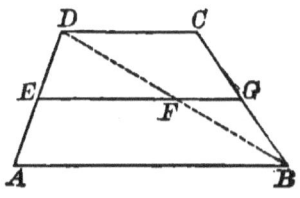

191. Cor. 4. *The median of a trapezoid is parallel to the bases, and is equal to half the sum of the bases.* For, draw the diagonal DB. In the △ ADB join E, the middle point of AD, to F, the middle point of DB. Then, by § 189, EF is ∥ to AB and $= \frac{1}{2} AB$. In the △ DBC join F to G, the middle point of BC. Then FG is ∥ to DC and $= \frac{1}{2} DC$. AB and FG, being ∥ to DC, are ∥ to each other. But only one line can be drawn through F ∥ to AB. Therefore FG is the prolongation of EF. Hence EFG is ∥ to AB and DC, and $= \frac{1}{2}(AB + DC)$.

EXERCISES.

30. The bisectors of the angles of a triangle meet in a point which is equidistant from the sides of the triangle.

HINT. Let the bisectors AD and BE intersect at O. Then O being in AD is equidistant from AC and AB. (Why?) And O being in BE is equidistant from BC and AB. Hence O is equidistant from AC and BC, and therefore is in the bisector CF. (Why?)

31. The perpendicular bisectors of the sides of a triangle meet in a point which is equidistant from the vertices of the triangle.

HINT. Let the ⊥ bisectors EE' and DD' intersect at O. Then O being in EE' is equidistant from A and C. (Why?) And O being in DD' is equidistant from A and B. Hence O is equidistant from B and C, and therefore is in the ⊥ bisector FF'. (Why?)

32. The perpendiculars from the vertices of a triangle to the opposite sides meet in a point.

HINT. Let the ⊥s be AH, BP, and CK. Through A, B, C suppose $B'C'$, $A'C'$, $A'B'$ drawn ∥ to BC, AC, AB, respectively. Then AH is ⊥ to $B'C'$. (Why?) Now $ABCB'$ and $ACBC'$ are ▱ (why?), and $AB' = BC$, and $AC' = BC$. (Why?) That is, A is the middle point of $B'C'$. In the same way, B and C are the middle points of $A'C'$ and $A'B'$, respectively. Therefore, AH, BP, and CK are the ⊥ bisectors of the sides of the $\triangle A'B'C'$. Hence they meet in a point. (Why?)

33. The medians of a triangle meet in a point which is two-thirds of the distance from each vertex to the middle of the opposite side.

HINT. Let the two medians AD and CE meet in O. Take F the middle point of OA, and G of OC. Join GF, FE, ED, and DG. In $\triangle AOC$, GF is ∥ to AC and equal to $\tfrac{1}{2} AC$. (Why?) DE is ∥ to AC and equal to $\tfrac{1}{2} AC$. (Why?) Hence $DGFE$ is a ▱. (Why?) Hence $AF = FO = OD$, and $CG = GO = OE$. (Why?)

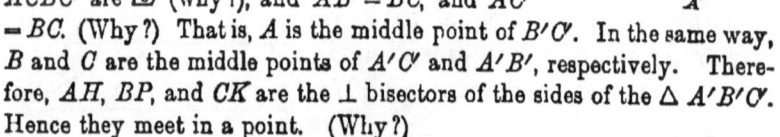

Hence, any median cuts off on any other median two-thirds of the distance from the vertex to the middle of the opposite side. Therefore the median from B will cut off AO, two-thirds of AD; that is, will pass through O.

Polygons in General.

192. A *polygon* is a plane figure bounded by straight lines.

The bounding lines are the *sides* of the polygon, and their sum is the *perimeter* of the polygon.

The *angles* which the adjacent sides make with each other are the angles of the polygon, and their vertices are the vertices of the polygon.

The number of sides of a polygon is evidently equal to the number of its angles.

193. A *diagonal* of a polygon is a line joining the vertices of two angles not adjacent; as AC, Fig. 1.

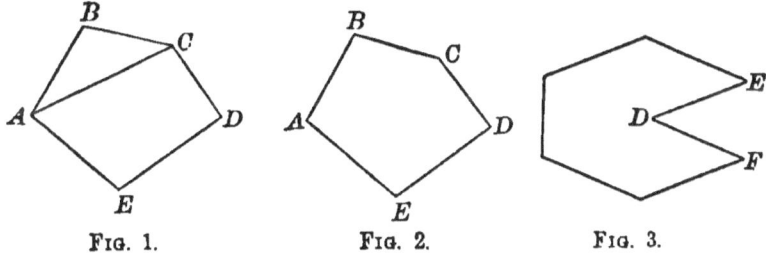

Fig. 1.   Fig. 2.   Fig. 3.

194. An *equilateral* polygon is a polygon which has all its sides equal.

195. An *equiangular* polygon is a polygon which has all its angles equal.

196. A *convex* polygon is a polygon of which no side, when produced, will enter the surface bounded by the perimeter.

197. Each angle of such a polygon is called a *salient* angle, and is less than a straight angle.

198. A *concave* polygon is a polygon of which two or more sides, when produced, will enter the surface bounded by the perimeter. Fig. 3.

199. The angle FDE is called a *re-entrant* angle, and is greater than a straight angle.

If the term polygon is used, a *convex* polygon is meant.

POLYGONS. 67

200. Two polygons are *equal* when they can be divided by diagonals into the same number of triangles, equal each to each, and similarly placed; for the polygons can be applied to each other, and the corresponding triangles will evidently coincide.

201. Two polygons are *mutually equiangular*, if the angles of the one are equal to the angles of the other, each to each, when taken in the same order. Figs. 1 and 2.

202. The equal angles in mutually equiangular polygons are called *homologous* angles; and the sides which lie *between* equal angles are called *homologous* sides.

203. Two polygons are *mutually equilateral*, if the sides of the one are equal to the sides of the other, each to each, when taken in the same order. Figs. 1 and 2.

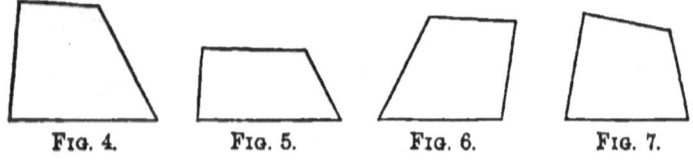

FIG. 4.   FIG. 5.   FIG. 6.   FIG. 7.

Two polygons may be mutually equiangular without being mutually equilateral; as, Figs. 4 and 5.

And, *except in the case of triangles*, two polygons may be mutually equilateral without being mutually equiangular; as, Figs. 6 and 7.

If two polygons are mutually equilateral and equiangular, *they are equal*, for they may be applied the one to the other so as to coincide.

204. A polygon of three sides is called a *trigon* or *triangle;* one of four sides, a *tetragon* or *quadrilateral;* one of five sides, a *pentagon;* one of six sides, a *hexagon;* one of seven sides, a *heptagon;* one of eight sides, an *octagon;* one of ten sides, a *decagon;* one of twelve sides, a *dodecagon.*

Proposition XLIV. Theorem.

205. *The sum of the interior angles of a polygon is equal to two right angles, taken as many times less two as the figure has sides.*

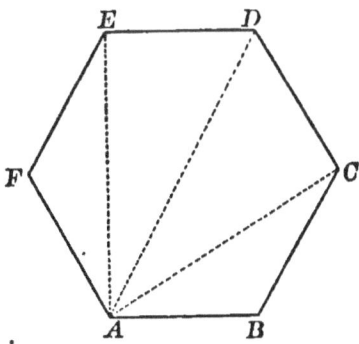

Let the figure $ABCDEF$ be a polygon having n sides.

To prove $\angle A + \angle B + \angle C$, etc. $= (n-2)\, 2$ rt. $\angle$.

Proof. From the vertex A draw the diagonals AC, AD, and AE.

The sum of the $\angle$ of the $\triangle$ = the sum of the $\angle$ of the polygon.

Now there are $(n-2)$ $\triangle$,

and the sum of the $\angle$ of each $\triangle = 2$ rt. $\angle$. § 138

∴ the sum of the $\angle$ of the $\triangle$, that is, the sum of the $\angle$ of the polygon $= (n-2)\, 2$ rt. $\angle$. Q.E.D.

206. Cor. *The sum of the angles of a quadrilateral equals two right angles taken $(4-2)$ times*, i.e., *equals 4 right angles; and if the angles are all equal, each angle is a right angle. In general, each angle of an equiangular polygon of n sides is equal to* $\dfrac{2(n-2)}{n}$ *right angles.*

POLYGONS. 69

PROPOSITION XLV. THEOREM.

207. *The exterior angles of a polygon, made by producing each of its sides in succession, are together equal to four right angles.*

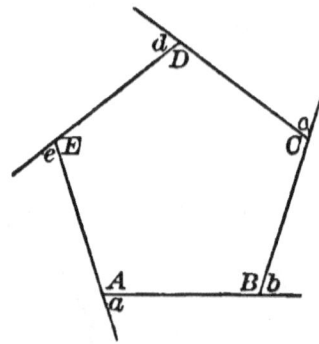

Let the figure ABCDE be a polygon, having its sides produced in succession.

To prove the sum of the ext. $\angle s = 4$ rt. $\angle s$.

Proof. Denote the int. $\angle s$ of the polygon by A, B, C, D, E, and the ext. $\angle s$ by a, b, c, d, e.

$$\angle A + \angle a = 2 \text{ rt. } \angle s, \qquad §\,90$$
and
$$\angle B + \angle b = 2 \text{ rt. } \angle s,$$
(*being sup.-adj. $\angle s$*).

In like manner each pair of adj. $\angle s = 2$ rt. $\angle s$.

∴ the sum of the interior and exterior $\angle s = 2$ rt. $\angle s$ taken as many times as the figure has sides,

or, $2\,n$ rt. $\angle s$.

But the interior $\angle s = 2$ rt. $\angle s$ taken as many times as the figure has sides less two, $= (n-2)\,2$ rt. $\angle s$,

or, $2\,n$ rt. $\angle s - 4$ rt. $\angle s$.

∴ the exterior $\angle s = 4$ rt. $\angle s$.

Q. E. D.

Proposition XLVI. Theorem.

208. *A quadrilateral which has two adjacent sides equal, and the other two sides equal, is symmetrical with respect to the diagonal joining the vertices of the angles formed by the equal sides, and the diagonals intersect at right angles.*

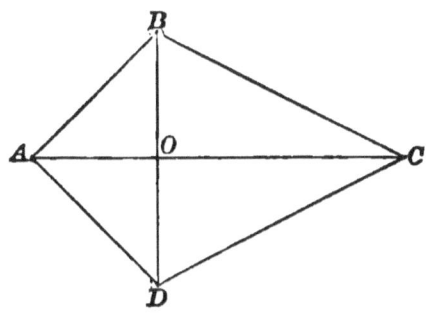

Let ABCD be a quadrilateral, having AB = AD, **and** CB = CD, **and having the diagonals** AC **and** BD.

To prove that the diagonal AC is an axis of symmetry, and is ⊥ to the diagonal BD.

Proof. In the △ ABC and ADC

$$AB = AD, \text{ and } BC = DC, \qquad \text{Hyp.}$$
and $$AC = AC. \qquad \text{Iden.}$$
$$\therefore \triangle ABC = \triangle ADC, \qquad \S\ 160$$

(*having three sides of the one equal to three sides of the other*).

$$\therefore \angle BAC = \angle DAC, \text{ and } \angle BCA = \angle DCA,$$

(*homologous ▲ of equal ▲*).

Hence, if ABC is turned on AC as an axis, AB will fall upon AD, CB on CD, and OB on OD.

Hence AC is an axis of symmetry, § 65, and is ⊥ to BD.

Q. E. D.

Proposition XLVII. Theorem.

209. *If a figure is symmetrical with respect to two axes perpendicular to each other, it is symmetrical with respect to their intersection as a centre.*

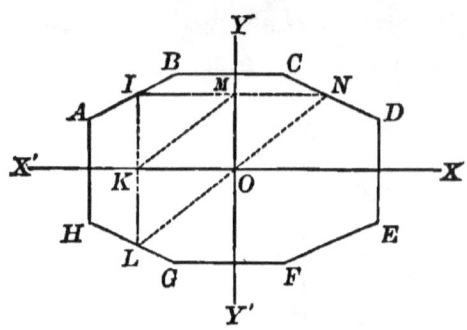

Let the figure $ABCDEFGH$ be symmetrical with respect to the two axes XX', YY', which intersect at right angles at O.

To prove O *the centre of symmetry of the figure.*

Proof. Let N be any point in the perimeter of the figure.

Draw $NMI \perp$ to YY' and $IKL \perp$ to XX'.

Join LO, ON, and KM.

Now $\qquad\qquad KI = KL,$ §61
(the figure being symmetrical with respect to XX').

But $\qquad\qquad KI = OM,$ §180
(∥s comprehended between ∥s are equal).

$\therefore KL = OM$, and $KLOM$ is a $\square$, §182
(having two sides equal and parallel).

$\therefore LO$ is equal and parallel to KM. §179

In like manner we may prove ON equal and parallel to KM.

Hence the points L, O, and N are in the same straight line drawn through the point O ∥ to KM; and $LO = ON$, since each is equal to KM.

$\therefore$ any straight line LON, drawn through O, is bisected at O.

$\therefore O$ is the centre of symmetry of the figure. §64

Q. E. D.

Exercises.

34. The median from the vertex to the base of an isosceles triangle is perpendicular to the base, and bisects the vertical angle.

35. State and prove the converse.

36. The bisector of an exterior angle of an isosceles triangle, formed by producing one of the legs through the vertex, is parallel to the base.

37. State and prove the converse.

38. The altitudes upon the legs of an isosceles triangle are equal.

39. State and prove the converse.

40. The medians drawn to the legs of an isosceles triangle are equal.

41. State and prove the converse. (See Ex. 33.)

42. The bisectors of the base angles of an isosceles triangle are equal.

43. State the converse and the opposite theorems.

44. The perpendiculars dropped from the middle point of the base of an isosceles triangle upon the legs are equal.

45. State and prove the converse.

46. If one of the legs of an isosceles triangle is produced through the vertex by its own length, the line joining the end of the leg produced to the nearer end of the base is perpendicular to the base.

47. Show that the sum of the interior angles of a hexagon is equal to eight right angles.

48. Show that each angle of an equiangular pentagon is $\frac{3}{5}$ of a right angle.

49. How many sides has an equiangular polygon, four of whose angles are together equal to seven right angles?

50. How many sides has a polygon, the sum of whose interior angles is equal to the sum of its exterior angles?

51. How many sides has a polygon, the sum of whose interior angles is double that of its exterior angles?

52. How many sides has a polygon, the sum of whose exterior angles is double that of its interior angles?

EXERCISES.

53. BAC is a triangle having the angle B double the angle A. If BD bisect the angle B, and meet AC in D, show that BD is equal to AD.

54. If from any point in the base of an isosceles triangle parallels to the legs are drawn, show that a parallelogram is formed whose perimeter is constant, and equal to the sum of the legs of the triangle.

55. The lines joining the middle points of the sides of a triangle divide the triangle into four equal triangles.

56. The lines joining the middle points of the side of a square, taken in order, enclose a square.

57. The lines joining the middle points of the sides of a rectangle, taken in order, enclose a rhombus.

58. The lines joining the middle points of the sides of a rhombus, taken in order, enclose a rectangle.

59. The lines joining the middle points of the sides of an isosceles trapezoid, taken in order, enclose a rhombus or a square.

60. The lines joining the middle points of the sides of any quadrilateral, taken in order, enclose a parallelogram.

61. The median of a trapezoid passes through the middle points of the two diagonals.

62. The line joining the middle points of the diagonals of a trapezoid is equal to half the difference of the bases.

63. In an isosceles trapezoid each base makes equal angles with the legs.
   HINT. Draw $CE \parallel DB$.

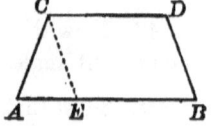

64. In an isosceles trapezoid the opposite angles are supplementary.

65. If the angles at the base of a trapezoid are equal, the other angles are equal, and the trapezoid is isosceles.

66. The diagonals of an isosceles trapezoid are equal.

67. If the diagonals of a trapezoid are equal, the trapezoid is isosceles.
   HINT. Draw CE and $DF \perp$ to CD. Show that $\triangle$ ADF and BCE are equal, that $\triangle$ COD and AOB are isosceles, and that $\triangle$ AOC and BOD are equal.

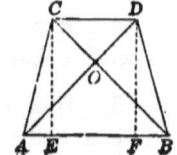

68. *ABCD* is a parallelogram, *E* and *F* the middle points of *AD* and *BC* respectively; show that *BE* and *DF* will trisect the diagonal *AC*.

69. If from the diagonal *BD* of a square *ABCD*, *BE* is cut off equal to *BC*, and *EF* is drawn perpendicular to *BD* to meet *DC* at *F*, show that *DE* is equal to *EF*, and also to *FC*.

70. The bisector of the vertical angle *A* of a triangle *ABC*, and the bisectors of the exterior angles at the base formed by producing the sides *AB* and *AC*, meet in a point which is equidistant from the base and the sides produced.

71. If the two angles at the base of a triangle are bisected, and through the point of meeting of the bisectors a line is drawn parallel to the base, the length of this parallel between the sides is equal to the sum of the segments of the sides between the parallel and the base.

72. If one of the acute angles of a right triangle is double the other, the hypotenuse is double the shortest side.

73. The sum of the perpendiculars dropped from any point in the base of an isosceles triangle to the legs is constant, and equal to the altitude upon one of the legs.

HINT. Let *PD* and *PE* be the two ⊥s, *BF* the altitude upon *AC*. Draw *PG* ⊥ to *BF*, and prove the △ *PBG* and *PBD* equal.

74. The sum of the perpendiculars dropped from any point within an equilateral triangle to the three sides is constant, and equal to the altitude.

HINT. Draw through the point a line ∥ to the base, and apply Ex. 73.

75. What is the locus of all points equidistant from a pair of intersecting lines?

76. In the triangle *CAB* the bisector of the angle *C* makes with the perpendicular from *C* to *AB* an angle equal to half the difference of the angles *A* and *B*.

77. If one angle of an isosceles triangle is equal to 60°, the triangle is equilateral.

BOOK II.

THE CIRCLE.

Definitions.

210. A *circle* is a portion of a plane bounded by a curved line called a *circumference*, all points of which are equally distant from a point within called the *centre*.

211. A *radius* is a straight line drawn from the centre to the circumference; and a *diameter* is a straight line drawn through the centre, having its extremities in the circumference.

By the definition of a circle, all its radii are equal. All its diameters are equal, since the diameter is equal to two radii.

212. A *secant* is a straight line which intersects the circumference in two points; as, AD, Fig. 1.

213. A *tangent* is a straight line which touches the circumference but does not intersect it; as, BC, Fig. 1. The point in which the tangent touches the circumference is called the *point of contact*, or *point of tangency*.

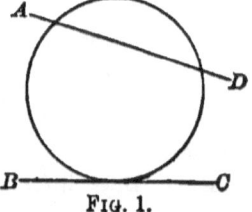

Fig. 1.

214. Two *circumferences* are tangent to each other when they are both tangent to a straight line at the same point; and are tangent *internally* or *externally*, according as one circumference lies wholly *within* or *without* the other.

215. An *arc* of a circle is any portion of the circumference. An arc equal to one-half the circumference is called a *semi-circumference*.

216. A *chord* is a straight line having its extremities in the circumference.

Every chord subtends two arcs whose sum is the circumference; thus, the chord AB (Fig. 3) subtends the smaller arc AB and the larger arc $BCDEA$. If a chord and its arc are spoken of, the less arc is meant unless it is otherwise stated.

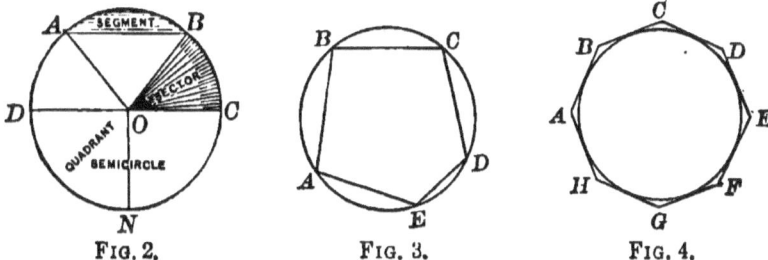

Fig. 2. Fig. 3. Fig. 4.

217. A *segment* of a circle is a portion of a circle bounded by an arc and its chord.

A segment equal to one-half the circle is called a *semicircle*.

218. A *sector* of a circle is a portion of the circle bounded by two radii and the arc which they intercept.

A sector equal to one-fourth of the circle is called a *quadrant*.

219. A straight line is *inscribed in a circle* if it is a chord.

220. An angle is *inscribed in a circle* if its vertex is in the circumference and its sides are chords.

221. An angle is *inscribed in a segment* if its vertex is on the arc of the segment and its sides pass through the extremities of the arc.

222. A polygon is *inscribed in a circle* if its sides are chords of the circle.

223. A circle is *inscribed in a polygon* if the circumference touches the sides of the polygon but does not intersect them.

224. A polygon is *circumscribed about a circle* if all the sides of the polygon are tangents to the circle.

225. A circle is *circumscribed about a polygon* if the circumference passes through all the vertices of the polygon.

226. Two circles are equal if they have equal radii; for they will coincide if one is applied to the other; conversely, two equal circles have equal radii.

Two circles are concentric if they have the same centre.

PROPOSITION I. THEOREM.

227. *The diameter of a circle is greater than any other chord; and bisects the circle and the circumference.*

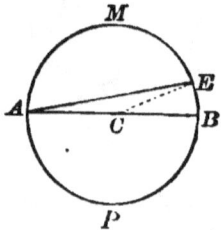

Let AB be the diameter of the circle $AMBP$, and AE any other chord.

To prove $AB > AE$, and AB bisects the circle and the circumference.

Proof. I. From C, the centre of the $\odot$, draw CE.

$$CE = CB,$$
(*being radii of the same circle*).

But $\qquad AC + CE > AE,$ §137
(*the sum of two sides of a $\triangle$ is $>$ the third side*).

Then $\quad AC + CB > AE$, or $AB > AE.$ Ax. 9

II. Fold over the segment AMB on AB as an axis until it falls upon APB, §59. The points A and B will remain fixed; therefore the arc AMB will coincide with the arc APB; because all points in each are equally distant from the centre C. §210

Hence the two figures coincide throughout and are equal. §59

Q. E. D.

PROPOSITION II. THEOREM.

228. *A straight line cannot intersect the circumference of a circle in more than two points.*

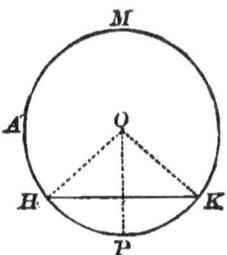

Let *HK* be any line cutting the circumference *AMP*.

To prove that *HK* can intersect the circumference in only two points.

Proof. If possible, let *HK* intersect the circumference in three points *H*, *P*, and *K*.

From *O*, the centre of the ⊙, draw *OH*, *OP*, and *OK*.

Then   *OH*, *OP*, and *OK* are equal,

(*being radii of the same circle*).

Hence, we have three equal straight lines *OH*, *OP*, and *OK* drawn from the same point to a given straight line. But this is impossible, § 120

(*only two equal straight lines can be drawn from a point to a straight line*).

Therefore, *HK* can intersect the circumference in only two points.   Q.E.D.

ARCS AND CHORDS. 79

PROPOSITION III. THEOREM.

229. *In the same circle, or equal circles, equal angles at the centre intercept equal arcs;* CONVERSELY, *equal arcs subtend equal angles at the centre.*

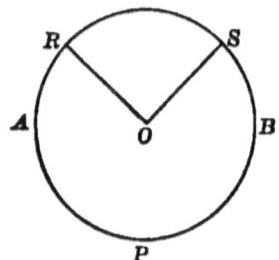 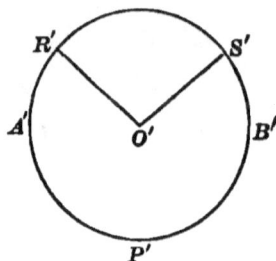

In the equal circles ABP and A'B'P' let ∠ O = ∠ O'.

To prove arc RS = arc $R'S'$.

Proof. Apply ⊙ ABP to ⊙ $A'B'P'$,

so that ∠ O shall coincide with ∠ O'.

R will fall upon R', and S upon S', § 226

(*for* $OR = O'R'$, *and* $OS = O'S'$, *being radii of equal* ⊙).

Then the arc RS will coincide with the arc $R'S'$,

since all points in the arcs are equidistant from the centre.

§ 210

∴ arc RS = arc $R'S'$.

CONVERSELY: **Let arc RS = arc $R'S'$.**

To prove ∠ O = ∠ O'.

Proof. Apply ⊙ ABP to ⊙ $A'B'P'$, so that arc RS shall fall upon arc $R'S'$, R falling upon R', S upon S', and O upon O'.

Then RO will coincide with $R'O'$, and SO with $S'O'$.

∴ ∠s O and O' coincide and are equal. Q. E. D.

Proposition IV. Theorem.

230. *In the same circle, or equal circles, if two chords are equal, the arcs which they subtend are equal;* CONVERSELY, *if two arcs are equal, the chords which subtend them are equal.*

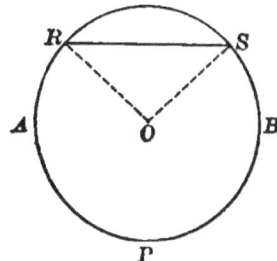 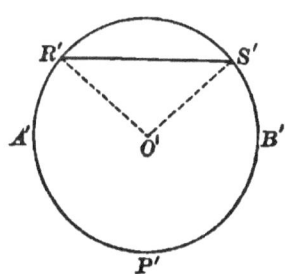

In the equal circles ABP and $A'B'P'$, let chord $RS =$ chord $R'S'$.

To prove   arc $RS =$ arc $R'S'$.

Proof.   Draw the radii OR, OS, $O'R'$, and $O'S'$.

In the $\triangle ORS$ and $O'R'S'$

$$RS = R'S', \qquad \text{Hyp.}$$

the radii OR and $OS =$ the radii $O'R'$ and $O'S'$.   § 226

$$\therefore \triangle ROS = \triangle R'O'S', \qquad § 160$$

(*three sides of the one being equal to three sides of the other*).

$$\therefore \angle O = \angle O',$$

$$\therefore \text{arc } RS = \text{arc } R'S', \qquad § 229$$

(*in equal ⊙, equal ∠ at the centre intercept equal arcs*).

CONVERSELY: **Let arc $RS =$ arc $R'S'$.**

To prove   chord $RS =$ chord $R'S'$.

Proof. $\angle O = \angle O',$ § 229

(*equal arcs in equal ⊙ subtend equal ∠ at the centre*),

and OR and $OS = O'R'$ and $O'S'$, respectively.   § 226

$$\therefore \triangle ORS = \triangle O'R'S', \qquad § 150$$

(*having two sides equal each to each and the included ∠ equal*).

$$\therefore \text{chord } RS = \text{chord } R'S'. \qquad \text{Q.E.D.}$$

Proposition V. Theorem.

231. *In the same circle, or equal circles, if two arcs are unequal, and each is less than a semi-circumference, the greater arc is subtended by the greater chord;* Conversely, *the greater chord subtends the greater arc.*

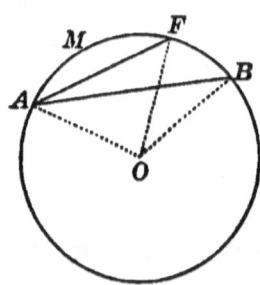

In the circle whose centre is O, let the arc AMB be greater than the arc AMF.

To prove   chord AB greater than chord AF.

Proof.   Draw the radii OA, OF, and OB.

Since F is between A and B, OF will fall between OA and OB, and $\angle AOB$ be greater than $\angle AOF$.

Hence, in the $\triangle$ AOB and AOF,

the radii OA and $OB =$ the radii OA and OF,

but $\angle AOB$ is greater than $\angle AOF$.

$$\therefore AB > AF, \qquad \S\ 152$$

(*the $\triangle$ having two sides equal each to each, but the included $\angle$ unequal*).

Conversely: **Let AB be greater than AF.**

To prove   arc AB greater than arc AF.

In the $\triangle$ AOB and AOF,

OA and $OB = OA$ and OF respectively.

But AB is greater than AF.   Hyp.

$$\therefore \angle AOB \text{ is greater than } \angle AOF, \qquad \S\ 153$$

(*the $\triangle$ having two sides equal each to each, but the third sides unequal*).

$\therefore OB$ falls without OF.

$\therefore$ arc AB is greater than arc AF.   q.e.d.

PROPOSITION VI. THEOREM.

232. *The radius perpendicular to a chord bisects the chord and the arc subtended by it.*

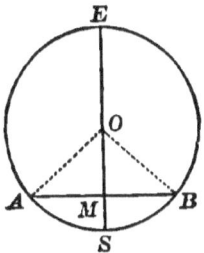

Let AB be the chord, and let the radius OS be perpendicular to AB at M.

To prove $AM = BM$, and arc $AS =$ arc BS.

Proof. Draw OA and OB from O, the centre of the circle.

In the rt. $\triangle$ OAM and OBM

the radius $OA =$ the radius OB,

and $OM = OM$.   Iden.

$\therefore \triangle OAM = \triangle OBM$,   § 161

(*having the hypotenuse and a side of one equal to the hypotenuse and a side of the other*).

$\therefore AM = BM$,

and $\angle AOS = \angle BOS$.

$\therefore$ arc $AS =$ arc BS,   § 229

(*equal $\triangle$ at the centre intercept equal arcs on the circumference*).

Q. E. D.

233. Cor. 1. *The perpendicular erected at the middle of a chord passes through the centre of the circle.* For the centre is equidistant from the extremities of a chord, and is therefore in the perpendicular erected at the middle of the chord. § 122

234. Cor. 2. *The perpendicular erected at the middle of a chord bisects the arcs of the chord.*

235. Cor. 3. *The locus of the middle points of a system of parallel chords is the diameter perpendicular to them.*

Proposition VII. Theorem.

236. *In the same circle, or equal circles, equal chords are equally distant from the centre;* AND CONVERSELY.

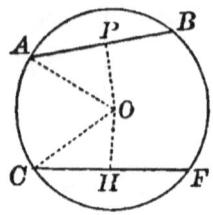

Let AB **and** CF **be equal chords of the circle** $ABFC$.
To prove AB and CF equidistant from the centre O.
Proof. Draw $OP \perp$ to AB, $OH \perp$ to CF, and join OA and OC.

OP and OH bisect AB and CF,   § 232
(*a radius $\perp$ to a chord bisects it*).

Hence, in the rt. $\triangle$ OPA and OHC

$$AP = CH,$$ Ax. 7

the radius $OA =$ the radius OC.

$$\therefore \triangle OPA = \triangle OHC,$$ § 161

(*having a side and hypotenuse of the one equal to a side and hypotenuse of the other*).

$$\therefore OP = OH.$$

$\therefore AB$ and CF are equidistant from O.

Conversely: **Let** $OP = OH$.
To prove $AB = CF$.
Proof. In the rt. $\triangle$ OPA and OHC
the radius $OA =$ the radius OC, and $OP = OH$.   Hyp.

$\therefore \triangle OPA$ and OHC are equal.   § 161

$$\therefore AP = CH.$$

$$\therefore AB = CF.$$ Ax. 6.

Q.E.D.

PROPOSITION VIII. THEOREM.

237. *In the same circle, or equal circles, if two chords are unequal, they are unequally distant from the centre, and the greater is at the less distance.*

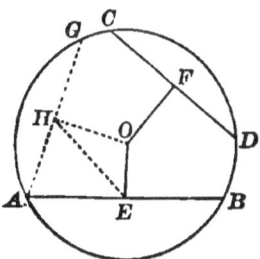

In the circle whose centre is O, let the chords AB and CD be unequal, and AB the greater; and let OE and OF be perpendicular to AB and CD respectively.

To prove $\qquad OE < OF.$

Proof. Suppose AG drawn equal to CD, and $OH \perp$ to AG.

$\qquad$ Then $OH = OF,$ $\qquad$ § 236

(*in the same ⊙ two equal chords are equidistant from the centre*).

$\qquad$ Join $EH.$

OE and OH bisect AB and AG, respectively, $\qquad$ § 232

(*a radius ⊥ to a chord bisects it*).

Since, by hypothesis, AB is greater than CD or its equal AG, AE, the half of AB, is greater than AH, the half of AG.

$\therefore$ the $\angle AHE$ is greater than the $\angle AEH,$ $\qquad$ § 158

(*the greater of two sides of a △ has the greater ∠ opposite to it*).

Therefore, the $\angle OHE$, the complement of the $\angle AHE$, is less than the $\angle OEH$, the complement of the $\angle AEH.$

$\qquad \therefore OE < OH,$ $\qquad$ § 159

(*the greater of two ⦟ of a △ has the greater side opposite to it*).

$\qquad \therefore OE < OF,$ the equal of $OH.$

Q. E. D.

PROPOSITION IX. THEOREM.

238. CONVERSELY: *In the same circle, or equal circles, if two chords are unequally distant from the centre, they are unequal, and the chord at the less distance is the greater.*

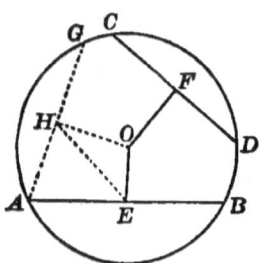

In the circle whose centre is O, let AB and CD be unequally distant from O; and let OE perpendicular to AB be less than OF perpendicular to CD.

To prove $AB > CD$.

Proof. Suppose AG drawn equal to CD, and $OH \perp$ to AG.

Then $OH = OF$, § 236

(*in the same ⊙ two equal chords are equidistant from the centre*).

Hence, $OE < OH$.

Join EH.

In the $\triangle OEH$ the $\angle OHE$ is less than the $\angle OEH$, § 158

(*the greater of two sides of a △ has the greater ∠ opposite to it*).

Therefore, the $\angle AHE$, the complement of the $\angle OHE$, is greater than the $\angle AEH$, the complement of the $\angle OEH$.

$\therefore AE > AH$, § 159

(*the greater of two ∠s of a △ has the greater side opposite to it*).

But $AE = \tfrac{1}{2} AB$, and $AH = \tfrac{1}{2} AG$.

$\therefore AB > AG$; hence $AB > CD$, the equal of AG.

Q. E. D.

PROPOSITION X. THEOREM.

239. *A straight line perpendicular to a radius at its extremity is a tangent to the circle.*

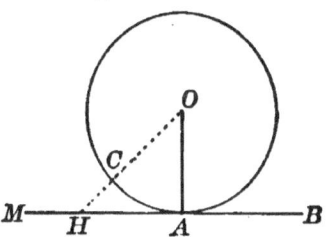

Let MB be perpendicular to the radius OA at A.
To prove   *MB tangent to the circle.*
Proof. From O draw any other line to MB, as OCH.
$$OH > OA, \qquad\qquad §\,114$$
(*a ⊥ is the shortest line from a point to a straight line*).

∴ the point H is without the circle.

Hence, every point, except A, of the line MB is without the circle, and therefore MB is a tangent to the circle at A. § 213
Q. E. D.

240. Cor. 1. *A tangent to a circle is perpendicular to the radius drawn to the point of contact.* For, if MB is tangent to the circle at A, every point of MB, except A, is without the circle. Hence, OA is the shortest line from O to MB, and is therefore perpendicular to MB (§ 114); that is, MB is perpendicular to OA.

241. Cor. 2. *A perpendicular to a tangent at the point of contact passes through the centre of the circle.* For a radius is perpendicular to a tangent at the point of contact, and therefore, by § 89, a perpendicular erected at the point of contact coincides with this radius and passes through the centre.

242. Cor. 3. *A perpendicular let fall from the centre of a circle upon a tangent to the circle passes through the point of contact.*

Proposition XI. Theorem.

243. *Parallels intercept equal arcs on a circumference.*

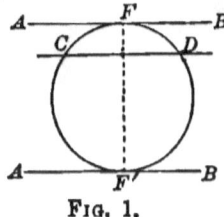
Fig. 1.

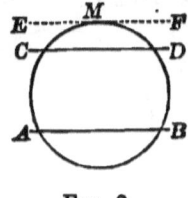
Fig. 2.

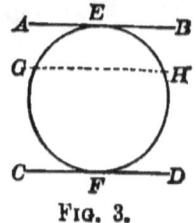
Fig. 3.

Let AB and CD be the two parallels.

Case I. *When AB is a tangent, and CD a secant.* Fig. 1.

Suppose AB touches the circle at F.

To prove   arc $CF =$ arc DF.

Proof. Suppose FF' drawn $\perp$ to AB.

This $\perp$ to AB at F is a diameter of the circle. § 241

It is also $\perp$ to CD.   § 102

∴ arc $CF =$ arc DF,   § 232

(*a radius $\perp$ to a chord bisects the chord and its subtended arc*).

Also, arc $FCF' =$ arc FDF',   § 227

∴ arc $(FCF' - FC) =$ arc $(FDF' - FD)$,   § 82

that is,   arc $CF' =$ arc DF'.

Case II. *When AB and CD are secants.* Fig. 2.

Suppose EF drawn ∥ to CD and tangent to the circle at M.

Then   arc $AM =$ arc BM

and   arc $CM =$ arc DM.   Case I.

∴ by subtraction, arc $AC =$ arc BD.

Case III. *When AB and CD are tangents.* Fig. 3.

Suppose AB tangent at E, CD at F, and GH ∥ to AB.

Then   arc $GE =$ arc EH

and   arc $GF =$ arc HF.   Case I.

∴ by addition, arc $EGF =$ arc EHF.

Q. E. D.

Proposition XII. Theorem.

244. *Through three points not in a straight line, one circumference, and only one, can be drawn.*

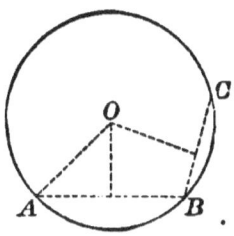

Let A, B, C be three points not in a straight line.

To prove that a circumference can be drawn through A, B, and C, and only one.

Proof. Join AB and BC.

At the middle points of AB and BC suppose ⊥s erected.

Since BC is not the prolongation of AB, these ⊥s will intersect in some point O.

The point O, being in the ⊥ to AB at its middle point, is equidistant from A and B; and being in the ⊥ to BC at its middle point, is equidistant from B and C, § 122
(*every point in the perpendicular-bisector of a straight line is equidistant from the extremities of the straight line*).

Therefore O is equidistant from A, B, and C; and a circumference described from O as a centre, with a radius OA, will pass through the three given points.

Only one circumference can be made to pass through these points. For the centre of a circumference passing through the three points must be in both perpendiculars, and hence at their intersection. As two straight lines can intersect in only one point, O is the centre of the only circumference that can pass through the three given points. Q.E.D.

245. Cor. *Two circumferences can intersect in only two points.* For, if two circumferences have three points common, they coincide and form one circumference.

Tangents.

Proposition XIII. Theorem.

246. *The tangents to a circle drawn from an exterior point are equal, and make equal angles with the line joining the point to the centre.*

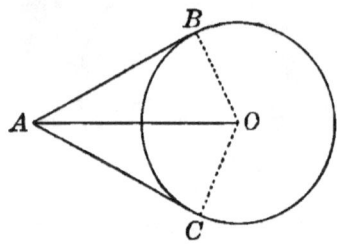

Let AB and AC be tangents from A to the circle whose centre is O, and AO the line joining A to O.

To prove $AB = AC$, and $\angle BAO = \angle CAO$.

Proof. Draw OB and OC.

AB is $\perp$ to OB, and $AC \perp$ to OC, § 240

(*a tangent to a circle is $\perp$ to the radius drawn to the point of contact*).

In the rt. $\triangle$ OAB and OAC

$OB = OC$,

(*radii of the same circle*).

$OA = OA$. Iden.

$\therefore \triangle OAB = \triangle OAC$, § 161

(*having a side and hypotenuse of the one equal to a side and hypotenuse of the other*).

$\therefore AB = AC$,

and $\angle BAO = \angle CAO$. Q. E. D.

247. Def. The line joining the centres of two circles is called the *line of centres*.

248. Def. A common tangent to two circles is called a *common exterior tangent* when it does not cut the line of centres, and a *common interior tangent* when it cuts the line of centres.

Proposition XIV. Theorem.

249. *If two circumferences intersect each other, the line of centres is perpendicular to their common chord at its middle point.*

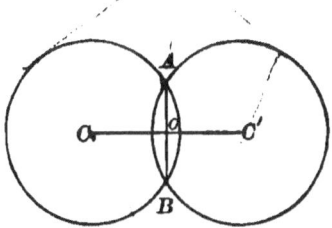

Let C and C' be the centres of two circumferences which intersect at A and B. Let AB be their common chord, and CC' join their centres.

To prove $CC' \perp$ to AB at its middle point.

Proof. A $\perp$ drawn through the middle of the chord AB passes through the centres C and C', § 233

(*a $\perp$ erected at the middle of a chord passes through the centre of the $\odot$*).

∴ the line CC', having two points in common with this $\perp$, must coincide with it.

∴ CC' is $\perp$ to AB at its middle point. Q.E.D.

Ex. 78. Describe the relative position of two circles if the line of centres:
  (i.) is greater than the sum of the radii;
  (ii.) is equal to the sum of the radii;
  (iii.) is less than the sum but greater than the difference of the radii;
  (iv.) is equal to the difference of the radii;
  (v.) is less than the difference of the radii.
  Illustrate each case by a figure.

TANGENTS. 91

Proposition XV. Theorem.

250. *If two circumferences are tangent to each other, the line of centres passes through the point of contact.*

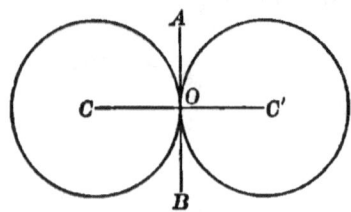

Let the two circumferences, whose centres are C and C', touch each other at O, in the straight line AB, and let CC' be the straight line joining their centres.

To prove O is in the straight line CC'.

Proof. A $\perp$ to AB, drawn through the point O, passes through the centres C and C',   § 241

(a $\perp$ to a tangent at the point of contact passes through the centre of the circle).

∴ the line CC', having two points in common with this $\perp$ must coincide with it.

∴ O is in the straight line CC'.   Q.E.D.

Ex. 79. The line joining the centre of a circle to the middle of a chord is perpendicular to the chord.

Ex. 80. The tangents drawn through the extremities of a diameter are parallel.

Ex. 81. The perimeter of an inscribed equilateral triangle is equal to half the perimeter of the circumscribed equilateral triangle.

Ex. 82. The sum of two opposite sides of a circumscribed quadrilateral is equal to the sum of the other two sides.

Measurement.

251. To *measure* a quantity of any kind is to find how *many times* it contains another known quantity of the *same kind*.

Thus, to measure a line is to find how many times it contains another known line, called the *linear unit*.

The *number* which expresses how many times a quantity contains the unit-quantity, is called the *numerical measure* of that quantity; as, 5 in 5 yards.

252. The magnitude of a quantity is always *relative* to the magnitude of another quantity of the *same kind*. No quantity is great or small except by comparison. This relative magnitude is called their *ratio*, and is expressed by the indicated quotient of their numerical measures when the same unit of measure is applied to both.

The ratio of a to b is written $\frac{a}{b}$, or $a:b$.

253. Two quantities that can be expressed in integers in terms of a common unit are said to be *commensurable*. The common unit is called a *common measure*, and each quantity is called a *multiple* of this common measure.

Thus, a common measure of $2\frac{1}{2}$ feet and $3\frac{2}{3}$ feet is $\frac{1}{6}$ of a foot, which is contained 15 times in $2\frac{1}{2}$ feet, and 22 times in $3\frac{2}{3}$ feet. Hence, $2\frac{1}{2}$ feet and $3\frac{2}{3}$ feet are multiples of $\frac{1}{6}$ of a foot, $2\frac{1}{2}$ feet being obtained by taking $\frac{1}{6}$ of a foot 15 times, and $3\frac{2}{3}$ feet by taking $\frac{1}{6}$ of a foot 22 times.

254. When two quantities are *incommensurable*, that is, have no common unit in terms of which *both* quantities can be expressed in *integers*, it is impossible to find a fraction that will indicate the exact value of the ratio of the given quantities. It is possible, however, by taking the unit sufficiently small, to find a fraction that shall differ from the true value of the ratio by as little as we please.

Thus, suppose a and b to denote two lines, such that

a———————— $\dfrac{a}{b} = \sqrt{2}.$
b————

Now $\sqrt{2} = 1.41421356....$, a value greater than 1.414213, but less than 1.414214.

If, then, a *millionth part* of b be taken as the unit, the value of the ratio $\dfrac{a}{b}$ lies between $\dfrac{1414213}{1000000}$ and $\dfrac{1414214}{1000000}$, and therefore differs from either of these fractions by less than $\dfrac{1}{1000000}$.

By carrying the decimal farther, a fraction may be found that will differ from the true value of the ratio by less than a *billionth, a trillionth, or any other assigned value whatever.*

Expressed generally, when a and b are incommensurable, and b is divided into any integral number (n) of equal parts, if one of these parts is contained in a more than m times, but less than $m+1$ times, then

$$\dfrac{a}{b} > \dfrac{m}{n}, \text{ but } < \dfrac{m+1}{n};$$

that is, the value of $\dfrac{a}{b}$ lies between $\dfrac{m}{n}$ and $\dfrac{m+1}{n}$.

The error, therefore, in taking either of these values for $\dfrac{a}{b}$ is less than $\dfrac{1}{n}$. But by *increasing n indefinitely*, $\dfrac{1}{n}$ can be made *to decrease indefinitely*, and to become *less than any assigned value, however small*, though it cannot be made *absolutely equal to zero.*

Hence, the ratio of two incommensurable quantities cannot be expressed *exactly* by figures, but it may be expressed *approximately* within any assigned measure of precision.

255. The ratio of two incommensurable quantities is called an *incommensurable ratio;* and is *a fixed value* toward which its successive approximate values constantly tend.

256. Theorem. *Two incommensurable ratios are equal if, when the unit of measure is indefinitely diminished, their approximate values constantly remain equal.*

Let $a:b$ and $a':b'$ be two incommensurable ratios whose true values lie between the approximate values $\dfrac{m}{n}$ and $\dfrac{m+1}{n}$, when the unit of measure is indefinitely diminished. Then they cannot differ so much as $\dfrac{1}{n}$.

Now the difference (if any) between the fixed values $a:b$ and $a':b'$, is a *fixed value*. Let d denote this difference.

Then $$d < \dfrac{1}{n}.$$

But if d has *any* value, *however small*, $\dfrac{1}{n}$, which by hypothesis can be indefinitely diminished, can be made less than d.

Therefore d cannot have any value; that is, $d = 0$, and there is no difference between the ratios $a:b$ and $a':b'$; therefore $a:b = a':b'$.

The Theory of Limits.

257. When a quantity is regarded as having a *fixed* value throughout the same discussion, it is called a *constant;* but when it is regarded, under the conditions imposed upon it, as having *different successive* values, it is called a *variable.*

When it can be shown that the value of a variable, measured at a series of definite intervals, can by continuing the series be made to differ from a given constant by less than any assigned quantity, however small, but cannot be made absolutely equal to the constant, that constant is called the *limit* of the variable, and the variable is said to *approach indefinitely to its limit.*

If the variable is increasing, its limit is called a *superior* limit; if decreasing, an *inferior* limit.

THEORY OF LIMITS. 95

Suppose a point to move from A toward B, under the conditions that the first second it shall move one-half the distance from A to B, that is, to M; the next second, one-half the remaining distance, that is, to M'; the next second, one-half the remaining distance, that is, to M''; and so on indefinitely.

Then it is evident that the moving point *may approach as near to B as we please, but will never arrive at B.* For, however near it may be to B at any instant, the next second it will pass over one-half the interval still remaining; it must, therefore, approach nearer to B, since *half* the interval still remaining is *some* distance, but will not reach B, since *half* the interval still remaining is not the *whole* distance.

Hence, the distance from A to the moving point is an increasing variable, which indefinitely approaches the constant AB as its *limit;* and the distance from the moving point to B is a decreasing variable, which indefinitely approaches the constant zero as its *limit.*

If the length of AB is two inches, and the variable is denoted by x, and the difference between the variable and its limit, by v:

after one second, $\quad x = 1, \quad\quad\quad v = 1;$
after two seconds, $\quad x = 1 + \frac{1}{2}, \quad\quad v = \frac{1}{2};$
after three seconds, $\quad x = 1 + \frac{1}{2} + \frac{1}{4}, \quad v = \frac{1}{4};$
after four seconds, $\quad x = 1 + \frac{1}{2} + \frac{1}{4} + \frac{1}{8}, \ v = \frac{1}{8};$
and so on indefinitely.

Now the sum of the series $1 + \frac{1}{2} + \frac{1}{4} + \frac{1}{8}$, etc., is less than 2; but by taking a great number of terms, the sum can be made to differ from 2 by as little as we please. Hence 2 is the limit of the sum of the series, when the number of the terms is increased indefinitely; and 0 is the limit of the difference between this variable sum and 2.

Consider the repetend 0.33333....., which may be written

$$\tfrac{3}{10} + \tfrac{3}{100} + \tfrac{3}{1000} + \tfrac{3}{10000} + \cdots$$

However great the number of terms of this series we take, the sum of these terms will be less than $\tfrac{1}{3}$; but the more terms we take the nearer does the sum approach $\tfrac{1}{3}$. Hence the sum of the series, as the number of terms is increased, approaches indefinitely the constant $\tfrac{1}{3}$ as a limit.

258. In the right triangle ACB, if the vertex A approaches indefinitely the base BC, the angle B diminishes, and approaches zero indefinitely; if the vertex A moves away from the base indefinitely, the angle B increases and approaches a right angle indefinitely; but B cannot become zero or a right angle, so long as ACB is a triangle; for if B becomes zero, the triangle becomes the straight line BC, and if B becomes a right angle, the triangle becomes two parallel lines AC and AB perpendicular to BC. Hence the value of B must lie between 0° and 90° as limits.

259. Again, suppose a square $ABCD$ inscribed in a circle, and E, F, H, K the middle points of the arcs subtended by the sides of the square. If we draw the straight lines AE, EB, BF, etc., we shall have an inscribed polygon of double the number of sides of the square.

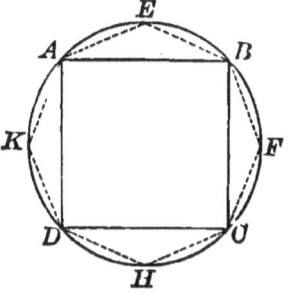

The length of the perimeter of this polygon, represented by the dotted lines, is greater than that of the square, since two sides replace each side of the square and form with it a triangle, and two sides of a triangle are together greater than the third side; but less than the length of the circumference, for it is made up of straight lines, each one of which is less than the part of the circumference between its extremities.

By continually repeating the process of doubling the number of sides of each resulting inscribed figure, the length of the perimeter will increase with the increase of the number of sides; but it cannot become equal to the length of the circumference, for the perimeter will continue to be made up of straight lines, each one of which is less than the part of the circumference between its extremities.

The length of the circumference is therefore the *limit* of the length of the perimeter as the number of sides of the inscribed figure is indefinitely increased.

260. Theorem. *If two variables are constantly equal and each approaches a limit, their limits are equal.*

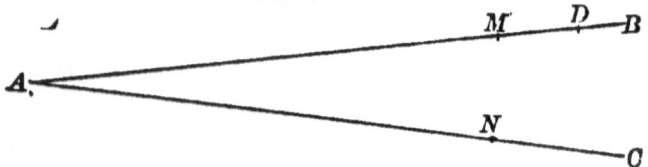

Let AM and AN be two variables which are constantly equal and which approach indefinitely AB and AC respectively as limits.

To prove $\qquad AB = AC.$

Proof. If possible, suppose $AB > AC$, and take $AD = AC$.

Then the variable AM may assume values between AD and AB, while the variable AN must always be less than AD. But this is contrary to the hypothesis that the variables should continue equal.

$\therefore AB$ cannot be $> AC.$

In the same way it may be proved that AC cannot be $> AB$.

$\therefore AB$ and AC are two values neither of which is greater than the other.

Hence $AB = AC.$

Q. E. D.

98 PLANE GEOMETRY. — BOOK II.

MEASURE OF ANGLES.

PROPOSITION XVI. THEOREM.

261. *In the same circle, or equal circles, two angles at the centre have the same ratio as their intercepted arcs.*

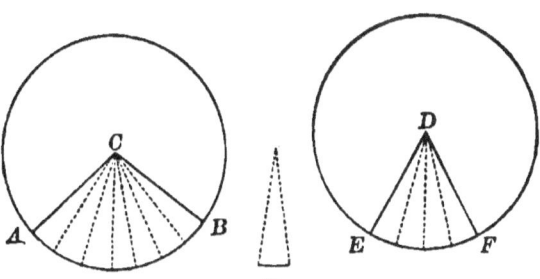

CASE I. *When the arcs are commensurable.*

In the circles whose centres are C and D, let ACB and EDF be the angles, AB and EF the intercepted arcs.

To prove $\dfrac{\angle ACB}{\angle EDF} = \dfrac{\text{arc } AB}{\text{arc } EF}$.

Proof. Let m be a common measure of AB and EF.

Suppose m to be contained in AB seven times, and in EF four times.

Then $\dfrac{\text{arc } AB}{\text{arc } EF} = \dfrac{7}{4}.$ (1)

At the several points of division on AB and EF draw radii. These radii will divide $\angle ACB$ into seven parts, and $\angle EDF$ into four parts, equal each to each, § 229
(*in the same ⊙, or equal ⊙, equal arcs subtend equal ⊿ at the centre*).

$\therefore \dfrac{\angle ACB}{\angle EDF} = \dfrac{7}{4}.$ (2)

From (1) and (2),

$\dfrac{\angle ACB}{\angle EDF} = \dfrac{\text{arc } AB}{\text{arc } EF}$ **Ax. 1**

MEASURE OF ANGLES.

CASE II. *When the arcs are incommensurable.*

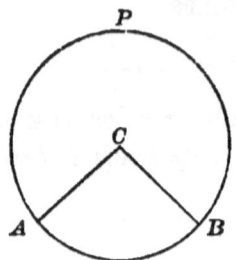 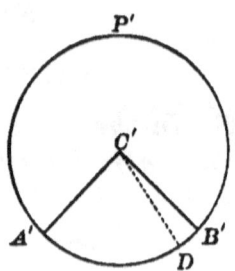

In the equal circles ABP and $A'B'P'$ let the angles ACB and $A'C'B'$ intercept the incommensurable arcs AB and $A'B'$.

To prove
$$\frac{\angle ACB}{\angle A'C'B'} = \frac{\text{arc } AB}{\text{arc } A'B'}.$$

Proof. Divide AB into any number of equal parts, and apply one of these parts as a unit of measure to $A'B'$ as many times as it will be contained in $A'B'$.

Since AB and $A'B'$ are incommensurable, a certain number of these parts will extend from A' to some point, as D, leaving a remainder DB' less than one of these parts.

Draw $C'D$.

Since AB and $A'D$ are commensurable,

$$\frac{\angle ACB}{\angle A'C'D} = \frac{\text{arc } AB}{\text{arc } A'D}. \qquad \text{Case I.}$$

If the unit of measure is indefinitely diminished, these ratios continue equal, and approach indefinitely the limiting ratios

$$\frac{\angle ACB}{\angle A'C'B'} \quad \text{and} \quad \frac{\text{arc } AB}{\text{arc } A'B'}.$$

Therefore
$$\frac{\angle ACB}{\angle A'C'B'} = \frac{\text{arc } AB}{\text{arc } A'B'}. \qquad \S\ 260$$

(*If two variables are constantly equal, and each approaches a limit, their limits are equal.*)

Q. E. D.

100   PLANE GEOMETRY. — BOOK II.

262. The circumference, like the angular magnitude about a point, is divided into 360 equal parts, called *degrees*. The arc-degree is subdivided into 60 equal parts, called *minutes;* and the minute into 60 equal parts, called *seconds.*

Since an angle at the centre has the same number of angle-degrees, minutes, and seconds as the intercepted arc has of arc-degrees, minutes, and seconds, we say: *An angle at the centre is measured by its intercepted arc;* meaning, An angle at the centre is such a part of the whole angular magnitude about the centre as its intercepted arc is of the whole circumference.

PROPOSITION XVII. THEOREM.

263. *An inscribed angle is measured by one-half the arc intercepted between its sides.*

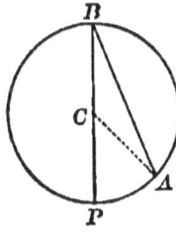
Fig. 1.
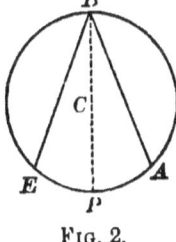
Fig. 2.
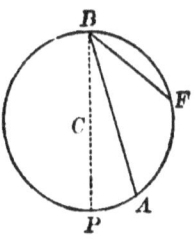
Fig. 3.

CASE I. *When one side of the angle is a diameter.*

In the circle PAB (Fig. 1), let the centre C be in one of the sides of the inscribed angle B.

To prove $\angle B$ is measured by $\tfrac{1}{2}$ arc PA.

Proof.   Draw CA.

Radius CA = radius CB.

$\therefore \angle B = \angle A$,   § 154

(*being opposite equal sides of the* △ *CAB*).

But $\angle PCA = \angle B + \angle A$,   § 145

(*the exterior* ∠ *of a* △ *is equal to the sum of the two opposite interior* ▲).

$\therefore \angle PCA = 2 \angle B$.

But $\angle PCA$ is measured by PA,   § 262

(*the* ∠ *at the centre is measured by the intercepted arc*).

$\therefore \angle B$ is measured by $\tfrac{1}{2} PA$.

MEASURE OF ANGLES. 101

Case II. *When the centre is within the angle.*

In the circle BAE (Fig. 2), let the centre C fall within the angle EBA.

To prove ∠ EBA is measured by ½ arc EA.
Proof.   Draw the diameter BCP.
            ∠ PBA is measured by ½ arc PA,   Case I.
            ∠ PBE is measured by ½ arc PE,   Case I.
∴ ∠ PBA + ∠ PBE is measured by ½ (arc PA + arc PE),
    or ∠ EBA is measured by ½ arc EA.

Case III. *When the centre is without the angle.*

In the circle BFP (Fig. 3), let the centre C fall without the angle ABF.

To prove ∠ ABF is measured by ½ arc AF.
Proof.   Draw the diameter BCP.
            ∠ PBF is measured by ½ arc PF,   Case I.
            ∠ PBA is measured by ½ arc PA.   Case I.
∴ ∠ PBF − ∠ PBA is measured by ½ (arc PF − arc PA),
    or ∠ ABF is measured by ½ arc AF.   Q.E.D.

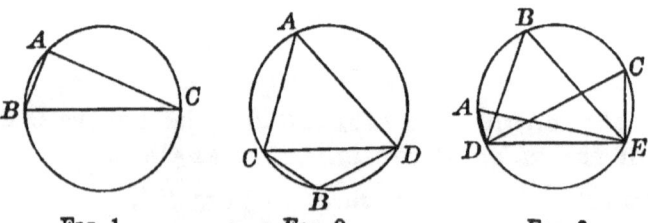

Fig. 1.   Fig. 2.   Fig. 3.

264. Cor. 1. *An angle inscribed in a semicircle is a right angle.* For it is measured by one-half a semi-circumference.

265. Cor. 2. *An angle inscribed in a segment greater than a semicircle is an acute angle.* For it is measured by an arc less than half a semi-circumference; as, ∠ CAD. Fig. 2.

266. Cor. 3. *An angle inscribed in a segment less than a semicircle is an obtuse angle.* For it is measured by an arc greater than half a semi-circumference; as, ∠ CBD. Fig. 2.

267. Cor. 4. *All angles inscribed in the same segment are equal.* For they are measured by half the same arc. Fig. 3.

PROPOSITION XVIII. THEOREM.

268. *An angle formed by two chords intersecting within the circumference is measured by one-half the sum of the intercepted arcs.*

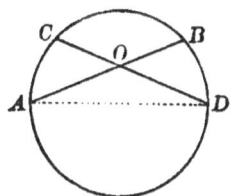

Let the angle AOC be formed by the chords AB and CD.

To prove $\angle AOC$ is measured by $\frac{1}{2}(AC+BD)$.

Proof.   Draw AD.

$$\angle COA = \angle D + \angle A, \qquad \S 145$$

(*the exterior $\angle$ of a $\triangle$ is equal to the sum of the two opposite interior $\angle$s*).

But $\angle D$ is measured by $\frac{1}{2}$ arc AC,   § 263

and $\angle A$ is measured by $\frac{1}{2}$ arc BD,

(*an inscribed $\angle$ is measured by $\frac{1}{2}$ the intercepted arc*).

∴ $\angle COA$ is measured by $\frac{1}{2}(AC+BD)$.

Q. E. D.

Ex. 83. The opposite angles of an inscribed quadrilateral are supplements of each other.

Ex. 84. If through a point within a circle two perpendicular chords are drawn, the sum of the opposite arcs which they intercept is equal to a semi-circumference.

Ex. 85. The line joining the centre of the square described upon the hypotenuse of a rt. $\triangle$, to the vertex of the rt. $\angle$, bisects the right angle.

HINT. Describe a circle upon the hypotenuse as diameter.

MEASURE OF ANGLES.   103

Proposition XIX.   Theorem.

269. *An angle formed by a tangent and a chord is measured by one-half the intercepted arc.*

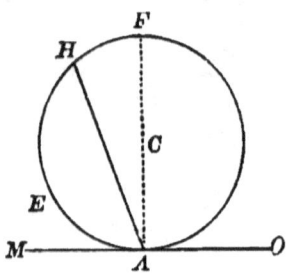

Let MAH be the angle formed by the tangent MO and chord AH.

To prove   ∠ *MAH is measured by* ½ *arc AEH.*

Proof.   Draw the diameter *ACF*.

∠ *MAF* is a rt. ∠,   § 240

(*the radius drawn to a tangent at the point of contact is* ⊥ *to it*).

∠ *MAF* being a rt. ∠, is measured by ½ the semi-circumference *AEF*.

But   ∠ *HAF* is measured by ½ arc *HF*,   § 263

(*an inscribed* ∠ *is measured by* ½ *the intercepted arc*).

∴ ∠ *MAF* − ∠ *HAF* is measured by ½ (*AEF* − *HF*);

or ∠ *MAH* is measured by ½ *AEH*.

Q. E. D.

Ex. 86. If two circles touch each other and two secants are drawn through the point of contact, the chords joining their extremities are parallel. Hint. Draw the common tangent.

104 PLANE GEOMETRY. — BOOK II.

PROPOSITION XX. THEOREM.

270. *An angle formed by two secants, two tangents, or a tangent and a secant, intersecting without the circumference, is measured by one-half the difference of the intercepted arcs.*

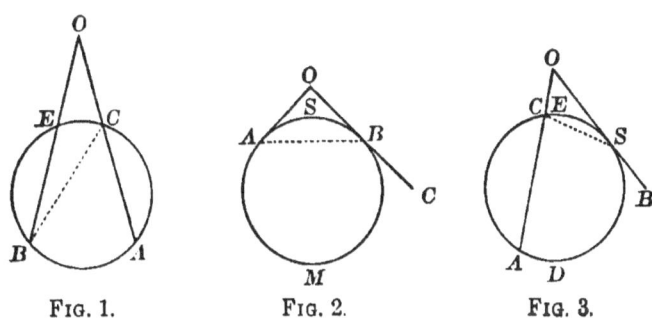

FIG. 1.　　FIG. 2.　　FIG. 3.

CASE I. *Angle formed by two secants.*

Let the angle O (Fig. 1) be formed by the two secants OA and OB.

To prove $\angle O$ is measured by $\frac{1}{2}(AB - EC)$.

Proof. Draw CB.

$$\angle ACB = \angle O + \angle B, \qquad \S\,145$$

(*the exterior $\angle$ of a $\triangle$ is equal to the sum of the two opposite interior $\angle$s*).

By taking away $\angle B$ from both sides,

$$\angle O = \angle ACB - \angle B.$$

But　　$\angle ACB$ is measured by $\frac{1}{2} AB$, 　　§ 263

and　　$\angle B$ is measured by $\frac{1}{2} CE$,

(*an inscribed $\angle$ is measured by $\frac{1}{2}$ the intercepted arc*).

∴ $\angle O$ is measured by $\frac{1}{2}(AB - CE)$.

MEASURE OF ANGLES.

CASE II. *Angle formed by two tangents.*

Let the angle O (Fig. 2) be formed by the two tangents OA and OB.

To prove $\angle O$ is measured by $\frac{1}{2}(AMB - ASB)$.

Proof. Draw AB.

$$\angle ABC = \angle O + \angle OAB, \qquad \S\ 145$$

(*the exterior $\angle$ of a $\triangle$ is equal to the sum of the two opposite interior $\angle$s*).

By taking away $\angle OAB$ from both sides,

$$\angle O = \angle ABC - \angle OAB.$$

But $\angle ABC$ is measured by $\frac{1}{2} AMB$, § 269

and $\angle OAB$ is measured by $\frac{1}{2} ASB$,

(*an $\angle$ formed by a tangent and a chord is measured by $\frac{1}{2}$ the intercepted arc*).

$\therefore \angle O$ is measured by $\frac{1}{2}(AMB - ASB)$.

CASE III. *Angle formed by a tangent and a secant.*

Let the angle O (Fig. 3) be formed by the tangent OB and the secant OA.

To prove $\angle O$ is measured by $\frac{1}{2}(ADS - CES)$.

Proof. Draw CS.

$$\angle ACS = \angle O + \angle CSO, \qquad \S\ 145$$

(*the exterior $\angle$ of a $\triangle$ is equal to the sum of the two opposite interior $\angle$s*).

By taking away $\angle CSO$ from both sides,

$$\angle O = \angle ACS - \angle CSO.$$

But $\angle ACS$ is measured by $\frac{1}{2} ADS$, § 263
  (*being an inscribed $\angle$*),

and $\angle CSO$ is measured by $\frac{1}{2} CES$, § 269
  (*being an $\angle$ formed by a tangent and a chord*).

$\therefore \angle O$ is measured by $\frac{1}{2}(ADS - CES)$.

Q. E. D.

PROBLEMS OF CONSTRUCTION.

PROPOSITION XXI. PROBLEM.

271. *At a given point in a straight line, to erect a perpendicular to that line.*

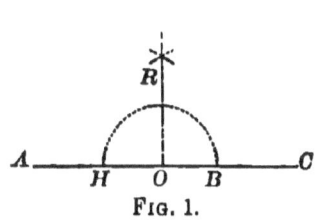
FIG. 1.

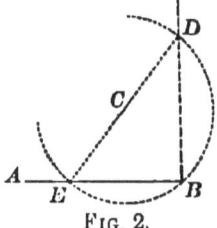
FIG. 2.

I. **Let O be the given point in AC. (Fig. 1).**

To erect a ⊥ to the line *AC* at the point *O*.

Construction. From *O* as a centre, with any radius *OB*, describe an arc intersecting *AC* in two points *H* and *B*.

From *H* and *B* as centres, with equal radii greater than *OB*, describe two arcs intersecting at *R*. Join *OR*.

Then the line *OR* is the ⊥ required.

Proof. Since *O* and *R* are two points at equal distances from *H* and *B*, they determine the position of a perpendicular to the line *HB* at its middle point *O*. § 123

II. *When the given point is at the end of the line.*

Let B be the given point. (Fig. 2).

To erect a ⊥ to the line *AB* at *B*.

Construction. Take any point *C* without *AB*; and from *C* as a centre, with the distance *CB* as a radius, describe an arc intersecting *AB* at *E*.

Draw *EC*, and prolong it to meet the arc again at *D*.

Join *BD*, and *BD* is the ⊥ required.

Proof. The ∠ *B* is inscribed in a semicircle, and is therefore a right angle. § 264

Hence *BD* is ⊥ to *AB*.

Q. E. F.

Proposition XXII. Problem.

272. *From a point without a straight line, to let fall a perpendicular upon that line.*

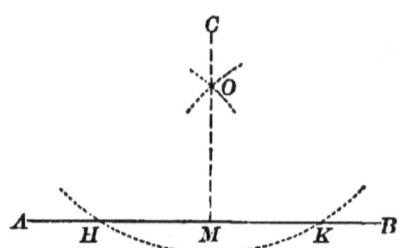

Let *AB* be the given straight line, and *C* the given point without the line.

To let fall a ⊥ to the line AB from the point C.

Construction. From *C* as a centre, with a radius sufficiently great, describe an arc cutting *AB* in two points, *H* and *K*.

From *H* and *K* as centres, with equal radii greater than ½ *HK*,

describe two arcs intersecting at *O*.

Draw *CO*,

and produce it to meet *AB* at *M*.

CM is the ⊥ required.

Proof. Since *C* and *O* are two points equidistant from *H* and *K*, they determine a ⊥ to *HK* at its middle point. § 123

Q. E. F.

Note. *Given* lines of the figures are full lines, *resulting* lines are long-dotted, and *auxiliary* lines are short-dotted.

Proposition XXIII. Problem.

273. *To bisect a given straight line.*

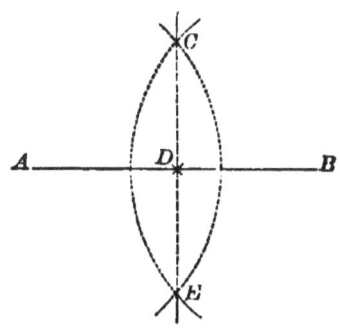

Let AB be the given straight line.

To bisect the line AB.

Construction. From A and B as centres, with equal radii greater than $\frac{1}{2} AB$, describe arcs intersecting at C and E.

Join CE.

Then the line CE bisects AB.

Proof. C and E are two points equidistant from A and B. Hence they determine a $\perp$ to the middle point of AB. § 123

Q. E. F.

Ex. 87. To find in a given line a point X which shall be equidistant from two given points.

Ex. 88. To find a point X which shall be equidistant from two given points and at a given distance from a third given point.

Ex. 89. To find a point X which shall be at given distances from two given points.

Ex. 90. To find a point X which shall be equidistant from three given points.

Proposition XXIV. Problem.

274. *To bisect a given arc.*

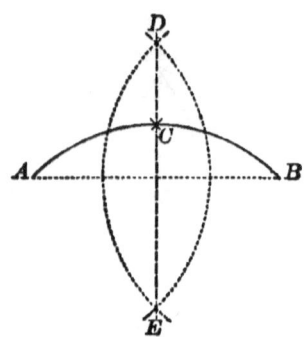

Let ACB be the given arc.

To bisect the arc ACB.

Construction.   Draw the chord AB.

From A and B as centres, with equal radii greater than $\frac{1}{2}AB$, describe arcs intersecting at D and E,

Draw DE.

DE bisects the arc ACB.

Proof. Since D and E are two points equidistant from A and B, they determine a ⊥ erected at the middle of chord AB. § 123

And a ⊥ erected at the middle of a chord passes through the centre of the ⊙, and bisects the arc of the chord.   § 234

Q. E. F.

Ex. 91. To construct a circle having a given radius and passing through two given points.

Ex. 92. To construct a circle having its centre in a given line and passing through two given points.

PROPOSITION XXV. PROBLEM.

275. *To bisect a given angle.*

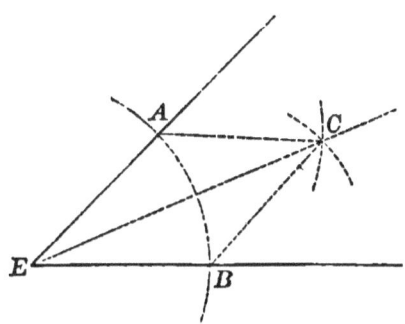

Let AEB be the given angle.

To bisect ∠ AEB.

Construction. From E as a centre, with any radius, as EA, describe an arc cutting the sides of the ∠ E at A and B.

From A and B as centres, with equal radii greater than one-half the distance from A to B, describe two arcs intersecting at C.

Join EC, AC, and BC.

EC bisects the ∠ E.

Proof. In the △ AEC and BEC

	$AE = BE$, and $AC = BC$,	Cons.
and	$EC = EC$.	Iden.
	∴ △ $AEC = $ △ BEC,	§ 160

(*having three sides equal each to each*).

∴ ∠ $AEC = $ ∠ BEC.

Q. E. F.

Ex. 93. To divide a right angle into three equal parts.

Ex. 94. To construct an equilateral triangle, having given one side.

Ex. 95. To find a point X which shall be equidistant from two given points and also equidistant from two given intersecting lines.

Proposition XXVI. Problem.

276. *At a given point in a given straight line, to construct an angle equal to a given angle.*

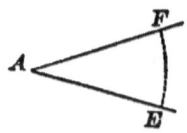 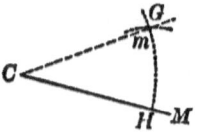

Let *C* be the given point in the given line *CM*, and *A* the given angle.

To construct an ∠ at *C* equal to the ∠ *A*.

Construction. From *A* as a centre, with any radius, as *AE*, describe an arc cutting the sides of the ∠ *A* at *E* and *F*.

From *C* as a centre, with a radius equal to *AE*,

describe an arc cutting *CM* at *H*.

From *H* as a centre, with a radius equal to the distance *EF*,

describe an arc intersecting the arc *HG* at *m*.

Draw *Cm*, and *HCm* is the required angle.

Proof. The chords *EF* and *Hm* are equal. Cons.

∴ arc *EF* = arc *Hm*, § 230

(*in equal ⊙ equal chords subtend equal arcs*).

∴ ∠ *C* = ∠ *A*, § 229

(*in equal ⊙ equal arcs subtend equal ∠ at the centre*). Q.E.F.

Ex. 96. In a triangle *ABC*, draw *DE* parallel to the base *BC*, cutting the sides of the triangle in *D* and *E*, so that *DE* shall equal *DB* + *EC*.

Ex. 97. If an interior point *O* of a triangle *ABC* is joined to the vertices *B* and *C*, the angle *BOC* is greater than the angle *BAC* of the triangle.

Proposition XXVII. Problem.

277. *Two angles of a triangle being given, to find the third angle.*

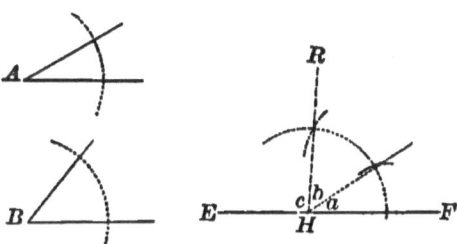

Let A and B be the two given angles of a triangle.

To find the third ∠ of the △.

Construction. Take any straight line, as EF, and at any point, as H,

construct ∠ a equal to ∠ A, § 276

and ∠ b equal to ∠ B.

Then ∠ c is the ∠ required.

Proof. Since the sum of the three ∠s of a △ = 2 rt. ∠s, § 138

and the sum of the three ∠s a, b, and c, = 2 rt. ∠s; § 92

and since two ∠s of the △ are equal to the ∠s a and b,

the third ∠ of the △ will be equal to the ∠ c. Ax. 3.

Q. E. F.

Ex. 98. In a triangle ABC, given angles A and B, equal respectively to 37° 13′ 32″ and 41° 17′ 56″. Find the value of angle C.

Proposition XXVIII. Problem.

278. *Through a given point, to draw a straight line parallel to a given straight line.*

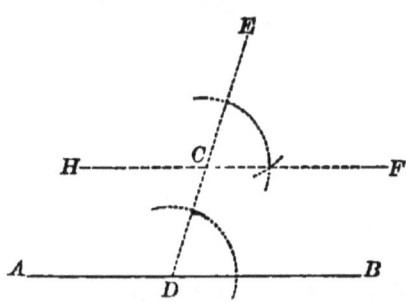

Let AB be the given line, and C the given point.

To draw through the point C a line parallel to the line AB.

Construction. Draw DCE, making the $\angle EDB$.

At the point C construct $\angle ECF = \angle EDB$. § 276

Then the line FCH is ∥ to AB.

Proof. $\angle ECF = \angle EDB$. Cons.

∴ HF is ∥ to AB, § 108

(*when two straight lines, lying in the same plane, are cut by a third straight line, if the ext.-int. ∠ are equal, the lines are parallel*).

Q. E. F.

Ex. 99. To find a point X equidistant from two given points and also equidistant from two given parallel lines.

Ex. 100. To find a point X equidistant from two given intersecting lines and also equidistant from two given parallels.

Proposition XXIX. Problem.

279. *To divide a given straight line into equal parts.*

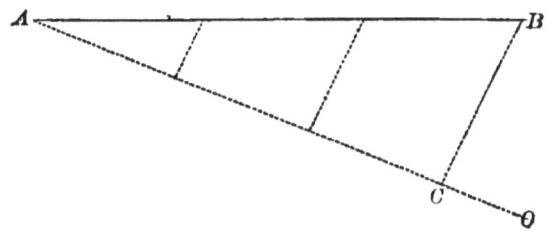

Let AB be the given straight line.

To divide AB into equal parts.

Construction. From A draw the line AO.

Take any convenient length, and apply it to AO as many times as the line AB is to be divided into parts.

From the last point thus found on AO, as C, draw CB.

Through the several points of division on AO draw lines ∥ to CB, and these lines divide AB into equal parts.

Proof. Since AC is divided into equal parts, AB is also, § 187

(*if three or more ∥s intercept equal parts on any transversal, they intercept equal parts on every transversal*).

Q. E. F.

Ex. 101. To divide a line into four equal parts by two different methods.

Ex. 102. To find a point X in one side of a given triangle and equidistant from the other two sides.

Ex. 103. Through a given point to draw a line which shall make equal angles with the two sides of a given angle.

Proposition XXX. Problem.

280. *Two sides and the included angle of a triangle being given, to construct the triangle.*

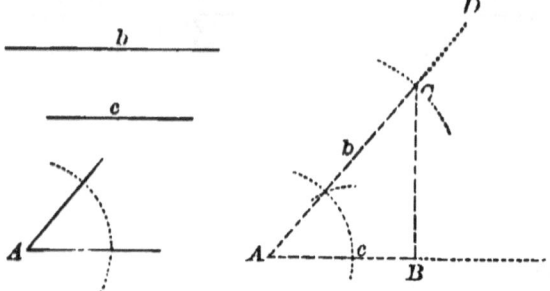

Let the two sides of the triangle be *b* and *c*, and the included angle *A*.

To construct a △ having two sides equal to *b* and *c* respectively, and the included ∠ = ∠ *A*.

Construction. Take AB equal to the side c.

At A, the extremity of AB, construct an angle equal to the given ∠ A. § 276

On AD take AC equal to b.

Draw CB.

Then △ ACB is the △ required.

Q. E. F.

Ex. 104. To construct an angle of 45°.

Ex. 105. To find a point X which shall be equidistant from two given intersecting lines and at a given distance from a given point.

Ex. 106. To draw through two sides of a triangle a line ∥ to the third side so that the part intercepted between the sides shall have a given length.

Proposition XXXI. Problem.

281. *A side and two angles of a triangle being given, to construct the triangle.*

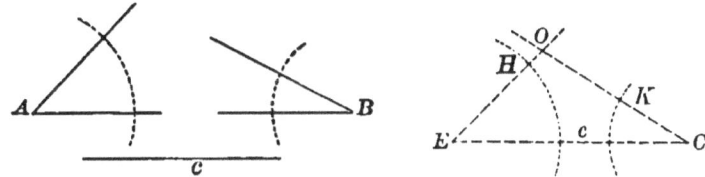

Let c be the given side, A and B the given angles.
To construct the triangle.

Construction.   Take EC equal to c.

At the point E construct the $\angle CEH$ equal to $\angle A$.   § 276

At the point C construct the $\angle ECK$ equal to $\angle B$.

Let the sides EH and CK intersect at O.

Then $\triangle COE$ is the $\triangle$ required.

Q. E. F.

Remark. If one of the given angles is opposite to the given side, find the third angle by § 277, and proceed as above.

Discussion. The problem is impossible when the two given angles are together equal to or greater than two right angles.

Ex. 107. To construct an angle of 150°.

Ex. 108. A straight railway passes two miles from a town. A place is four miles from the town and one mile from the railway. To find by construction how many places answer this description.

Ex. 109. If in a circle two equal chords intersect, the segments of one chord are equal to the segments of the other, each to each.

Ex. 110. AB is any chord and AC is tangent to a circle at A, CDE a line cutting the circumference in D and E and parallel to AB; show that the triangles ACD and EAB are mutually equiangular.

PROBLEMS. 117

Proposition XXXII. Problem.

282. *The three sides of a triangle being given, to construct the triangle.*

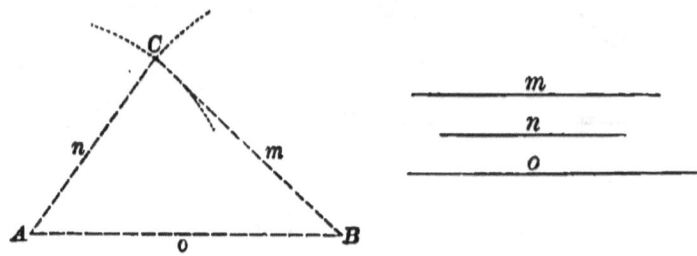

Let the three sides be *m*, *n*, and *o*.

To construct the triangle.

Construction. Draw AB equal to o.

From A as a centre, with a radius equal to n, describe an arc;

and from B as a centre, with a radius equal to m, describe an arc intersecting the former arc at C.

Draw CA and CB.

Then △ CAB is the △ required.

Q. E. F.

Discussion. The problem is impossible when one side is equal to or greater than the sum of the other two.

Ex. 111. The base, the altitude, and an angle at the base, of a triangle being given, to construct the triangle.

Ex. 112. Show that the bisectors of the angles contained by the opposite sides (produced) of an inscribed quadrilateral intersect at right angles.

Ex. 113. Given two perpendiculars, AB and CD, intersecting in O, and a straight line intersecting these perpendiculars in E and F; to construct a square, one of whose angles shall coincide with one of the right angles at O, and the vertex of the opposite angle of the square shall lie in EF. (Two solutions.)

Proposition XXXIII. Problem.

283. *Two sides of a triangle and the angle opposite one of them being given, to construct the triangle.*

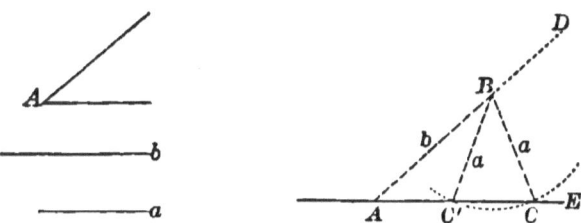

Case I. *If the side opposite the given angle is less than the other given side.*

Let b be greater than a, and A the given angle.
To construct the triangle.

Construction. Construct $\angle DAE =$ to the given $\angle A$. § 276

On AD take $AB = b$.

From B as a centre, with a radius equal to a,

describe an arc intersecting the line AE at C and C'.

Draw BC and BC'.

Then both the $\triangle ABC$ and ABC' fulfil the conditions, and hence we have two constructions. This is called the *ambiguous* case.

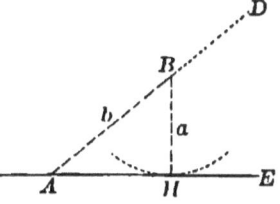

Discussion. If the side a is equal to the $\perp BH$, the arc described from B will touch AE, and there will be but one construction, the right triangle ABH.

If the given side a is less than the $\perp$ from B, the arc described from B will not intersect or touch AE, and hence the problem is impossible.

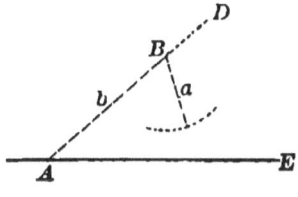

If the ∠ A is right or obtuse, the problem is impossible; for the side opposite a right or obtuse angle is the greatest side. § 159

CASE II. *If a is equal to b.*

If the ∠ A is acute, and $a = b$, the arc described from B as a centre, and with a radius equal to a, will cut the line AE at the points A and C. There is therefore but one solution: the isosceles △ ABC.

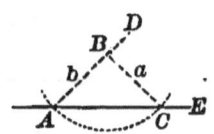

Discussion. If the ∠ A is right or obtuse, the problem is impossible; for equal sides of a △ have equal ⦞ opposite them, and a △ cannot have two right ⦞ or two obtuse ⦞.

CASE III. *If a is greater than b.*

If the given ∠ A is acute, the arc described from B will cut the line ED on opposite sides of A, at C and C'. The △ ABC answers the required conditions, but the △ ABC' does not, for it does not contain the acute ∠ A. There is then only one solution; namely, the △ ABC.

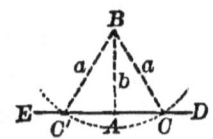

If the ∠ A is right, the arc described from B cuts the line ED on opposite sides of A, and we have two *equal* right ⦞ which fulfil the required conditions.

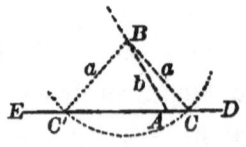

If the ∠ A is obtuse, the arc described from B cuts the line ED on opposite sides of A, at the points C and C'. The △ ABC answers the required conditions, but the △ ABC' does not, for it does not contain the obtuse ∠ A. There is then only one solution; namely, the △ ABC.

Q. E. F.

PROPOSITION XXXIV. PROBLEM.

284. *Two sides and an included angle of a parallelogram being given, to construct the parallelogram.*

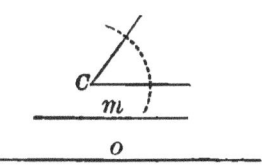 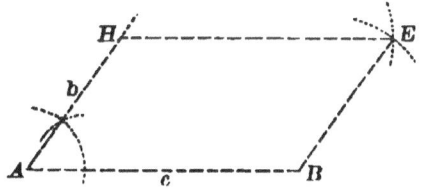

Let *m* and *o* be the two sides, and *C* the included angle.

To construct a parallelogram.

Construction. Draw AB equal to *o*.

At A construct the $\angle A$ equal to $\angle C$,   § 276

and take AH equal to *m*.

From H as a centre, with a radius equal to *o*, describe an arc.

From B as a centre, with a radius equal to *m*,

describe an arc, intersecting the former arc at E.

Draw EH and EB.

The quadrilateral $ABEH$ is the □ required.

Proof. $AB = HE$,   Cons.

$AH = BE$.   Cons.

∴ the figure $ABEH$ is a □,   § 183

(*having its opposite sides equal*).

Q. E. F.

Proposition XXXV. Problem.

285. *To circumscribe a circle about a given triangle.*

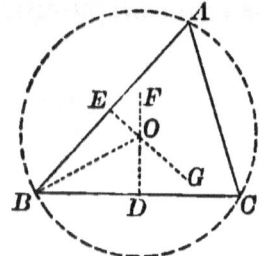

Let ABC be the given triangle.
To circumscribe a circle about ABC.

Construction.   Bisect AB and BC.   § 273

At the points of bisection erect ⊥s.   § 271

Since BC is not the prolongation of AB, these ⊥s will intersect at some point O.

From O, with a radius equal to OB, describe a circle.

⊙ ABC is the ⊙ required.

Proof.   The point O is equidistant from A and B,

and also is equidistant from B and C,   § 122

(*every point in the ⊥ erected at the middle of a straight line is equidistant from the extremities of that line*).

∴ the point O is equidistant from A, B, and C,

and a ⊙ described from O as a centre, with a radius equal to OB, will pass through the vertices A, B, and C.   Q.E.F.

286. Scholium. The same construction serves to describe a circumference which shall pass through the three points not in the same straight line; also to find the centre of a given circle or of a given arc,

PROPOSITION XXXVI. PROBLEM.

287. *Through a given point, to draw a tangent to a given circle.*

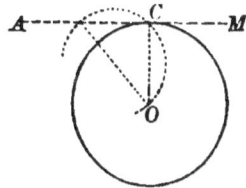
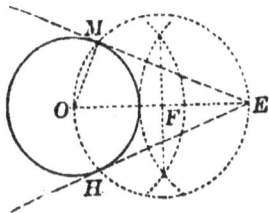

CASE I. *When the given point is on the circle.*
Let C be the given point on the circle.
To draw a tangent to the circle at C.

Construction. From the centre O draw the radius OC.
Through C draw $AM \perp$ to OC. § 271
Then AM is the tangent required.

Proof. A straight line $\perp$ to a radius at its extremity is tangent to the circle. § 239

CASE II. *When the given point is without the circle.*
Let O be the centre of the given circle, E the given point without the circle.
To draw a tangent to the given circle from the point E.

Construction. Join OE.

On OE as a diameter, describe a circumference intersecting the given circumference at the points M and H.
Draw OM and EM.
Then EM is the tangent required.

Proof. $\angle OME$ is a right angle, § 264
(*being inscribed in a semicircle*).
∴ EM is tangent to the circle at M. § 239
In like manner, we may prove HE tangent to the given ⊙.

Q. E. F.

PROPOSITION XXXVII. PROBLEM.

288. *To inscribe a circle in a given triangle.*

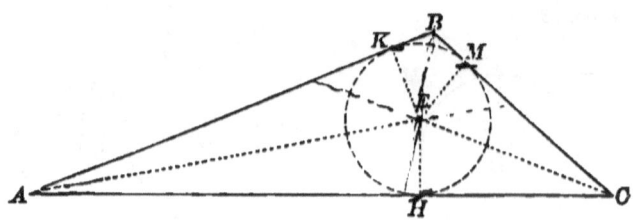

Let *ABC* be the given triangle.
To inscribe a circle in the △ *ABC*.

Construction. Bisect ∠s *A* and *C*. § 275

From *E*, the intersection of these bisectors,
draw *EH* ⊥ to the line *AC*. § 272

From *E*, with radius *EH*, describe the ⊙ *KMH*.

The ⊙ *KHM* is the ⊙ required.

Proof. Since *E* is in the bisector of the ∠ *A*, it is equidistant from the sides *AB* and *AC*; and since *E* is in the bisector of the ∠ *C*, it is equidistant from the sides *AC* and *BC*, § 162

(*every point in the bisector of an ∠ is equidistant from the sides of the ∠*).

∴ a ⊙ described from *E* as centre, with a radius equal to *EH*, will touch the sides of the △ and be inscribed in it.

Q. E. F.

289. Scholium. The intersections of the bisectors of exterior angles of a triangle, formed by producing the sides of the triangle, are the centres of three circles, each of which will touch one side of the triangle, and the two other sides produced. These three circles are called *escribed* circles.

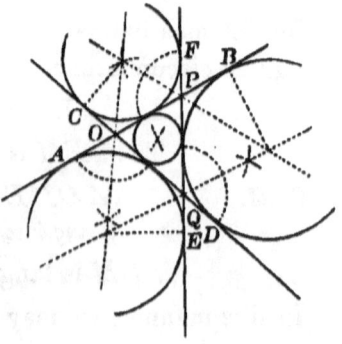

PROPOSITION XXXVIII. PROBLEM.

290. *Upon a given straight line, to describe a segment of a circle which shall contain a given angle.*

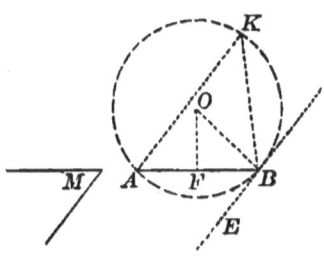

Let AB be the given line, and M the given angle.

To describe a segment upon AB which shall contain $\angle M$.

Construction. Construct $\angle ABE$ equal to $\angle M$. § 276

    Bisect the line AB by the $\perp FO$. § 273

    From the point B draw $BO \perp$ to EB. § 271

From O, the point of intersection of FO and BO, as a centre, with a radius equal to OB, describe a circumference.

    The segment AKB is the segment required.

Proof. The point O is equidistant from A and B, § 122
(*every point in a $\perp$ erected at the middle of a straight line is equidistant from the extremities of that line*).

    ∴ the circumference will pass through A.

But BE is $\perp$ to OB.   Cons.

    ∴ BE is tangent to the $\odot$, § 239
(*a straight line $\perp$ to a radius at its extremity is tangent to the $\odot$*).

    ∴ $\angle ABE$ is measured by $\tfrac{1}{2}$ arc AB, § 269
(*being an $\angle$ formed by a tangent and a chord*).

An $\angle$ inscribed in the segment AKB is measured by $\tfrac{1}{2} AB$. § 263

    ∴ segment AKB contains $\angle M$.   Ax. 1

Q. E. F.

PROPOSITION XXXIX. PROBLEM.

291. *To find the ratio of two commensurable straight lines.*

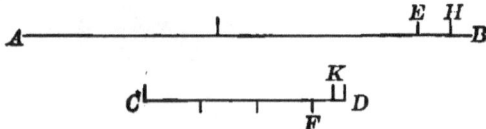

Let AB and CD be two straight lines.
To find the ratio of AB and CD.

Apply CD to AB as many times as possible.
Suppose twice, with a remainder EB.
Then apply EB to CD as many times as possible.
Suppose three times, with a remainder FD.
Then apply FD to EB as many times as possible.
Suppose once, with a remainder HB.
Then apply HB to FD as many times as possible.
Suppose once, with a remainder KD.
Then apply KD to HB as many times as possible.
Suppose KD is contained just twice in HB.

The measure of each line, referred to KD as a unit, will then be as follows:

$$HB = 2\,KD;$$
$$FD = HB + KD = 3\,KD;$$
$$EB = FD + HB = 5\,KD;$$
$$CD = 3\,EB + FD = 18\,KD;$$
$$AB = 2\,CD + EB = 41\,KD;$$
$$\therefore \frac{AB}{CD} = \frac{41\,KD}{18\,KD};$$
$$\therefore \text{the ratio } \frac{AB}{CD} = \frac{41}{18}.$$

Q. E. F.

Theorems.

114. The shortest line and the longest line which can be drawn from a given exterior point to a given circumference pass through the centre.

115. If through a point within a circle a diameter and a chord ⊥ to the diameter are drawn, the chord is the shortest cord that can be drawn through the given point.

116. In the same circle, or in equal circles, if two arcs are each greater than a semi-circumference, the greater arc subtends the *less* chord, and conversely.

117. If ABC is an inscribed equilateral triangle, and P is any point in the arc BC, then $PA = PB + PC$.

HINT. On PA take PM equal to PB, and join BM.

118. In what kinds of parallelograms can a circle be inscribed? Prove your answer.

119. The radius of the circle inscribed in an equilateral triangle is equal to one-third of the altitude of the triangle.

120. A circle can be circumscribed about a rectangle.

121. A circle can be circumscribed about an isosceles trapezoid.

122. The tangents drawn through the vertices of an inscribed rectangle enclose a rhombus.

123. The diameter of the circle inscribed in a rt. $\triangle$ is equal to the difference between the sum of the legs and the hypotenuse.

124. From a point A without a circle, a straight line AOB is drawn through the centre, and also a secant ACD, so that the part AC without the circle is equal to the radius. Prove that $\angle DAB$ equals one-third the $\angle DOB$.

125. All chords of a circle which touch an interior concentric circle are equal, and are bisected at the points of contact.

126. If two circles intersect, and a secant is drawn through each point of intersection, the chords which join the extremities of the secants are parallel. HINT. By drawing the common chord, two inscribed quadrilaterals are obtained.

127. If an equilateral triangle is inscribed in a circle, the distance of each side from the centre of the circle is equal to half the radius.

128. Through one of the points of intersection of two circles a diameter of each circle is drawn. Prove that the straight line joining the ends of the diameters passes through the other point of intersection.

129. A circle touches two sides of an angle BAC at B, C; through any point D in the arc BC a tangent is drawn, meeting AB at E and AC at F. Prove (i.) that the perimeter of the triangle AEF is constant for all positions of D in BC; (ii.) that the angle EOF is also constant.

Loci.

130. Find the locus of a point at three inches from a given point.

131. Find the locus of a point at a given distance from a given circumference.

132. Prove that the locus of the vertex of a right triangle, having a given hypotenuse as base, is the circumference described upon the given hypotenuse as diameter.

133. Prove that the locus of the vertex of a triangle, having a given base and a given angle at the vertex, is the arc which forms with the base a segment capable of containing the given angle.

134. Find the locus of the middle points of all chords of a given length that can be drawn in a given circle.

135. Find the locus of the middle points of all chords that can be drawn through a given point A in a given circumference.

136. Find the locus of the middle points of all straight lines that can be drawn from a given exterior point A to a given circumference.

137. A straight line moves so that it remains parallel to a given line, and touches at one end a given circumference. Find the locus of the other end.

138. A straight rod moves so that its ends constantly touch two fixed rods which are $\perp$ to each other. Find the locus of its middle point.

139. In a given circle let AOB be a diameter, OC any radius, CD the perpendicular from C to AB. Upon OC take $OM = CD$. Find the locus of the point M as OC turns about O.

Construction of Polygons.

To construct an equilateral $\triangle$, having given:

140. The perimeter.   **141.** The radius of the circumscribed circle.
142. The altitude.   **143.** The radius of the inscribed circle.

To construct an isosceles triangle, having given:

144. The angle at the vertex and the base.

145. The angle at the vertex and the altitude.
146. The base and the radius of the circumscribed circle.
147. The base and the radius of the inscribed circle.
148. The perimeter and the altitude.

HINTS. Let ABC be the $\triangle$ required, and EF the given perimeter. The altitude CD passes through the middle of EF, and the $\triangle$ AEC, BFC are isosceles.

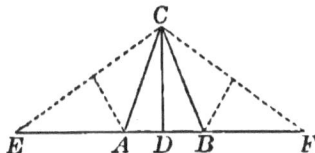

To construct a right triangle, having given:
149. The hypotenuse and one leg.
150. The hypotenuse and the altitude upon the hypotenuse.
151. One leg and the altitude upon the hypotenuse as base.
152. The median and the altitude drawn from the vertex of the rt. $\angle$.
153. The radius of the inscribed circle and one leg.
154. The radius of the inscribed circle and an acute angle.
155. An acute angle and the sum of the legs.
156. An acute angle and the difference of the legs.

To construct a triangle, having given:
157. The base, the altitude, and the $\angle$ at the vertex.
158. The base, the corresponding median, and the $\angle$ at the vertex.
159. The perimeter and the angles.
160. One side, an adjacent $\angle$, and the sum of the other sides.
161. One side, an adjacent $\angle$, and the difference of the other sides.
162. The sum of two sides and the angles.
163. One side, an adjacent $\angle$, and radius of circumscribed $\odot$.
164. The angles and the radius of the circumscribed $\odot$.
165. The angles and the radius of the inscribed $\odot$.
166. An angle, the bisector, and the altitude drawn from the vertex.
167. Two sides and the median corresponding to the other side.
168. The three medians.

To construct a square, having given:
169. The diagonal.   170. The sum of the diagonal and one side.

EXERCISES.

To construct a rectangle, having given:
171. One side and the ∠ formed by the diagonals.
172. The perimeter and the diagonal.
173. The perimeter and the ∠ of the diagonals.
174. The difference of the two adjacent sides and the ∠ of the diagonals.

To construct a rhombus, having given:
175. The two diagonals.
176. One side and the radius of the inscribed circle.
177. One angle and the radius of the inscribed circle.
178. One angle and one of the diagonals.

To construct a rhomboid, having given:
179. One side and the two diagonals.
180. The diagonals and the ∠ formed by them.
181. One side, one ∠, and one diagonal.
182. The base, the altitude, and one angle.

To construct an isosceles trapezoid, having given:
183. The bases and one angle.   184. The bases and the altitude.
185. The bases and the diagonal.
186. The bases and the radius of the circumscribed circle.

To construct a trapezoid, having given:
187. The four sides.   188. The two bases and the two diagonals.
189. The bases, one diagonal, and the ∠ formed by the diagonals.

CONSTRUCTION OF CIRCLES.

Find the locus of the centre of a circle:
190. Which has a given radius r and passes through a given point P.
191. Which has a given radius r and touches a given straight line AB.
192. Which passes through two given points P and Q.
193. Which touches a given straight line AB at a given point P.
194. Which touches each of two given parallels.
195. Which touches each of two given intersecting lines.

To construct a circle which has the radius r and which also:
196. Touches each of two intersecting lines AB and CD.
197. Touches a given line AB and a given circle K.
198. Passes through a given point P and touches a given line AB.
199. Passes through a given point P and touches a given circle K.

To construct a circle which shall:
200. Touch two given parallels and pass through a given point P.
201. Touch three given lines two of which are parallel.
202. Touch a given line AB at P and pass through a given point Q.
203. Touch a given circle at P and pass through a given point Q.
204. Touch two given lines and touch one of them at a given point P.
205. Touch a given line and touch a given circle at a point P.
206. Touch a given line AB at P and also touch a given circle.
207. To inscribe a circle in a given sector.
208. To construct within a given circle three equal circles, so that each shall touch the other two and also the given circle.
209. To describe circles about the vertices of a given triangle as centres, so that each shall touch the two others.

Construction of Straight Lines.

210. To draw a common tangent to two given circles.
211. To bisect the angle formed by two lines, without producing the lines to their point of intersection.
212. To draw a line through a given point, so that it shall form with the sides of a given angle an isosceles triangle.
213. Given a point P between the sides of an angle BAC. To draw through P a line terminated by the sides of the angle and bisected at P.
214. Given two points P, Q, and a line AB; to draw lines from P and Q which shall meet on AB and make equal angles with AB.

Hint. Make use of the point which forms with P a pair of points symmetrical with respect to AB.

215. To find the shortest path from P to Q which shall touch a line AB.
216. To draw a tangent to a given circle, so that it shall be parallel to a given straight line.

BOOK III.

PROPORTIONAL LINES AND SIMILAR POLYGONS.

The Theory of Proportion.

292. A *proportion* is an expression of equality between two equal ratios.

A proportion may be expressed in any one of the following forms:

$$\frac{a}{b} = \frac{c}{d}; \quad a:b = c:d; \quad a:b :: c:d;$$

and is read, "the ratio of a to b equals the ratio of c to d."

293. The *terms* of a proportion are the four quantities compared; the *first* and *third* terms are called the *antecedents*, the *second* and *fourth* terms, the *consequents*; the *first* and *fourth* terms are called the *extremes*, the *second* and *third* terms, the *means*.

294. In the proportion $a:b = c:d$, d is a *fourth proportional* to a, b, and c.

In the proportion $a:b = b:c$, c is a *third proportional* to a and b.

In the proportion $a:b = b:c$, b is a *mean proportional* between a and c.

PLANE GEOMETRY. — BOOK III.

Proposition I.

295. *In every proportion the product of the extremes is equal to the product of the means.*

Let $a : b = c : d.$

To prove $\quad ad = bc.$

Now $\quad \dfrac{a}{b} = \dfrac{c}{d},$

whence, by multiplying both sides by bd,
$$ad = bc. \qquad \text{Q.E.D.}$$

Proposition II.

296. *A mean proportional between two quantities is equal to the square root of their product.*

In the proportion $a : b = b : c,$
$$b^2 = ac, \qquad \S\ 295$$
(*the product of the extremes is equal to the product of the means*).

Whence, extracting the square root,
$$b = \sqrt{ac}. \qquad \text{Q.E.D.}$$

Proposition III.

297. *If the product of two quantities is equal to the product of two others, either two may be made the extremes of a proportion in which the other two are made the means.*

Let $ad = bc.$

To prove $\quad a : b = c : d.$

Divide both members of the given equation by bd.

Then $\quad \dfrac{a}{b} = \dfrac{c}{d},$

or, $\quad a : b = c : d. \qquad \text{Q.E.D.}$

Proposition IV.

298. *If four quantities of the same kind are in proportion, they will be in proportion by* **alternation**; *that is, the first term will be to the third as the second to the fourth.*

$$\text{\textit{Let }} a:b = c:d.$$

To prove $\quad\quad a:c = b:d.$

Now $\quad\quad\quad \dfrac{a}{b} = \dfrac{c}{d}.$

Multiply each member of the equation by $\dfrac{b}{c}$.

Then $\quad\quad\quad \dfrac{a}{c} = \dfrac{b}{d},$

or, $\quad\quad\quad a:c = b:d.$

Q.E.D.

Proposition V.

299. *If four quantities are in proportion, they will be in proportion by* **inversion**; *that is, the second term will be to the first as the fourth to the third.*

$$\text{\textit{Let }} a:b = c:d.$$

To prove $\quad\quad b:a = d:c.$

Now $\quad\quad\quad bc = ad.$ § 295

Divide each member of the equation by ac.

Then $\quad\quad\quad \dfrac{b}{a} = \dfrac{d}{c},$

or, $\quad\quad\quad b:a = d:c.$

Q.E.D.

Proposition VI.

300. *If four quantities are in proportion, they will be in proportion by* **composition;** *that is, the sum of the first two terms will be to the second term as the sum of the last two terms to the fourth term.*

Let $a:b=c:d$.

To prove $\quad a+b:b=c+d:d$.

Now $\quad\dfrac{a}{b}=\dfrac{c}{d}.$

Add 1 to each member of the equation.

Then $\quad\dfrac{a}{b}+1=\dfrac{c}{d}+1;$

that is, $\quad\dfrac{a+b}{b}=\dfrac{c+d}{d},$

or, $\quad a+b:b=c+d:d.$

In like manner, $a+b:a=c+d:c.$

Q. E. D.

Proposition VII.

301. *If four quantities are in proportion, they will be in proportion by* **division;** *that is, the difference of the first two terms will be to the second term as the difference of the last two terms to the fourth term.*

Let $a:b=c:d$.

To prove $\quad a-b:b=c-d:d$.

Now $\quad\dfrac{a}{b}=\dfrac{c}{d}.$

Subtract 1 from each member of the equation.

Then $\quad\dfrac{a}{b}-1=\dfrac{c}{d}-1;$

that is, $\quad\dfrac{a-b}{b}=\dfrac{c-d}{d},$

or, $\quad a-b:b=c-d:d.$

In like manner, $a-b:a=c-d:c.$

Q.E.D.

Proposition VIII.

302. *In any proportion the terms are in proportion by* **composition and division;** *that is, the sum of the first two terms is to their difference as the sum of the last two terms to their difference.*

$$\text{Let } a:b=c:d.$$

Then, by § 300, $\dfrac{a+b}{a}=\dfrac{c+d}{c}.$

And, by § 301, $\dfrac{a-b}{a}=\dfrac{c-d}{c}.$

By division, $\dfrac{a+b}{a-b}=\dfrac{c+d}{c-d},$

or, $a+b:a-b=c+d:c-d.$

Q. E. D.

Proposition IX.

303. *In a series of equal ratios, the sum of the antecedents is to the sum of the consequents as any antecedent is to its consequent.*

$$\text{Let } a:b=c:d=e:f=g:h.$$

To prove $a+c+e+g:b+d+f+h=a:b.$

Denote each ratio by r.

Then $r=\dfrac{a}{b}=\dfrac{c}{d}=\dfrac{e}{f}=\dfrac{g}{h}.$

Whence, $a=br,\ c=dr,\ e=fr,\ g=hr.$

Add these equations.

Then $a+c+e+g=(b+d+f+h)r.$

Divide by $(b+d+f+h).$

Then $\dfrac{a+c+e+g}{b+d+f+h}=r=\dfrac{a}{b},$

or, $a+c+e+g:b+d+f+h=a:b.$

Q. E. D.

Proposition X.

304. *The products of the corresponding terms of two or more proportions are in proportion.*

Let $a:b = c:d,\ e:f = g:h,\ k:l = m:n.$

To prove $\qquad aek : bfl = cgm : dhn.$

Now $\qquad \dfrac{a}{b} = \dfrac{c}{d},\ \dfrac{e}{f} = \dfrac{g}{h},\ \dfrac{k}{l} = \dfrac{m}{n}.$

Whence, by multiplication,
$$\frac{aek}{bfl} = \frac{cgm}{dhn},$$
or, $\qquad aek : bfl = cgm : dhn.$

Q.E.D.

Proposition XI.

305. *Like powers, or like roots, of the terms of a proportion are in proportion.*

Let $a:b = c:d.$

To prove $\qquad a^n : b^n = c^n : d^n,$

and $\qquad a^{\frac{1}{n}} : b^{\frac{1}{n}} = c^{\frac{1}{n}} : d^{\frac{1}{n}}.$

Now $\qquad \dfrac{a}{b} = \dfrac{c}{d}$

By raising to the nth power,
$$\frac{a^n}{b^n} = \frac{c^n}{d^n};\ \text{or}\ a^n : b^n = c^n : d^n.$$

By extracting the nth root,
$$\frac{a^{\frac{1}{n}}}{b^{\frac{1}{n}}} = \frac{c^{\frac{1}{n}}}{d^{\frac{1}{n}}};\ \text{or,}\ a^{\frac{1}{n}} : b^{\frac{1}{n}} = c^{\frac{1}{n}} : d^{\frac{1}{n}}.$$

Q.E.D.

306. *Equimultiples* of two quantities are the products obtained by multiplying each of them by the same number. Thus, ma and mb are equimultiples of a and b.

Proposition XII.

307. *Equimultiples of two quantities are in the same ratio as the quantities themselves.*

Let a and b be any two quantities.

To prove $\qquad ma : mb = a : b.$

Now $\qquad\qquad \dfrac{a}{b} = \dfrac{a}{b}.$

Multiply both terms of first fraction by m.

Then $\qquad\qquad \dfrac{ma}{mb} = \dfrac{a}{b},$

or, $\qquad\qquad ma : mb = a : b.$

Q.E.D.

308. Scholium. In the treatment of proportion it is assumed that fractions may be found which will *represent* the ratios. It is evident that the ratio of two quantities may be represented by a fraction when the two quantities compared can be expressed in *integers* in terms of a *common unit*. But when there is no unit in terms of which both quantities can be expressed in *integers*, it is possible to find a fraction that will represent the ratio to *any required degree of accuracy*. (See §§ 251–256.)

Hence, in speaking of the product of two quantities, as for instance, the product of two lines, we mean simply *the product of the numbers which represent them when referred to a common unit*.

An interpretation of this kind must be given to the product of any two quantities throughout the Geometry.

PLANE GEOMETRY. — BOOK III.

PROPORTIONAL LINES.

PROPOSITION I. THEOREM.

309. *If a line is drawn through two sides of a triangle parallel to the third side, it divides those sides proportionally.*

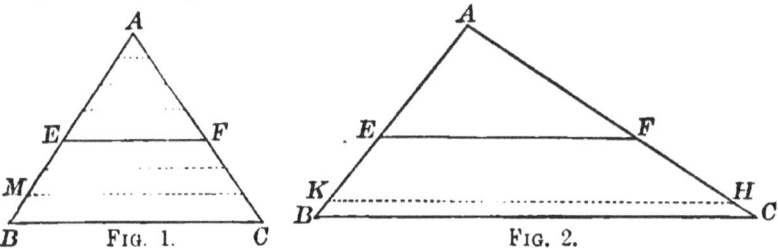

FIG. 1.   FIG. 2.

In the triangle ABC let EF be drawn parallel to BC.

To prove $\dfrac{EB}{AE} = \dfrac{FC}{AF}$.

CASE I. *When AE and EB* (Fig. 1) *are commensurable.*

Find a common measure of AE and EB, as BM.

Suppose BM to be contained in BE three times,

and in AE four times.

Then $\dfrac{EB}{AE} = \dfrac{3}{4}$. (1)

At the several points of division on BE and AE draw straight lines ∥ to BC.

These lines will divide AC into seven equal parts, of which FC will contain three, and A will contain four,   § 187
(*if parallels intercept equal parts on any transversal, they intercept equal parts on every transversal*).

$$\therefore \dfrac{FC}{AF} = \dfrac{3}{4}.$$ (2)

Compare (1) and (2),

$$\dfrac{EB}{AE} = \dfrac{FC}{AF}.$$ Ax. 1.

CASE II. *When AE and EB* (Fig. 2) *are incommensurable.*

Divide AE into any number of equal parts, and apply one of these parts as a unit of measure to EB as many times as it will be contained in EB.

Since AE and EB are incommensurable, a certain number of these parts will extend from E to a point K, leaving a remainder KB less than the unit of measure.

Draw KH ∥ to BC.

Then $$\frac{EK}{AE} = \frac{FH}{AF}.$$ Case I.

Suppose the unit of measure indefinitely diminished, the ratios $\frac{EK}{AE}$ and $\frac{FH}{AF}$ continue equal; and approach indefinitely the limiting ratios $\frac{EB}{AE}$ and $\frac{FC}{AF}$, respectively.

Therefore $$\frac{EB}{AE} = \frac{FC}{AF}.$$ §260

Q. E. D.

310. COR. 1. *One side of a triangle is to either part cut off by a straight line parallel to the base as the other side is to the corresponding part.*

For $EB : AE = FC : AF$, by the theorem.

∴ $EB + AE : AE = FC + AF : AF$, §300

or $AB : AE = AC : AF$.

311. COR. 2. *If two lines are cut by any number of parallels, the corresponding intercepts are proportional.*

Let the lines be AB and CD.

Draw AN ∥ to CD, cutting the ∥s at L, M, and N. Then

$AL = CG$, $LM = GK$, $MN = KD$. §187

By the theorem,

$AH : AM = AF : AL = FH : LM = HB : MN$.

That is, $AF : CG = FH : GK = HB : KD$.

If the two lines AB and CD were parallel, the corresponding intercepts would be equal, and the above proportion be true.

PROPOSITION II. THEOREM.

312. *If a straight line divides two sides of a triangle proportionally, it is parallel to the third side.*

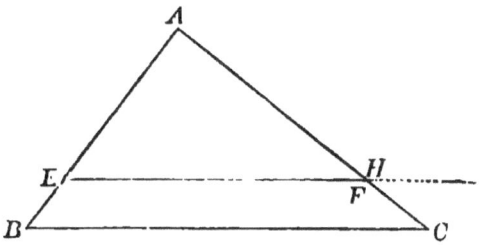

In the triangle ABC let EF be drawn so that

$$\frac{AB}{AE} = \frac{AC}{AF}.$$

To prove $\quad\quad EF \parallel$ to BC.

Proof. $\quad$ From E draw $EH \parallel$ to BC.

Then $\quad\quad AB : AE = AC : AH,$ $\quad\quad$ § 310

(*one side of a △ is to either part cut off by a line ∥ to the base, as the other side is to the corresponding part*).

But $\quad\quad AB : AE = AC : AF.$ $\quad\quad$ Hyp.

The last two proportions have the first three terms equal, each to each; therefore the fourth terms are equal; that is,

$$AF = AH.$$

∴ EF and EH coincide.

But $\quad\quad EH$ is $\parallel$ to BC. $\quad\quad$ Cons.

∴ EF, which coincides with EH, is $\parallel$ to BC.

Q. E. D.

Proposition III. Theorem.

313. *The bisector of an angle of a triangle divides the opposite side into segments proportional to the other two sides.*

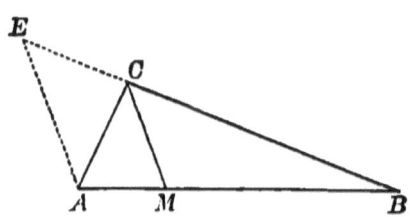

Let CM bisect the angle C of the triangle CAB.

To prove $\qquad MA : MB = CA : CB.$

Proof. Draw $AE \parallel$ to MC to meet BC produced at E.

Since MC is $\parallel$ to AE of the $\triangle BAE$, we have $\qquad$ § 309

$$MA : MB = CE : CB. \qquad (1)$$

Since MC is $\parallel$ to AE,

$\qquad\qquad \angle ACM = \angle CAE, \qquad\qquad$ § 104

$\qquad\qquad$ (*being alt.-int. ▵ of* $\parallel$ *lines*);

and $\qquad\qquad \angle BCM = \angle CEA, \qquad\qquad$ § 106

$\qquad\qquad$ (*being ext.-int. ▵ of* $\parallel$ *lines*).

But $\qquad\qquad$ the $\angle ACM = \angle BCM.$ $\qquad\qquad$ Hyp.

$\qquad\qquad \therefore$ the $\angle CAE = \angle CEA.$ $\qquad\qquad$ Ax. 1

$\qquad\qquad \therefore CE = CA,$ $\qquad\qquad$ § 156

(*if two ▵ of a △ are equal, the opposite sides are equal*).

Putting CA for CE in (1), we have

$$MA : MB = CA : CB.$$

Q.E.D.

PROPOSITION IV. THEOREM.

314. *The bisector of an exterior angle of a triangle meets the opposite side produced at a point the distances of which from the extremities of this side are proportional to the other two sides.*

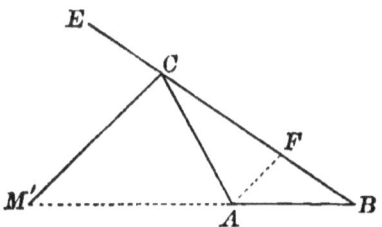

Let CM' **bisect the exterior angle** ACE **of the triangle** CAB, **and meet** BA **produced at** M'.

To prove $\qquad M'A : M'B = CA : CB$.

Proof. Draw $AF \parallel$ to CM' to meet BC at F.

Since AF is $\parallel$ to CM' of the $\triangle BCM'$, we have §309
$$M'A : M'B = CF : CB. \qquad (1)$$

Since AF is $\parallel$ to CM',

$\qquad$ the $\angle M'CE = \angle AFC$, §106
$\qquad\qquad$ (*being ext.-int. $\triangleleft$ of $\parallel$ lines*);

and $\qquad$ the $\angle M'CA = \angle CAF$, §104
$\qquad\qquad$ (*being alt.-int. $\triangleleft$ of $\parallel$ lines*).

Since CM' bisects the $\angle ECA$,
$$\angle M'CE = \angle M'CA.$$

∴ the $\angle AFC = \angle CAF$. Ax. 1

∴ $CA = CF$, §156

(*if two $\triangleleft$ of a $\triangle$ are equal, the opposite sides are equal*).

Putting CA **for** CF **in** (1), we have
$$M'A : M'B = CA : CB.$$

Q. E. D.

315. Scholium. If a given line AB is divided at M, a point between the extremities A and B, it is said to be divided *internally* into the segments MA and MB; and if it is divided at M', a point in the prolongation of AB, it is said to be divided *externally* into the segments $M'A$ and $M'B$.

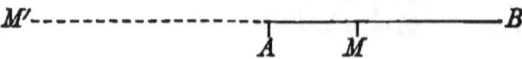

In either case the segments are the *distances* from the point of division to the extremities of the line. If the line is divided internally, the *sum* of the segments is equal to the line; and if the line is divided externally, the *difference* of the segments is equal to the line.

Suppose it is required to divide the given line AB internally and externally in the *same ratio;* as, for example, the ratio of the two numbers 3 and 5.

We divide AB into $5+3$, or 8, equal parts, and take 3 parts from A; we then have the point M, such that

$$MA : MB = 3 : 5. \qquad (1)$$

Secondly, we divide AB into two equal parts, and lay off on the prolongation of AB, to the left of A, three of these equal parts; we then have the point M', such that

$$M'A : M'B = 3 : 5. \qquad (2)$$

Comparing (1) and (2),

$$MA : MB = M'A : M'B.$$

316. If a given straight line is divided internally and externally into segments having the same ratio, the line is said to be *divided harmonically.*

317. Cor. 1. *The bisectors of an interior angle and an exterior angle at one vertex of a triangle divide the opposite side harmonically.* For, by §§ 313 and 314, each bisector divides the opposite side into segments proportional to the other two sides of the triangle.

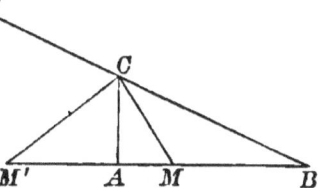

318. Cor. 2. *If the points M and M' divide the line AB harmonically, the points A and B divide the line MM' harmonically.*

For, if $\quad MA : MB = M'A : M'B$,
by alternation, $\quad MA : M'A = MB : M'B$. § 298

That is, the ratio of the distances of A from M and M' is equal to the ratio of the distances of B from M and M'.

The four points A, B, M, and M' are called *harmonic points*, and the two pairs, A, B, and M, M', are called *conjugate harmonic points*.

Similar Polygons.

319. *Similar* polygons are polygons that have their homologous angles equal, and their homologous sides proportional.

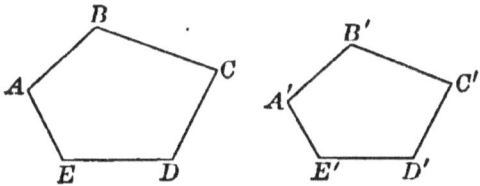

Thus, if the polygons $ABCDE$ and $A'B'C'D'E'$ are similar

the $\angle$ A, B, C, etc., are equal to $\angle$ A', B', C', etc.

and $\quad \dfrac{AB}{A'B'} = \dfrac{BC}{B'C'} = \dfrac{CD}{C'D'}$, etc.

320. In two similar polygons, the ratio of any two homologous sides is called the *ratio of similitude* of the polygons.

SIMILAR TRIANGLES.

Proposition V. Theorem.

321. *Two mutually equiangular triangles are similar.*

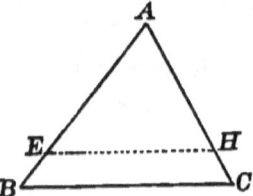
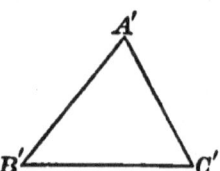

In the triangles ABC and $A'B'C'$ let angles A, B, C be equal to angles A', B', C' respectively.

To prove   △ ABC and $A'B'C'$ similar.

Proof.   Apply the △ $A'B'C'$ to the △ ABC,

so that $\angle A'$ shall coincide with $\angle A$.

Then the △ $A'B'C'$ will take the position of △ AEH.

Now $\angle AEH$ (same as $\angle B'$) $= \angle B$.

     ∴ EH is ∥ to BC,   § 108

(when two straight lines, lying in the same plane, are cut by a third straight line, if the ext.-int. ▵ are equal the lines are parallel).

     ∴ $AB : AE = AC : AH$,   § 310

or $AB : A'B' = AC : A'C'$.

In like manner, by applying △ $A'B'C'$ to △ ABC, so that $\angle B'$ shall coincide with $\angle B$, we may prove that

$$AB : A'B' = BC : B'C'.$$

Therefore   the two △ are similar.   § 319

Q. E. D.

322. Cor. 1. *Two triangles are similar if two angles of the one are equal respectively to two angles of the other.*

323. Cor. 2. *Two right triangles are similar if an acute angle of the one is equal to an acute angle of the other.*

PROPOSITION VI. THEOREM.

324. *If two triangles have their sides respectively proportional, they are similar.*

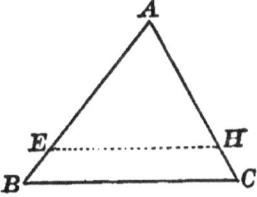 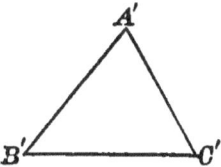

In the triangles ABC and $A'B'C'$ let
$$\frac{AB}{A'B'} = \frac{AC}{A'C'} = \frac{BC}{B'C'}.$$

To prove   △ ABC and $A'B'C'$ similar.

Proof.   Take $AE = A'B'$, and $AH = A'C'$.

Draw EH.

Then from the given proportion,

$$\frac{AB}{AE} = \frac{AC}{AH}.$$

∴ EH is ∥ to BC,   § 312

(*if a line divide two sides of a △ proportionally, it is ∥ to the third side*).

Hence in the △ ABC and AEH

∠ ABC = ∠ AEH,   § 106

and   ∠ ACB = ∠ AHE,

(*being ext.-int. ∠ of ∥ lines*).

∴ △ ABC and AEH are similar,   § 322

(*two △ are similar if two ∠ of one are equal respectively to two ∠ of the other*).

∴ $AB : AE = BC : EH$;

that is, $AB : A'B' = BC : EH$.

SIMILAR TRIANGLES. 147

But by hypothesis,
$$AB : A'B' = BC : B'C'.$$

The last two proportions have the first three terms equal, each to each; therefore the fourth terms are equal; that is,
$$EH = B'C'.$$

Hence in the $\triangle\ AEH$ and $A'B'C'$,
$$EH = B'C',\ AE = A'B',\ \text{and}\ AH = A'C'.$$
$$\therefore \triangle\ AEH = \triangle\ A'B'C', \qquad \S\ 160$$
(*having three sides of the one equal respectively to three sides of the other*).

But $\quad \triangle\ AEH$ is similar to $\triangle\ ABC$.

$\therefore \triangle\ A'B'C'$ is similar to $\triangle\ ABC$. q.e.d.

325. Scholium. The primary idea of similarity is *likeness of form*; and the two conditions necessary to similarity are:

I. For every angle in one of the figures there must be an equal angle in the other, and

II. The homologous sides must be in proportion.

In the case of *triangles*, either condition involves the other, but in the case of *other polygons*, it does not follow that if one condition exist the other does also.

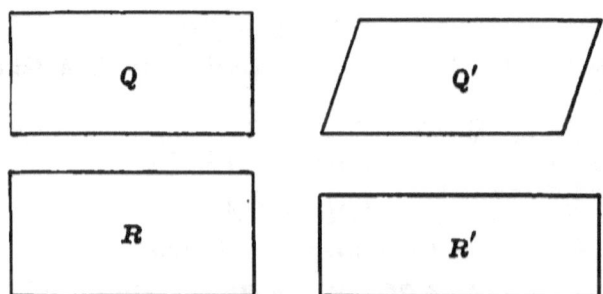

Thus in the quadrilaterals Q and Q', the homologous sides are proportional, but the homologous angles are not equal.

In the quadrilaterals R and R' the homologous angles are equal, but the sides are not proportional.

Proposition VII. Theorem.

326. *If two triangles have an angle of the one equal to an angle of the other, and the including sides proportional, they are similar.*

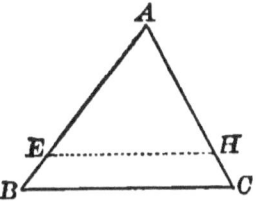
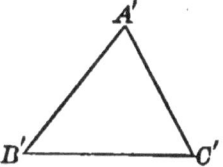

In the triangles ABC **and** $A'B'C'$, **let** $\angle A = \angle A'$, **and**
$$\frac{AB}{A'B'} = \frac{AC}{A'C'}.$$

To prove $\triangle ABC$ and $A'B'C'$ similar.

Proof. Apply the $\triangle A'B'C'$ to the $\triangle ABC$, so that $\angle A'$ shall coincide with $\angle A$.

Then the $\triangle A'B'C'$ will take the position of $\triangle AEH$.

Now $\qquad\qquad \dfrac{AB}{A'B'} = \dfrac{AC}{A'C'}.\qquad\qquad$ Hyp.

That is, $\qquad\quad \dfrac{AB}{AE} = \dfrac{AC}{AH}.$

Therefore the line EH divides the sides AB and AC proportionally;

$\qquad\qquad\qquad \therefore EH$ is $\parallel$ to BC, $\qquad\qquad$ § 312

(*if a line divide two sides of a* $\triangle$ *proportionally, it is* $\parallel$ *to the third side*).

Hence the $\triangle ABC$ and AEH are mutually equiangular and similar.

$\qquad\qquad \therefore \triangle A'B'C'$ is similar to $\triangle ABC.$

Q. E. D.

Proposition VIII. Theorem.

327. *If two triangles have their sides respectively parallel, or respectively perpendicular, they are similar.*

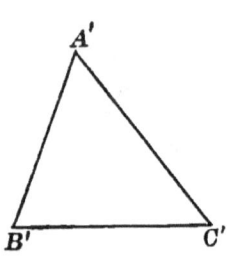
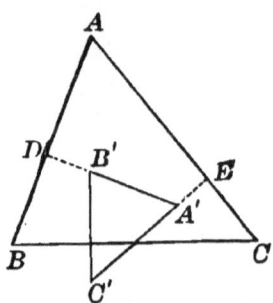

In the triangles $A'B'C'$ and ABC let $A'B'$, $A'C'$, $B'C'$ be respectively parallel, or respectively perpendicular, to AB, AC, BC.

To prove . △ $A'B'C'$ and ABC similar.

Proof. The corresponding ⦨ are either equal or supplements of each other, §§ 112, 113

(*if two ⦨ have their sides ||, or ⊥, they are equal or supplementary*).

Hence we may make three suppositions:

1st. $A + A' = 2$ rt. ⦨, $B + B' = 2$ rt. ⦨, $C + C' = 2$ rt. ⦨.
2d. $A = A'$, $B + B' = 2$ rt. ⦨, $C + C' = 2$ rt. ⦨.
3d. $A = A'$, $B = B'$, ∴ $C = C'$. § 140

Since the sum of the ⦨ of the two △ cannot exceed *four right angles*, the third supposition only is admissible. § 138

∴ the two △ ABC and $A'B'C'$ are similar, § 321

(*two mutually equiangular △ are similar*).

Q. E. D.

PROPOSITION IX. THEOREM.

328. *The homologous altitudes of two similar triangles have the same ratio as any two homologous sides.*

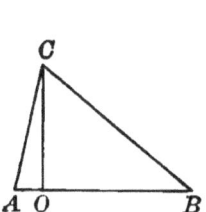
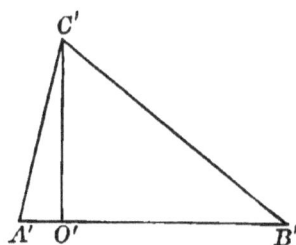

In the two similar triangles ABC **and** $A'B'C'$, **let the altitudes be** CO **and** $C'O'$.

To prove $\quad \dfrac{CO}{C'O'} = \dfrac{AC}{A'C'} = \dfrac{AB}{A'B'}.$

Proof. In the rt. $\triangle$ COA and $C'O'A'$,

$$\angle A = \angle A', \qquad \text{§ 319}$$

(*being homologous* $\angle$ *of the similar* $\triangle$ *ABC and A'B'C'*).

$\therefore \triangle COA$ and $C'O'A'$ are similar, §323

(*two rt.* $\triangle$ *having an acute* $\angle$ *of the one equal to an acute* $\angle$ *of the other are similar*).

$$\therefore \dfrac{CO}{C'O'} = \dfrac{AC}{A'C'}. \qquad \text{§ 319}$$

In the similar $\triangle$ ABC and $A'B'C'$,

$$\dfrac{AC}{A'C'} = \dfrac{AB}{A'B'}.$$

Therefore, $\quad \dfrac{CO}{C'O'} = \dfrac{AC}{A'C'} = \dfrac{AB}{A'B'}.$

Q. E. D.

SIMILAR TRIANGLES. 151

Proposition X. Theorem.

329. *Straight lines drawn through the same point intercept proportional segments upon two parallels.*

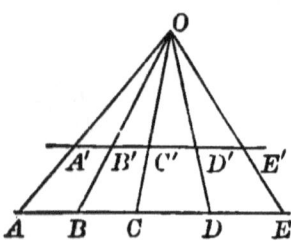

Let the two parallels AE and $A'E'$ cut the straight lines OA, OB, OC, OD, and OE.

To prove $\quad \dfrac{AB}{A'B'} = \dfrac{BC}{B'C'} = \dfrac{CD}{C'D'} = \dfrac{DE}{D'E'}.$

Proof. Since $A'E'$ is ∥ to AE, the pairs of △ OAB and $OA'B'$, OBC and $OB'C'$, etc., are mutually equiangular and similar,

$$\therefore \dfrac{AB}{A'B'} = \dfrac{OB}{OB'} \text{ and } \dfrac{BC}{B'C'} = \dfrac{OB}{OB'}. \qquad \text{§ 319}$$

(*homologous sides of similar △ are proportional*).

$$\therefore \dfrac{AB}{A'B'} = \dfrac{BC}{B'C'}. \qquad \text{Ax. 1}$$

In a similar way it may be shown that

$$\dfrac{BC}{B'C'} = \dfrac{CD}{C'D'} \text{ and } \dfrac{CD}{C'D'} = \dfrac{DE}{D'E'}.$$

Q. E. D.

Remark. A condensed form of writing the above is

$$\dfrac{AB}{A'B'} = \left(\dfrac{OB}{OB'}\right) = \dfrac{BC}{B'C'} = \left(\dfrac{OC}{OC'}\right) = \dfrac{CD}{C'D'} = \left(\dfrac{OD}{OD'}\right) = \dfrac{DE}{D'E'},$$

where a parenthesis about a ratio signifies that this ratio is used to prove the equality of the ratios immediately preceding and following it.

Proposition XI. Theorem.

330. CONVERSELY: *If three or more non-parallel straight lines intercept proportional segments upon two parallels, they pass through a common point.*

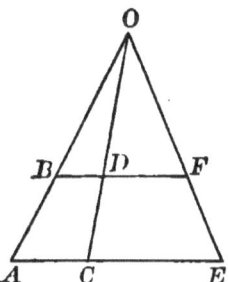

Let AB, CD, EF, cut the parallels AE and BF so that $AC : BD = CE : DF$.

To prove that AB, CD, EF prolonged meet in a point.

Proof. Prolong AB and CD until they meet in O.

Join OE.

If we designate by F' the point where OE cuts BF, we shall have by § 329,
$$AC : BD = CE : DF'.$$
But by hypothesis
$$AC : BD = CE : DF.$$

These proportions have the first three terms equal, each to each; therefore the fourth terms are equal; that is,
$$DF' = DF.$$
$\therefore F'$ coincides with F.

$\therefore EF$ prolonged passes through O.

$\therefore AB$, CD, and EF prolonged meet in the point O.
Q.E.D.

Similar Polygons.

Proposition XII. Theorem.

331. *If two polygons are composed of the same number of triangles, similar each to each, and similarly placed, the polygons are similar.*

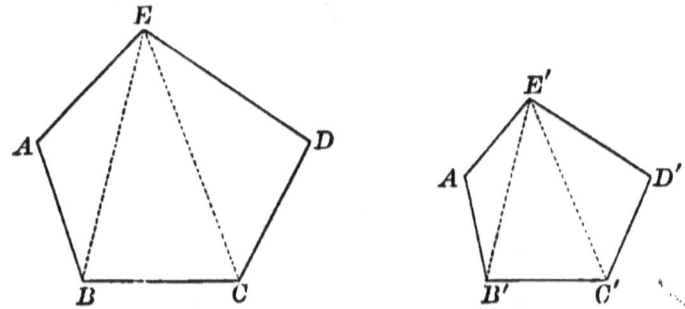

In the two polygons $ABCDE$ and $A'B'C'D'E'$, let the triangles AEB, BEC, CED be similar respectively to the triangles $A'E'B'$, $B'E'C'$, $C'E'D'$.

To prove $ABCDE$ similar to $A'B'C'D'E'$.

Proof. $\angle A = \angle A'$, § 319
(being homologous ∠ of similar △).

Also, $\angle ABE = \angle A'B'E'$, § 319
and $\angle EBC = \angle E'B'C'$.

By adding, $\angle ABC = \angle A'B'C'$.

In like manner we may prove $\angle BCD = \angle B'C'D'$, etc.
Hence the two polygons are mutually equiangular.
Now
$$\frac{AE}{A'E'} = \frac{AB}{A'B'} = \left(\frac{EB}{E'B'}\right) = \frac{BC}{B'C'} = \left(\frac{EC}{E'C'}\right) = \frac{CD}{C'D'} = \frac{ED}{E'D'},$$
(the homologous sides of similar △ are proportional).

Hence the homologous sides of the polygons are proportional.

Therefore the polygons are similar, § 319
(having their homologous ∠ equal, and their homologous sides proportional).

Q. E. D.

Proposition XIII. Theorem.

332. *If two polygons are similar, they are composed of the same number of triangles, similar each to each, and similarly placed.*

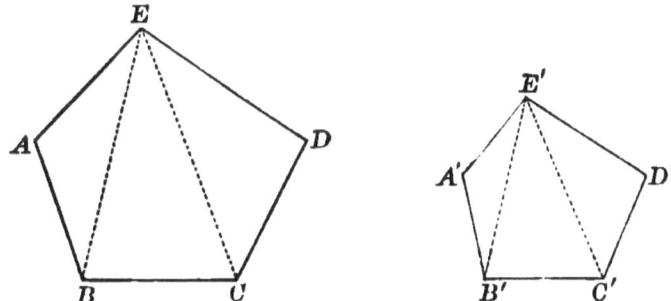

Let the polygons $ABCDE$ **and** $A'B'C'D'E'$ **be similar.**

From two homologous vertices, as E and E', draw diagonals EB, EC, and $E'B'$, $E'C'$.

To prove △ EAB, EBC, ECD
similar respectively to △ $E'A'B'$, $E'B'C'$, $E'C'D'$.

Proof. In the △ EAB and $E'A'B'$,

$$\angle A = \angle A',$$ § 319

(*being homologous △ of similar polygons*);

and $$\frac{AE}{A'E'} = \frac{AB}{A'B'},$$ § 319

(*being homologous sides of similar polygons*).

∴ △ EAB and $E'A'B'$ are similar, § 326

(*having an ∠ of the one equal to an ∠ of the other, and the including sides proportional*).

Also, $\angle ABC = \angle A'B'C'$, (1)

(*being homologous △ of similar polygons*).

And $\angle ABE = \angle A'B'E'$, (2)

(*being homologous △ of similar △*).

Subtract (2) from (1),

$\angle EBC = \angle E'B'C'$. Ax. 3

SIMILAR POLYGONS. 155

Now $$\frac{EB}{E'B'} = \frac{AB}{A'B'},$$
(*being homologous sides of similar △*).

And $$\frac{BC}{B'C'} = \frac{AB}{A'B'},$$
(*being homologous sides of similar polygons*).

$$\therefore \frac{EB}{E'B'} = \frac{BC}{B'C'}. \qquad \text{Ax. 1}$$

∴ △ EBC and $E'B'C'$ are similar, § 326
(*having an ∠ of the one equal to an ∠ of the other, and the including sides proportional*).

In like manner we may prove △ ECD and $E'C'D'$ similar.
Q. E. D.

PROPOSITION XIV. THEOREM.

333. *The perimeters of two similar polygons have the same ratio as any two homologous sides.*

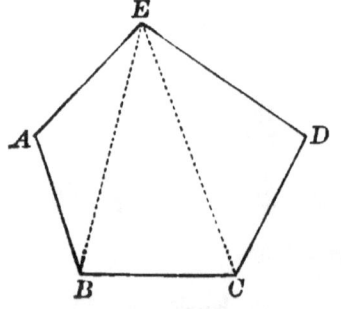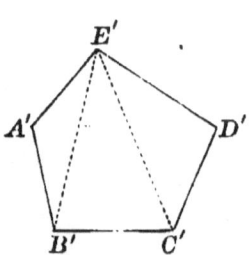

Let the two similar polygons be $ABCDE$ and $A'B'C'D'E'$, and let P and P' represent their perimeters.

To prove $\qquad P : P' = AB : A'B'$.

$AB : A'B' = BC : B'C' = CD : C'D'$, etc., § 319
(*the homologous sides of similar polygons are proportional*).

∴ $AB + BC$, etc. : $A'B' + B'C'$, etc. $= AB : A'B'$, § 303
(*in a series of equal ratios the sum of the antecedents is to the sum of the consequents as any antecedent is to its consequent*).

That is, $\qquad P : P' = AB : A'B'$.
Q. E. D.

NUMERICAL PROPERTIES OF FIGURES.

PROPOSITION XV. THEOREM.

334. *If in a right triangle a perpendicular is drawn from the vertex of the right angle to the hypotenuse:*

I. *The perpendicular is a mean proportional between the segments of the hypotenuse.*

II. *Each leg of the right triangle is a mean proportional between the hypotenuse and its adjacent segment.*

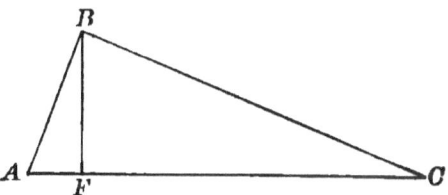

In the right triangle ABC, let BF be drawn from the vertex of the right angle B, perpendicular to AC.

I. To prove $\quad AF : BF = BF : FC$.

Proof. In the rt. △ BAF and BAC
$\qquad$ the acute $\angle A$ is common.
$\qquad$ Hence the △ are similar. $\qquad$ § 323

In the rt. △ BCF and BCA
$\qquad$ the acute $\angle C$ is common.
$\qquad$ Hence the △ are similar. $\qquad$ § 323

Now as the rt. △ ABF and CBF are both similar to ABC, they are similar to each other.

In the similar △ ABF and CBF,
$\qquad AF$, the shortest side of the one,
$\qquad : BF$, the shortest side of the other,
$\qquad :: BF$, the medium side of the one,
$\qquad : FC$, the medium side of the other.

II. To prove $\quad AC : AB = AB : AF$,
and $\qquad\qquad AC : BC = BC : FC$.

In the similar △ ABC and ABF,
  AC, the longest side of the one,
   : AB, the longest side of the other,
   :: AB, the shortest side of the one,
    : AF, the shortest side of the other.
Also in the similar △ ABC and FBC,
  AC, the longest side of the one,
   : BC, the longest side of the other,
   :: BC, the medium side of the one,
    : FC, the medium side of the other.   Q. E. D.

335. Cor. 1. *The squares of the two legs of a right triangle are proportional to the adjacent segments of the hypotenuse.*

The proportions in II. give, by § 295,
$$\overline{AB}^2 = AC \times AF, \text{ and } \overline{BC}^2 = AC \times CF.$$
By dividing one by the other, we have
$$\frac{\overline{AB}^2}{\overline{BC}^2} = \frac{AC \times AF}{AC \times CF} = \frac{AF}{CF}.$$

336. Cor. 2. *The squares of the hypotenuse and either leg are proportional to the hypotenuse and the adjacent segment.*

For
$$\frac{\overline{AC}^2}{\overline{AB}^2} = \frac{AC \times AC}{AC \times AF} = \frac{AC}{AF}.$$

337. Cor. 3. An angle inscribed in a semicircle is a right angle (§ 264). Therefore,

I. *The perpendicular from any point in the circumference to the diameter of a circle is a mean proportional between the segments of the diameter.*

II. *The chord drawn from the point to either extremity of the diameter is a mean proportional between the diameter and the adjacent segment.*

Remark. The pairs of corresponding sides in similar triangles may be called *longest, shortest, medium,* to enable the beginner to see quickly these pairs; but he must not forget that two sides are homologous, not because they appear to be the longest or the shortest sides, but because they lie opposite corresponding equal angles.

PROPOSITION XVI. THEOREM.

338. *The sum of the squares of the two legs of a right triangle is equal to the square of the hypotenuse.*

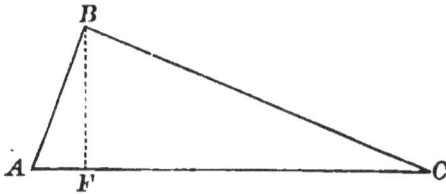

Let ABC be a right triangle with its right angle at B.
To prove $\overline{AB}^2 + \overline{BC}^2 = \overline{AC}^2$.
Proof. Draw $BF \perp$ to AC.
Then $\overline{AB}^2 = AC \times AF$ § 334
and $\overline{BC}^2 = AC \times CF$
By adding, $\overline{AB}^2 + \overline{BC}^2 = AC(AF + CF) = \overline{AC}^2$. Q.E.D.

339. Cor. *The square of either leg of a right triangle is equal to the difference of the squares of the hypotenuse and the other leg.*

340. Scholium. The ratio of the diagonal of a square to the side is the incommensurable number $\sqrt{2}$. For if AC is the diagonal of the square $ABCD$, then

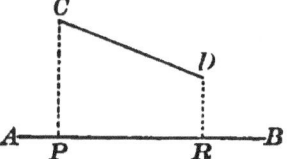

$$\overline{AC}^2 = \overline{AB}^2 + \overline{BC}^2, \text{ or } \overline{AC}^2 = 2\overline{AB}^2.$$

Divide by $\overline{AB}^2$, we have $\dfrac{\overline{AC}^2}{\overline{AB}^2} = 2$, or $\dfrac{AC}{AB} = \sqrt{2}$.

Since the square root of 2 is incommensurable, the diagonal and side of a square are two incommensurable lines.

341. *The projection of a line CD upon a straight line AB is* that part of the line AB comprised between the perpendiculars CP and DR let fall from the extremities of CD. Thus, PR is the projection of CD upon AB.

Proposition XVII. Theorem.

342. *In any triangle, the square of the side opposite an acute angle is equal to the sum of the squares of the other two sides diminished by twice the product of one of those sides and the projection of the other upon that side.*

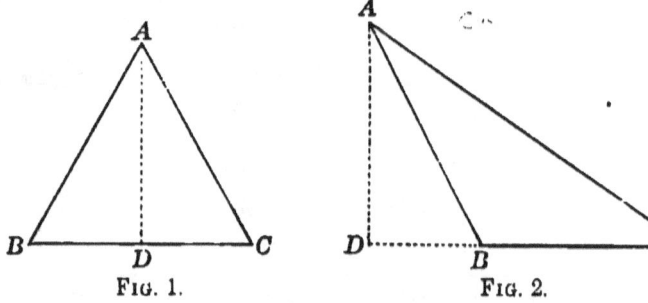

Fig. 1.   Fig. 2.

Let C be an acute angle of the triangle ABC, and DC the projection of AC upon BC.

To prove $\overline{AB}^2 = \overline{BC}^2 + \overline{AC}^2 - 2\,BC \times DC.$

Proof. If D fall upon the base (Fig. 1),
$$DB = BC - DC;$$
If D fall upon the base produced (Fig. 2),
$$DB = DC - BC.$$
In either case,
$$\overline{DB}^2 = \overline{BC}^2 + \overline{DC}^2 - 2\,BC \times DC.$$
Add $\overline{AD}^2$ to both sides of this equality, and we have
$$\overline{AD}^2 + \overline{DB}^2 = \overline{BC}^2 + \overline{AD}^2 + \overline{DC}^2 - 2\,BC \times DC.$$
But $\overline{AD}^2 + \overline{DB}^2 = \overline{AB}^2,$ § 338
and $\overline{AD}^2 + \overline{DC}^2 = \overline{AC}^2,$

(*the sum of the squares of the two legs of a rt. △ is equal to the square of the hypotenuse*).

Put $\overline{AB}^2$ and $\overline{AC}^2$ for their equals in the above equality,
$$\overline{AB}^2 = \overline{BC}^2 + \overline{AC}^2 - 2\,BC \times DC.$$

Q. E. D.

Proposition XVIII. Theorem.

343. *In any obtuse triangle, the square of the side opposite the obtuse angle is equal to the sum of the squares of the other two sides increased by twice the product of one of those sides and the projection of the other upon that side.*

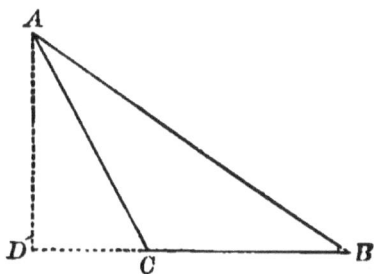

Let C be the obtuse angle of the triangle ABC, and CD be the projection of AC upon BC produced.

To prove $\overline{AB}^2 = \overline{BC}^2 + \overline{AC}^2 + 2\,BC \times DC$.

Proof. $\qquad DB = BC + DC.$

Squaring, $\overline{DB}^2 = \overline{BC}^2 + \overline{DC}^2 + 2\,BC \times DC.$

Add $\overline{AD}^2$ to both sides, and we have

$$\overline{AD}^2 + \overline{DB}^2 = \overline{BC}^2 + \overline{AD}^2 + \overline{DC}^2 + 2\,BC \times DC.$$

But $\qquad \overline{AD}^2 + \overline{DB}^2 = \overline{AB}^2,$ §338

and $\qquad \overline{AD}^2 + \overline{DC}^2 = \overline{AC}^2,$

(*the sum of the squares of the two legs of a rt. △ is equal to the square of the hypotenuse*).

Put $\overline{AB}^2$ and $\overline{AC}^2$ for their equals in the above equality,

$$\overline{AB}^2 = \overline{BC}^2 + \overline{AC}^2 + 2\,BC \times DC.$$

Q.E.D.

Note. The last three theorems enable us to compute the lengths of the altitudes if the lengths of the three sides of a triangle are known.

Proposition XIX. Theorem.

344. I. *The sum of the squares of two sides of a triangle is equal to twice the square of half the third side increased by twice the square of the median upon that side.*

II. *The difference of the squares of two sides of a triangle is equal to twice the product of the third side by the projection of the median upon that side.*

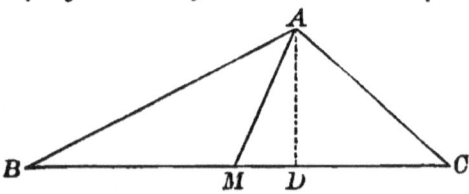

In the triangle ABC let AM be the median, and MD the projection of AM upon the side BC. Also let AB be greater than AC.

To prove I. $\overline{AB}^2 + \overline{AC}^2 = 2\,\overline{BM}^2 + 2\,\overline{AM}^2$.

II. $\overline{AB}^2 - \overline{AC}^2 = 2\,BC \times MD$.

Proof. Since $AB > AC$, the $\angle AMB$ will be obtuse, and the $\angle AMC$ will be acute. § 152

Then $\quad \overline{AB}^2 = \overline{BM}^2 + \overline{AM}^2 + 2\,BM \times MD$, § 343

(*in any obtuse △ the square of the side opposite the obtuse ∠ is equal to the sum of the squares of the other two sides increased by twice the product of one of those sides and the projection of the other on that side*);

and $\quad \overline{AC}^2 = \overline{MC}^2 + \overline{AM}^2 - 2\,MC \times MD$, § 342

(*in any △ the square of the side opposite an acute ∠ is equal to the sum of the squares of the other two sides diminished by twice the product of one of those sides and the projection of the other upon that side*).

Add these two equalities, and observe that $BM = MC$.

Then $\quad \overline{AB}^2 + \overline{AC}^2 = 2\,\overline{BM}^2 + 2\,\overline{AM}^2$.

Subtract the second equality from the first.

Then $\quad \overline{AB}^2 - \overline{AC}^2 = 2\,BC \times MD$. Q.E.D.

Note. This theorem enables us to compute the lengths of the medians if the lengths of the three sides of the triangle are known.

PROPOSITION XX. THEOREM.

345. *If any chord is drawn through a fixed point within a circle, the product of its segments is constant in whatever direction the chord is drawn.*

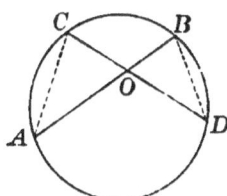

Let any two chords *AB* **and** *CD* **intersect at** *O*.
To prove $OA \times OB = OD \times OC$.
Proof. Draw *AC* and *BD*.
In the △ *AOC* and *BOD*,
$$\angle C = \angle B, \qquad \S\ 263$$
(*each being measured by* ½ *arc AD*).
$$\angle A = \angle D, \qquad \S\ 263$$
(*each being measured by* ½ *arc BC*).
∴ the △ are similar, § 322
(*two △ are similar when two ⩘ of the one are equal to two ⩘ of the other*).

Whence   *OA*, the longest side of the one,
: *OD*, the longest side of the other,
:: *OC*, the shortest side of the one,
: *OB*, the shortest side of the other.
∴ $OA \times OB = OD \times OC$. § 295

Q. E. D.

346. SCHOLIUM. This proportion may be written

$$\frac{OA}{OD} = \frac{OC}{OB}, \text{ or } \frac{OA}{OD} = \frac{1}{\frac{OB}{OC}};$$

that is, the ratio of two corresponding segments is equal to the *reciprocal* of the ratio of the other two corresponding segments. In this case the segments are said to be *reciprocally proportional*.

Proposition XXI. Theorem.

347. *If from a fixed point without a circle a secant is drawn, the product of the secant and its external segment is constant in whatever direction the secant is drawn.*

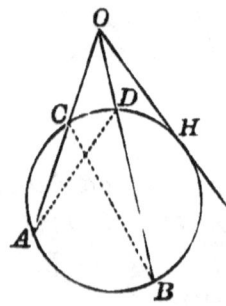

Let OA and OB be two secants drawn from point O.
To prove $\qquad OA \times OC = OB \times OD$.
Proof. $\qquad$ Draw BC and AD.
In the $\triangle$ OAD and OBC
$\qquad\qquad \angle O$ is common,
$\qquad\qquad\quad \angle A = \angle B, \qquad\qquad\qquad$ § 263
$\qquad$ (*each being measured by $\frac{1}{2}$ arc CD*).
$\qquad\qquad \therefore$ the two $\triangle$ are similar, $\qquad\qquad$ § 322
(*two $\triangle$ are similar when two $\angle$ of the one are equal to two $\angle$ of the other*).
Whence $\qquad OA$, the longest side of the one,
$\qquad\qquad : OB$, the longest side of the other,
$\qquad\qquad :: OD$, the shortest side of the one,
$\qquad\qquad : OC$, the shortest side of the other.
$\qquad\qquad \therefore OA \times OC = OB \times OD. \qquad\qquad$ § 295
$\hfill$ Q. E. D.

Remark. The above proportion continues true if the secant OB turns about O until B and D approach each other indefinitely. Therefore, by the theory of limits, it is true when B and D coincide at H. Whence, $OA \times OC = \overline{OH}^2$.
$\qquad$ This truth is demonstrated directly in the next theorem.

PROPOSITION XXII. THEOREM.

348. *If from a point without a circle a secant and a tangent are drawn, the tangent is a mean proportional between the whole secant and the external segment.*

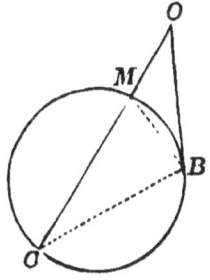

Let *OB* be a tangent and *OC* a secant drawn from the point *O* to the circle *MBC*.

To prove $OC : OB = OB : OM$.

Proof. Draw BM and BC.

In the $\triangle\, OBM$ and OBC

$\angle\, O$ is common.

$\angle\, OBM$ is measured by $\tfrac{1}{2}$ arc MB, § 269
(*being an $\angle$ formed by a tangent and a chord*).

$\angle\, C$ is measured by $\tfrac{1}{2}$ arc BM, § 263
(*being an inscribed $\angle$*).

$\therefore \angle\, OBM = \angle\, C$.

$\therefore \triangle\, OBC$ and OBM are similar, § 322
(*having two $\triangle$ of the one equal to two $\triangle$ of the other*).

Whence OC, the longest side of the one,
: OB, the longest side of the other,
:: OB, the shortest side of the one,
: OM, the shortest side of the other.

Q. E. D.

Proposition XXIII. Theorem.

349. *The square of the bisector of an angle of a triangle is equal to the product of the sides of this angle diminished by the product of the segments determined by the bisector upon the third side of the triangle.*

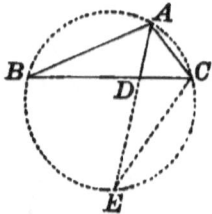

Let AD **bisect the angle** BAC **of the triangle** ABC.

To prove $\quad \overline{AD}^2 = AB \times AC - DB \times DC$.

Proof. Circumscribe the $\odot ABC$ about the $\triangle ABC$. § 285
Produce AD to meet the circumference in E, and draw EC.
Then in the $\triangle ABD$ and AEC,

$\angle BAD = \angle CAE$, Hyp.
$\angle B = \angle E$, § 263
(each being measured by $\frac{1}{2}$ the arc AC).

$\therefore \triangle ABD$ and AEC are similar, § 322
(two $\triangle$ are similar if two $\triangle$ of the one are equal respectively to two $\triangle$ of the other).

Whence $\quad AB$, the longest side of the one,
$\quad : AE$, the longest side of the other,
$\quad :: AD$, the shortest side of the one,
$\quad : AC$, the shortest side of the other.

$$\therefore AB \times AC = AD \times AE \quad \text{§ 295}$$
$$= AD(AD + DE)$$
$$= \overline{AD}^2 + AD \times DE.$$

But $\quad AD \times DE = DB \times DC$, § 345
(the product of the segments of a chord drawn through a fixed point in a $\odot$ is constant).

$$\therefore AB \times AC = \overline{AD}^2 + DB \times DC.$$

Whence $\quad \overline{AD}^2 = AB \times AC - DB \times DC.$ Q.E.D.

Note. This theorem enables us to compute the lengths of the bisectors of the angles of a triangle if the lengths of the sides are known.

PROPOSITION XXIV. THEOREM.

350. *In any triangle the product of two sides is equal to the product of the diameter of the circumscribed circle by the altitude upon the third side.*

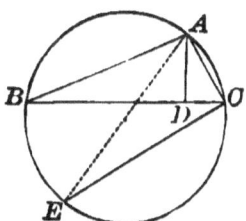

Let *ABC* **be a triangle,** *AD* **the altitude, and** *ABC* **the circle circumscribed about the triangle** *ABC*.

Draw the diameter AE, and draw EC.

To prove $\qquad AB \times AC = AE \times AD.$

Proof. In the △ ABD and AEC,

$\qquad\qquad \angle BDA$ is a rt. $\angle$, $\qquad\qquad$ Cons.

$\qquad\qquad \angle ECA$ is a rt. $\angle$, $\qquad\qquad$ § 264

$\qquad$(*being inscribed in a semicircle*),

$\qquad\qquad$ and $\angle B = \angle E$. $\qquad\qquad$ § 263

$\therefore$ △ ABD and AEC are similar, $\qquad$ § 323

(*two rt. △ having an acute $\angle$ of the one equal to an acute $\angle$ of the other are similar*).

Whence $\quad AB$, the longest side of the one,

$\qquad$: AE, the longest side of the other,

$\qquad$ :: AD, the shortest side of the one,

$\qquad$: AC, the shortest side of the other.

$\qquad\therefore AB \times AC = AE \times AD.$ $\qquad\qquad$ § 295

Q. E. D.

Note. This theorem enables us to compute the length of the radius of a circle circumscribed about a triangle, if the lengths of the three sides of the triangle are known.

Problems of Construction.

Proposition XXV. Problem.

351. *To divide a given straight line into parts proportional to any number of given lines.*

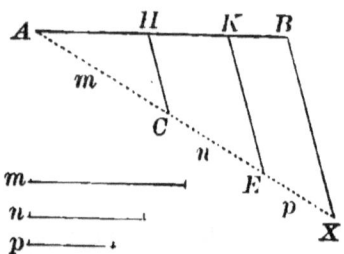

Let *AB*, *m*, *n*, and *p*, be given straight lines.
To divide *AB* into parts proportional to *m*, *n*, and *p*.

Construction. Draw AX, making an acute $\angle$ with AB.

On AX take $AC = m$, $CE = n$, $EX = p$.

Draw BX.

From E and C draw EK and CH ∥ to BX.

K and H are the division points required.

Proof. $\left(\dfrac{AK}{AE}\right) = \dfrac{AH}{AC} = \dfrac{HK}{CE} = \dfrac{KB}{EX},$ § 309

(*a line drawn through two sides of a △ ∥ to the third side divides those sides proportionally*).

∴ $AH : HK : KB = AC : CE : EX$.

Substitute *m*, *n*, and *p* for their equals AC, CE, and EX.

Then $AH : HK : KB = m : n : p$.

Q. E. F.

Proposition XXVI. Problem.

352. *To find a fourth proportional to three given straight lines.*

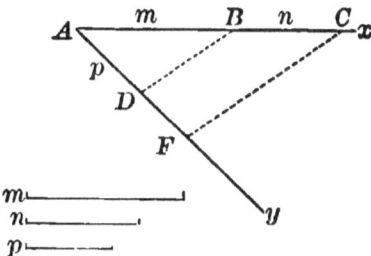

Let the three given lines be m, n, and p.

To find a fourth proportional to m, n, and p.

Draw Ax and Ay containing any acute angle.

Construction. On Ax take AB equal to m, $BC = n$.

On Ay take $AD = p$.

Draw BD.

From C draw $CF \parallel$ to BD, to meet Ay at F.

DF is the fourth proportional required.

Proof. $\qquad AB : BC = AD : DF,$ §309

(*a line drawn through two sides of a △ ∥ to the third side divides those sides proportionally*).

Substitute m, n, and p for their equals AB, BC, and AD.

Then $\qquad m : n = p : DF.$

Q. E. F.

Proposition XXVII. Problem.

353. *To find a third proportional to two given straight lines.*

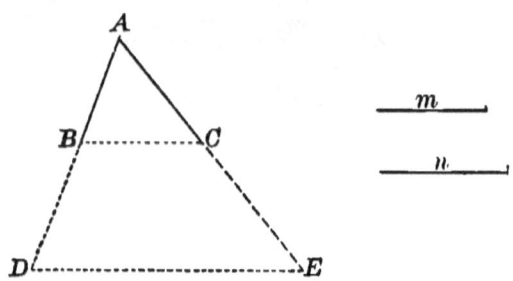

Let *m* and *n* be the two given straight lines.

To find a third proportional to *m* and *n*.

Construction. Construct any acute angle A,

and take $AB = m$, $AC = n$.

Produce AB to D, making $BD = AC$.

Join BC.

Through D draw DE ∥ to BC to meet AC produced at E.

CE is the third proportional to AB and AC.

Proof. $\quad AB : BD = AC : CE.$ §309

(*a line drawn through two sides of a △ ∥ to the third side divides those sides proportionally*).

Substitute, in the above proportion, AC for its equal BD.

Then $AB : AC = AC : CE.$

That is, $m : n = n : CE.$

Q. E. F.

Ex. 217. Construct x, if (1) $x = \dfrac{ab}{c}$, (2) $x = \dfrac{a^2}{c}$.

Special Cases: (1) $a = 2$, $b = 3$, $c = 4$; (2) $a = 3$, $b = 7$, $c = 11$; (3) $a = 2$, $c = 3$; (4) $a = 3$, $c = 5$; (5) $a = 2c$.

Proposition XXVIII. Problem.

354. *To find a mean proportional between two given straight lines.*

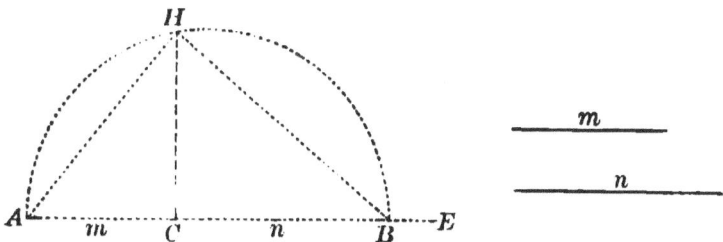

Let the two given lines be m and n.

To find a mean proportional between m and n.

Construction.   On the straight line AE

take $AC = m$, and $CB = n$.

On AB as a diameter describe a semi-circumference.

At C erect the $\perp$ CH to meet the circumference at H.

CH is a mean proportional between m and n.

Proof. $\therefore AC : CH = CH : CB,$ § 337

(*the $\perp$ let fall from a point in a circumference to the diameter of a circle is a mean proportional between the segments of the diameter*).

Substitute for AC and CB their equals m and n.

Then $m : CH = CH : n.$

Q. E. F.

355. A straight line is said to be divided *in extreme and mean ratio*, when the whole line is to the greater segment as the greater segment is to the less.

Ex. 218. Construct x if $x = \sqrt{ab}$.
Special Cases : (1) $a = 2,\ b = 3$; (2) $a = 1,\ b = 5$; (3) $a = 3,\ b = 7.$

Proposition XXIX. Problem.

356. *To divide a given line in extreme and mean ratio.*

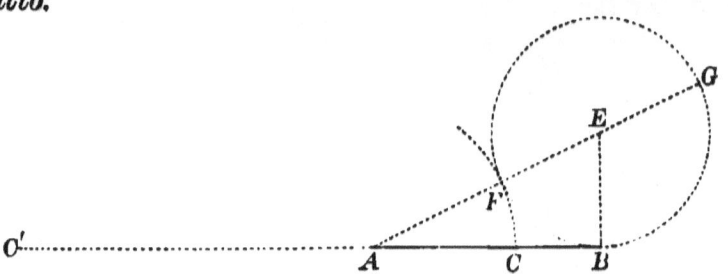

Let AB be the given line.
To divide AB in extreme and mean ratio.

Construction. At B erect a $\perp BE$ equal to one-half of AB.
From E as a centre, with a radius equal to EB, describe a $\odot$.
Draw AE, meeting the circumference in F and G.
On AB take $AC = AF$.
On BA produced take $AC' = AG$.

Then AB is divided internally at C and externally at C' in extreme and mean ratio.

Proof. $\qquad AG : AB = AB : AF,$ §348

(*if from a point without a $\odot$ a secant and a tangent are drawn, the tangent is a mean proportional between the whole secant and the external segment*).

Then by § 301 and § 300,
$$AG - AB : AB = AB - AF : AF, \qquad (1)$$
$$AG + AB : AG = AB + AF : AB. \qquad (2)$$

By construction $FG = 2EB = AB$.
$\therefore AG - AB = AG - FG = AF = AC.$

Hence (1) becomes
$$AC : AB = BC : AC;$$
or, by inversion, $\quad AB : AC = AC : BC.$ §299

Again, since $\quad C'A = AG = AB + AF,$
(2) becomes $\quad C'B : C'A = C'A : AB.$

Q. E. F.

PROPOSITION XXX. PROBLEM.

357. *Upon a given line homologous to a given side of a given polygon, to construct a polygon similar to the given polygon.*

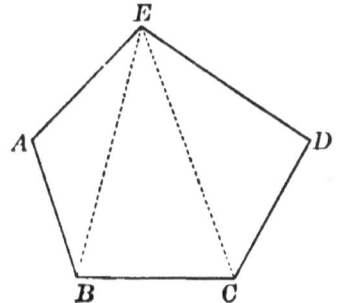
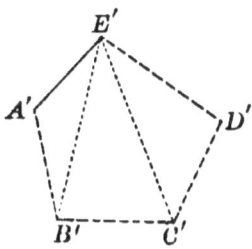

Let $A'E'$ be the given line homologous to AE of the given polygon $ABCDE$.

To construct on $A'E'$ a polygon similar to the given polygon.

Construction. From E draw the diagonals EB and EC.

From E' draw $E'B'$, $E'C'$, and $E'D'$,
making $\triangle A'E'B'$, $B'E'C'$, and $C'E'D'$ equal respectively to
$\triangle AEB$, BEC, and CED.

From A' draw $A'B'$, making $\angle E'A'B' = \angle EAB$,
and meeting $E'B'$ at B'.

From B' draw $B'C'$, making $\angle E'B'C' = \angle EBC$,
and meeting $E'C'$ at C'.

From C' draw $C'D'$, making $\angle E'C'D' = \angle ECD$,
and meeting $E'D'$ at D'.

Then $A'B'C'D'E'$ is the required polygon.

Proof. The corresponding $\triangle ABE$ and $A'B'E'$, EBC and $E'B'C'$, ECD and $E'C'D'$ are similar, § 322
(*two $\triangle$ are similar if they have two $\angle$ of the one equal respectively to two $\angle$ of the other*).

Then the two polygons are similar, § 331
(*two polygons, composed of the same number of $\triangle$ similar to each other and similarly placed, are similar*).

Q. E. F.

Problems of Computation.

219. To compute the altitudes of a triangle in terms of its sides.

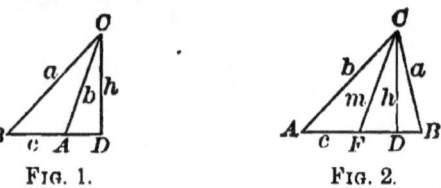

Fig. 1.   Fig. 2.

At least one of the angles A or B is acute. Suppose it is the angle B.

In the $\triangle CDB$, $\qquad h^2 = a^2 - \overline{BD}^2$. $\qquad\qquad$ § 338
In the $\triangle ABC$, $\qquad b^2 = a^2 + c^2 - 2c \times BD$. $\qquad$ § 342

Whence, $\qquad BD = \dfrac{a^2 + c^2 - b^2}{2c}$.

Hence $\quad h^2 = a^2 - \dfrac{(a^2 + c^2 - b^2)^2}{4c^2} = \dfrac{4a^2c^2 - (a^2 + c^2 - b^2)^2}{4c^2}$

$\qquad = \dfrac{(2ac + a^2 + c^2 - b^2)(2ac - a^2 - c^2 + b^2)}{4c^2}$

$\qquad = \dfrac{\{(a+c)^2 - b^2\}\{b^2 - (a-c)^2\}}{4c^2}$

$\qquad = \dfrac{(a+b+c)(a+c-b)(b+a-c)(b-a+c)}{4c^2}.$

Let $\qquad a + b + c = 2s$.
Then $\qquad a + c - b = 2(s - b)$,
$\qquad\qquad b + a - c = 2(s - c)$,
$\qquad\qquad b - a + c = 2(s - a)$.

Hence $\quad h^2 = \dfrac{2s \times 2(s-a) \times 2(s-b) \times 2(s-c)}{4c^2}.$

By simplifying, and extracting the square root,

$$h = \frac{2}{c}\sqrt{s(s-a)(s-b)(s-c)}.$$

220. To compute the medians of a triangle in terms of its sides.

By § 344, $\qquad a^2 + b^2 = 2m^2 + 2\left(\dfrac{c}{2}\right)^2$. $\qquad$ (Fig. 2)

Whence $\qquad 4m^2 = 2(a^2 + b^2) - c^2$.

$\qquad\qquad \therefore m = \tfrac{1}{2}\sqrt{2(a^2 + b^2) - c^2}.$

221. To compute the bisectors of a triangle in terms of the sides.

By § 349, $\quad t^2 = ab - AD \times BD.$

By § 313, $\quad \dfrac{AD}{b} = \dfrac{BD}{a} = \dfrac{AD + BD}{a + b} = \dfrac{c}{a+b}.$

$\therefore AD = \dfrac{bc}{a+b},$ and $BD = \dfrac{ac}{a+b}.$

Whence $\quad t^2 = ab - \dfrac{abc^2}{(a+b)^2}$

$\qquad = ab\left(1 - \dfrac{c^2}{(a+b)^2}\right)$

$\qquad = \dfrac{ab\{(a+b)^2 - c^2\}}{(a+b)^2}$

$\qquad = \dfrac{ab(a+b+c)(a+b-c)}{(a+b)^2}$

$\qquad = \dfrac{ab \times 2s \times 2(s-c)}{(a+b)^2}.$

Whence $\quad t = \dfrac{2}{a+b} \sqrt{abs(s-c)}.$

222. To compute the radius of the circle circumscribed about a triangle in terms of the sides of the triangle.

By § 350, $\quad AB \times AC = AE \times AD,$
or $\qquad bc = 2R \times AD.$
But $\qquad AD = \dfrac{2}{a}\sqrt{s(s-a)(s-b)(s-c)}.$
Whence $\quad R = \dfrac{abc}{4\sqrt{s(s-a)(s-b)(s-c)}}.$

223. If the sides of a triangle are 3, 4, and 5, is the angle opposite 5 right, acute, or obtuse?

224. If the sides of a triangle are 7, 9, and 12, is the angle opposite 12 right, acute, or obtuse?

225. If the sides of a triangle are 7, 9, and 11, is the angle opposite 11 right, acute, or obtuse?

226. The legs of a right triangle are 8 inches and 12 inches; find the lengths of the projections of these legs upon the hypotenuse, and the distance of the vertex of the right angle from the hypotenuse.

227. If the sides of a triangle are 6 inches, 9 inches, and 12 inches, find the lengths (1) of the altitudes; (2) of the medians; (3) of the bisectors; (4) of the radius of the circumscribed circle.

Theorems.

228. Any two altitudes of a triangle are inversely proportional to the corresponding bases.

229. Two circles touch at P. Through P three lines are drawn, meeting one circle in A, B, C, and the other in A', B', C', respectively. Prove that the triangles ABC, $A'B'C'$ are similar.

230. Two chords AB, CD intersect at M, and A is the middle point of the arc CD. Prove that the product $AB \times AM$ remains the same if the chord AB is made to turn about the fixed point A.

HINT. Draw the diameter AE, join BE, and compare the triangles thus formed.

231. The sum of the squares of the segments of two perpendicular chords is equal to the square of the diameter of the circle.

HINT. If AB, CD are the chords, draw the diameter BE, join AC, ED, BD, and prove that $AC = ED$. Apply § 338.

232. In a parallelogram $ABCD$, a line DE is drawn, meeting the diagonal AC in F, the side BC in G, and the side AB produced in E. Prove that $\overline{DF}^2 = FG \times FE$.

233. The tangents to two intersecting circles drawn from any point in their common chord produced, are equal. (§ 348.)

234. The common chord of two intersecting circles, if produced, will bisect their common tangents. (§ 348.)

235. If two circles touch each other, their common tangent is a mean proportional between their diameters.

HINT. Let AB be the common tangent. Draw the diameters AC, BD. Join the point of contact P to A, B, C, and D. Show that APD and BPC are straight lines ⊥ to each other, and compare ▲ ABC, ABD.

236. If three circles intersect one another, the common chords all pass through the same point.

HINT. Let two of the chords AB and CD meet at O. Join the point of intersection E to O, and suppose that EO produced meets the same two circles at two different points P and Q. Then prove that $OP = OQ$; hence, that the points P and Q coincide.

237. If two circles are tangent internally, all chords of the greater circle drawn from the point of contact are divided proportionally by the circumference of the smaller circle.

HINT. Draw any two of the chords, join the points where they meet the circumferences, and prove that the △ thus formed are similar.

238. In an inscribed quadrilateral, the product of the diagonals is equal to the sum of the products of the opposite sides.

HINT. Draw DE, making $\angle CDE = \angle ADB$. The △ ABD and CDE are similar. Also the △ BCD and ADE are similar.

239. The sum of the squares of the four sides of any quadrilateral is equal to the sum of the squares of the diagonals, increased by four times the square of the line joining the middle points of the diagonals.

HINT. Join the middle points F, E, of the diagonals. Draw EB and ED. Apply § 344 to the △ ABC and ADC, add the results, and eliminate $\overline{BE}^2 + \overline{DE}^2$ by applying § 343 to the △ BDE.

240. The square of the bisector of an exterior angle of a triangle is equal to the product of the external segments determined by the bisector upon one of the sides, diminished by the product of the other two sides.

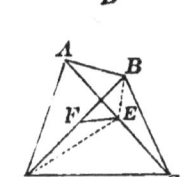

HINT. Let CD bisect the exterior $\angle BCH$ of the △ ABC. Circumscribe a ⊙ about the △, produce DC to meet the circumference in F, and draw BF. Prove △ ACD, BCF similar. Apply § 347.

241. If a point O is joined to the vertices of a triangle ABC, and through any point A' in OA a line parallel to AB is drawn, meeting OB at B', and then through B' a line parallel to BC, meeting OC at C', and C' is joined to A', the triangle $A'B'C'$ will be similar to the triangle ABC.

242. If the line of centres of two circles meets the circumferences at the points A, B, C, D, and meets the common exterior tangent at P, then $PA \times PD = PB \times PC$.

243. The line of centres of two circles meets the common exterior tangent at P, and a secant is drawn from P, cutting the circles at the consecutive points E, F, G, H. Prove that $PE \times PH = PF \times PG$.

Numerical Exercises.

244. A line is drawn parallel to a side AB of a triangle ABC, and cutting AC in D, BC in E. If $AD : DC = 2 : 3$, and $AB = 20$ inches, find DE.

245. The sides of a triangle are 9, 12, 15. Find the segments made by bisecting the angles. (§ 313.)

246. A tree casts a shadow 90 feet long, when a vertical rod 6 feet high casts a shadow 4 feet long. How high is the tree?

247. The bases of a trapezoid are represented by a, b, and the altitude by h. Find the altitudes of the two triangles formed by producing the legs till they meet.

248. The sides of a triangle are 6, 7, 8. In a similar triangle the side homologous to 8 is equal to 40. Find the other two sides.

249. The perimeters of two similar polygons are 200 feet and 300 feet. If a side of the first polygon is 24 feet, find the homologous side of the second polygon.

250. How long must a ladder be to reach a window 24 feet high, if the lower end of the ladder is 10 feet from the side of the house?

251. If the side of an equilateral triangle $= a$, find the altitude.

252. If the altitude of an equilateral triangle $= h$, find the side.

253. Find the lengths of the longest and the shortest chord that can be drawn through a point 6 inches from the centre of a circle whose radius is equal to 10 inches.

254. The distance from the centre of a circle to a chord 10 inches long is 12 inches. Find the distance from the centre to a chord 24 inches long.

255. The radius of a circle is 5 inches. Through a point 3 inches from the centre a diameter is drawn, and also a chord perpendicular to the diameter. Find the length of this chord, and the distance from one end of the chord to the ends of the diameter.

256. The radius of a circle is 6 inches. Through a point 10 inches from the centre tangents are drawn. Find the lengths of the tangents, and also of the chord joining the points of contact.

257. If a chord 8 inches long is 3 inches distant from the centre of the circle, find the radius and the distances from the end of the chord to the ends of the diameter which bisects the chord.

258. The radius of a circle is 13 inches. Through a point 5 inches from the centre any chord is drawn. What is the product of the two segments of the chord? What is the length of the shortest chord that can be drawn through the point?

259. From the end of a tangent 20 inches long a secant is drawn through the centre of the circle. If the exterior segment of this secant is 8 inches, find the radius of the circle.

260. The radius of a circle is 9 inches; the length of a tangent is 12 inches. Find the length of a secant drawn from the extremity of the tangent to the centre of the circle.

261. The radii of two circles are 8 inches and 3 inches, and the distance between their centres is 15 inches. Find the lengths of their common tangents.

262. Find the segments of a line 10 inches long divided in extreme and mean ratio.

263. The sides of a triangle are 4, 5, 6. Is the largest angle acute, right, or obtuse?

PROBLEMS.

264. To divide one side of a given triangle into segments proportional to the adjacent sides. (§ 313.)

265. To produce a line AB to a point C so that $AB : AC = 3 : 5$.

266. To find in one side of a given triangle a point whose distances from the other sides shall be to each other in a given ratio.

267. Given an obtuse triangle; to draw a line from the vertex of the obtuse angle to the opposite side which shall be a mean proportional between the segments of that side.

268. Through a given point P within a given circle to draw a chord AB so that $AP : BP = 2 : 3$.

269. To draw through a given point P in the arc subtended by a chord AB a chord which shall be bisected by AB.

270. To draw through a point P, exterior to a given circle, a secant PAB so that $PA : AB = 4 : 3$.

271. To draw through a point P, exterior to a given circle, a secant PAB so that $\overline{AB}^2 = PA \times PB$.

272. To find a point P in the arc subtended by a given chord AB so that $PA : PB = 3 : 1$.

EXERCISES. 179

273. To draw through one of the points of intersection of two circles a secant so that the two chords that are formed shall be to each other in the ratio of 3 : 5.

274. To divide a line into three parts proportional to $2, \frac{3}{4}, \frac{1}{2}$.

275. Having given the greater segment of a line divided in extreme and mean ratio, to construct the line.

276. To construct a circle which shall pass through two given points and touch a given straight line.

277. To construct a circle which shall pass through a given point and touch two given straight lines.

278. To inscribe a square in a semicircle.

279. To inscribe a square in a given triangle.

HINT. Suppose the problem solved, and $DEFG$ the inscribed square. Draw $CM \parallel$ to AB, and let AF produced meet CM in M. Draw CH and $MN \perp$ to AB, and produce AB to meet MN at N. The $\triangle ACM$, AGF are similar; also the $\triangle AMN, AFE$ are similar. By these triangles show that the figure $CMNH$ is a square. By constructing this square, the point F can be found.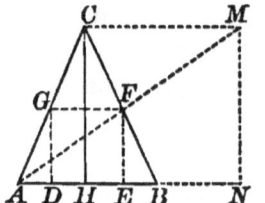

280. To inscribe in a given triangle a rectangle similar to a given rectangle.

281. To inscribe in a circle a triangle similar to a given triangle.

282. To inscribe in a given semicircle a rectangle similar to a given rectangle.

283. To circumscribe about a circle a triangle similar to a given triangle.

284. To construct the expression, $x = \dfrac{2abc}{de}$; that is, $\dfrac{2ab}{d} \times \dfrac{c}{e}$.

285. To construct two straight lines, having given their sum and their ratio.

286. To construct two straight lines, having given their difference and their ratio.

287. Having given two circles, with centres O and O', and a point A in their plane, to draw through the point A a straight line, meeting the circumferences at B and C, so that $AB : AC = 1 : 2$.

HINT. Suppose the problem solved, join OA and produce it to D, making $OA : AD = 1 : 2$. Join DC; $\triangle OAB, ADC$ are similar.

BOOK IV.

AREAS OF POLYGONS.

358. The *area* of a surface is the *numerical measure* of the surface referred to the *unit of surface*.

The unit of surface is a square whose side is a *unit of length;* as the *square inch*, the *square foot*, etc.

359. *Equivalent figures* are figures having equal areas.

PROPOSITION I. THEOREM.

360. *The areas of two rectangles having equal altitudes are to each other as their bases.*

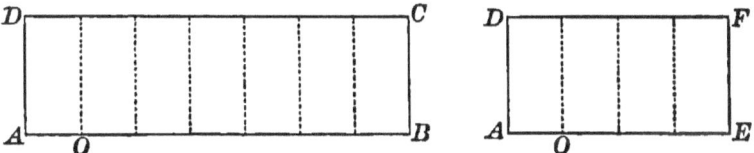

Let the two rectangles be AC and AF, having the same altitude AD.

To prove $\dfrac{\text{rect. } AC}{\text{rect. } AF} = \dfrac{AB}{AE}$.

Proof. CASE I. *When AB and AE are commensurable.*

Suppose AB and AE have a common measure, as AO, which is contained in AB seven times and in AE four times.

Then $\dfrac{AB}{AE} = \dfrac{7}{4}$. (1)

Apply this measure to AB and AE, and at the several points of division erect ⊥s.

The rect. AC will be divided into seven rectangles, and the rect. AF will be divided into four rectangles.

AREAS OF POLYGONS.   181

These rectangles are all equal.   § 186

Hence $\dfrac{\text{rect. } AC}{\text{rect. } AF} = \dfrac{7}{4}.$ (2)

From (1) and (2) $\dfrac{\text{rect. } AC}{\text{rect. } AF} = \dfrac{AB}{AE}.$ Ax. 1

CASE II. *When AB and AE are incommensurable.*

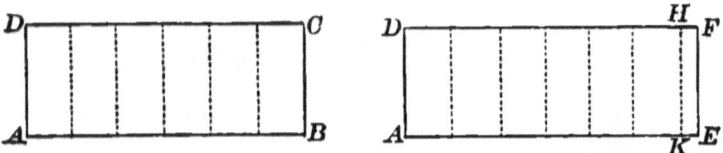

Divide AB into any number of equal parts, and apply one of them to AE as often as it will be contained in AE.

Since AB and AE are incommensurable, a certain number of these parts will extend from A to a point K, leaving a remainder KE less than one of the parts.

Draw $KH \parallel$ to EF.

Since AB and AK are commensurable,

$$\dfrac{\text{rect. } AH}{\text{rect. } AC} = \dfrac{AK}{AB}.$$ Case I.

These ratios continue equal, as the unit of measure is indefinitely diminished, and approach indefinitely the limiting ratios $\dfrac{\text{rect. } AF}{\text{rect. } AC}$ and $\dfrac{AE}{AB}$ respectively.

$$\therefore \dfrac{\text{rect. } AF}{\text{rect. } AC} = \dfrac{AE}{AB},$$ § 260

(*if two variables are constantly equal, and each approaches a limit, the limits are equal*).   Q. E. D.

361. COR. *The areas of two rectangles having equal bases are to each other as their altitudes.* For AB and AE may be considered as the altitudes, AD and AD as the bases.

NOTE. In propositions relating to *areas*, the words "rectangle," "triangle," etc., are often used for "area of rectangle," "area of triangle," etc.

Proposition II. Theorem.

362. *The areas of two rectangles are to each other as the products of their bases by their altitudes.*

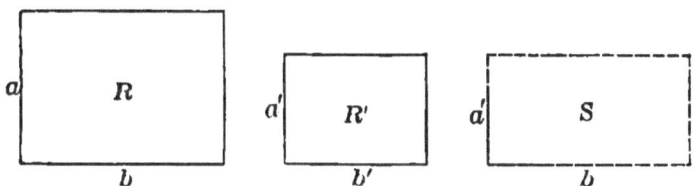

Let R and R' be two rectangles, having for their bases b and b', and for their altitudes a and a'.

To prove $\qquad \dfrac{R}{R'} = \dfrac{a \times b}{a' \times b'}.$

Proof. Construct the rectangle S, with its base the same as that of R, and its altitude the same as that of R'.

Then $\qquad \dfrac{R}{S} = \dfrac{a}{a'},$ §361

(*rectangles having equal bases are to each other as their altitudes*);

and $\qquad \dfrac{S}{R'} = \dfrac{b}{b'},$ §360

(*rectangles having equal altitudes are to each other as their bases*).

By multiplying these two equalities,

$$\dfrac{R}{R'} = \dfrac{a \times b}{a' \times b'}.$$

Q. E. D.

Ex. 288. Find the ratio of a rectangular lawn 72 yards by 49 yards to a grass turf 18 inches by 14 inches.

Ex. 289. Find the ratio of a rectangular courtyard 18½ yards by 15½ yards to a flagstone 31 inches by 18 inches.

Ex. 290. A square and a rectangle have the same perimeter, 100 yards. The length of the rectangle is 4 times its breadth. Compare their areas.

Ex. 291. On a certain map the linear scale is 1 inch to 5 miles. How many acres are represented on this map by a square the perimeter of which is 1 inch?

AREAS OF POLYGONS.

Proposition III. Theorem.

363. *The area of a rectangle is equal to the product of its base and altitude.*

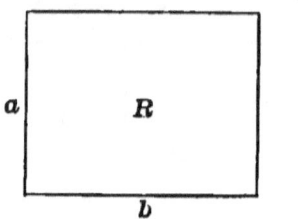

Let R be the rectangle, b the base, and a the altitude; and let U be a square whose side is equal to the linear unit.

To prove the area of $R = a \times b$.

$$\frac{R}{U} = \frac{a \times b}{1 \times 1} = a \times b, \qquad \S\ 362$$

(*two rectangles are to each other as the product of their bases and altitudes*).

But $\dfrac{R}{U} =$ the area of R. § 358

∴ the area of $R = a \times b$. Q. E. D.

364. Scholium. When the base and altitude each contain the linear unit an integral number of times, this proposition is rendered evident by dividing the figure into squares, each

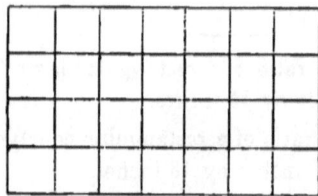

equal to the unit of measure. Thus, if the base contain seven linear units, and the altitude four, the figure may be divided into twenty-eight squares, each equal to the unit of measure; and the area of the figure equals 7×4 units of surface.

184 PLANE GEOMETRY. — BOOK IV.

PROPOSITION IV. THEOREM.

365. *The area of a parallelogram is equal to the product of its base and altitude.*

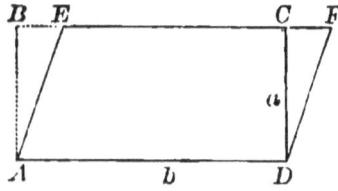 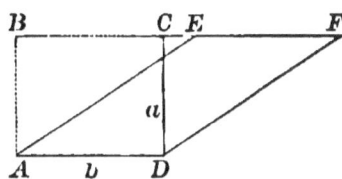

Let $AEFD$ be a parallelogram, AD its base, and CD its altitude.

To prove the area of the $\square$ $AEFD = AD \times CD$.

Proof. From A draw $AB \parallel$ to DC to meet FE produced.

Then the figure $ABCD$ will be a rectangle, with the same base and altitude as the $\square$ $AEFD$.

In the rt. $\triangle$ ABE and DCF

$AB = CD$ and $AE = DF$, § 179
(*being opposite sides of a $\square$*).

$\therefore \triangle ABE = \triangle DCF$, § 161

(*two rt. $\triangle$ are equal when the hypotenuse and a side of the one are equal respectively to the hypotenuse and a side of the other*).

Take away the $\triangle$ DCF, and we have left the rect. $ABCD$.

Take away the $\triangle$ ABE, and we have left the $\square$ $AEFD$.

$\therefore$ rect. $ABCD \Leftrightarrow \square AEFD$. Ax. 3

But the area of the rect. $ABCD = a \times b$, § 363

$\therefore$ the area of the $\square$ $AEFD = a \times b$. Ax. 1

Q. E. D.

366. Cor. 1. *Parallelograms having equal bases and equal altitudes are equivalent.*

367. Cor. 2. *Parallelograms having equal bases are to each other as their altitudes; parallelograms having equal altitudes are to each other as their bases; any two parallelograms are to each other as the products of their bases by their altitudes.*

Areas of Polygons.

Proposition V. Theorem.

368. *The area of a triangle is equal to one-half the product of its base by its altitude.*

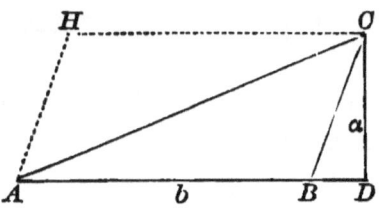

Let ABC **be a triangle,** AB **its base, and** DC **its altitude.**

To prove the area of the $\triangle ABC = \frac{1}{2} AB \times DC$.

Proof. From C draw CH ∥ to BA.

From A draw AH ∥ to BC.

The figure $ABCH$ is a parallelogram, § 168
(*having its opposite sides parallel*),

and AC is its diagonal.

∴ $\triangle ABC = \triangle AHC$, § 178

(*the diagonal of a ▱ divides it into two equal △*).

The area of the ▱ $ABCH$ is equal to the product of its base by its altitude. § 365

Therefore the area of one-half the ▱, that is, the area of the $\triangle ABC$, is equal to one-half the product of its base by its altitude.

Hence, the area of the $\triangle ABC = \frac{1}{2} AB \times DC$.

Q. E. D.

369. Cor. 1. *Triangles having equal bases and equal altitudes are equivalent.*

370. Cor. 2. *Triangles having equal bases are to each other as their altitudes; triangles having equal altitudes are to each other as their bases; any two triangles are to each other as the products of their bases by their altitudes.*

Proposition VI. Theorem.

371. *The area of a trapezoid is equal to one-half the sum of the parallel sides multiplied by the altitude.*

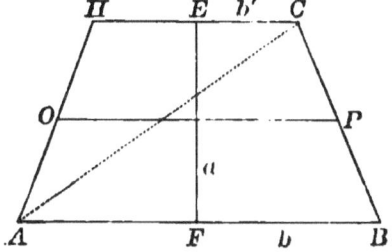

Let ABCH be a trapezoid, and EF the altitude.

To prove area of $ABCH = \frac{1}{2}(HC + AB) EF$

Proof. Draw the diagonal AC.

Then the area of the $\triangle ABC = \frac{1}{2}(AB \times EF)$, § 368
and the area of the $\triangle AHC = \frac{1}{2}(HC \times EF)$.
By adding, area of $ABCH = \frac{1}{2}(AB + HC) EF$.   Q.E.D.

372. Cor. *The area of a trapezoid is equal to the product of the median by the altitude.* For, by § 191, OP is equal to $\frac{1}{2}(HC + AB)$; and hence

the area of $ABCH = OP \times EF$.

373. Scholium. The area of an irregular polygon may be found by dividing the polygon into triangles, and by finding the area of each of these triangles separately. But the method generally employed in practice is to draw the longest diagonal, 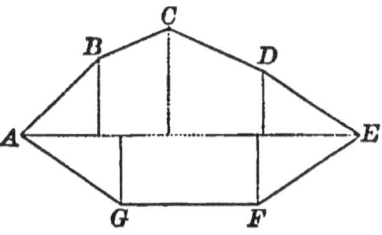 and to let fall perpendiculars upon this diagonal from the other angular points of the polygon.

The polygon is thus divided into right triangles and trapezoids; the sum of the areas of these figures will be the area of the polygon.

AREAS OF POLYGONS.

PROPOSITION VII. THEOREM.

374. *The areas of two triangles which have an angle of the one equal to an angle of the other are to each other as the products of the sides including the equal angles.*

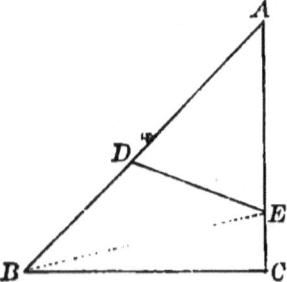

Let the triangles ABC **and** ADE **have the common angle** A.

To prove $\quad \dfrac{\triangle ABC}{\triangle ADE} = \dfrac{AB \times AC}{AD \times AE}.$

Proof. $\qquad$ Draw BE.

Now $\qquad \dfrac{\triangle ABC}{\triangle ABE} = \dfrac{AC}{AE},$

and $\qquad \dfrac{\triangle ABE}{\triangle ADE} = \dfrac{AB}{AD},$ $\qquad$ § 370

(△ *having the same altitude are to each other as their bases*).

By multiplying these equalities,

$$\dfrac{\triangle ABC}{\triangle ADE} = \dfrac{AB \times AC}{AD \times AE}.$$

Q. E. D.

Ex. 292. The areas of two triangles which have an angle of the one supplementary to an angle of the other are to each other as the products of the sides including the supplementary angles.

Comparison of Polygons.

Proposition VIII. Theorem.

375. *The areas of two similar triangles are to each other as the squares of any two homologous sides.*

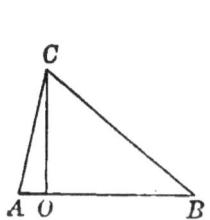 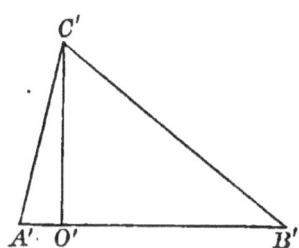

Let the two triangles be ACB and $A'C'B'$.

To prove $\quad \dfrac{\triangle ACB}{\triangle A'C'B'} = \dfrac{\overline{AB}^2}{\overline{A'B'}^2}.$

Draw the perpendiculars CO and $C'O'$.

Then $\quad \dfrac{\triangle ACB}{\triangle A'C'B'} = \dfrac{AB \times CO}{A'B' \times C'O'} = \dfrac{AB}{A'B'} \times \dfrac{CO}{C'O'},\qquad$ § 370

(*two △ are to each other as the products of their bases by their altitudes*).

But $\quad \dfrac{AB}{A'B'} = \dfrac{CO}{C'O'},\qquad$ § 328

(*the homologous altitudes of similar △ have the same ratio as their homologous bases*).

Substitute, in the above equality, for $\dfrac{CO}{C'O'}$ its equal $\dfrac{AB}{A'B'}$;

then $\quad \dfrac{\triangle ACB}{\triangle A'C'B'} = \dfrac{AB}{A'B'} \times \dfrac{AB}{A'B'} = \dfrac{\overline{AB}^2}{\overline{A'B'}^2}.$

Q. E. D.

Comparison of Polygons.

Proposition IX. Theorem.

376. *The areas of two similar polygons are to each other as the squares of any two homologous sides.*

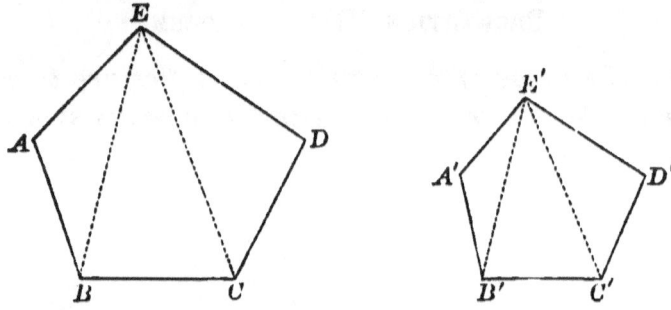

Let S and S' denote the areas of the two similar polygons ABC etc., and $A'B'C'$ etc.

To prove $S : S' = \overline{AB}^2 : \overline{A'B'}^2$.

Proof. By drawing all the diagonals from the homologous vertices E and E', the two similar polygons are divided into triangles similar and similarly placed. § 332

$$\therefore \frac{\overline{AB}^2}{\overline{A'B'}^2} = \frac{\triangle ABE}{\triangle A'B'E'} = \left(\frac{\overline{BE}^2}{\overline{B'E'}^2}\right) = \frac{\triangle BCE}{\triangle B'C'E'}$$

$$= \left(\frac{\overline{CE}^2}{\overline{C'E'}^2}\right) = \frac{\triangle CDE}{\triangle C'D'E'}, \S 375$$

(*similar △ are to each other as the squares of any two homologous sides*).

That is, $\dfrac{\triangle ABE}{\triangle A'B'E'} = \dfrac{\triangle BCE}{\triangle B'C'E'} = \dfrac{\triangle CDE}{\triangle C'D'E'}$.

$$\therefore \frac{\triangle ABE + BCE + CDE}{\triangle A'B'E' + B'C'E' + C'D'E'} = \frac{\triangle ABE}{\triangle A'B'E'} = \frac{\overline{AB}^2}{\overline{A'B'}^2}, \S 303$$

(*in a series of equal ratios the sum of the antecedents is to the sum of the consequents as any antecedent is to its consequent*).

$$\therefore S : S' = \overline{AB}^2 : \overline{A'B'}^2. \text{Q.E.D.}$$

377. Cor. 1. *The areas of two similar polygons are to each other as the squares of any two homologous lines.*

378. Cor. 2. *The homologous sides of two similar polygons have the same ratio as the square roots of their areas.*

Proposition X. Theorem.

379. *The square described on the hypotenuse of a right triangle is equivalent to the sum of the squares on the other two sides.*

Let BE, CH, AF, be squares on the three sides of the right triangle ABC.

To prove $\overline{BC}^2 = \overline{AB}^2 + \overline{AC}^2$.

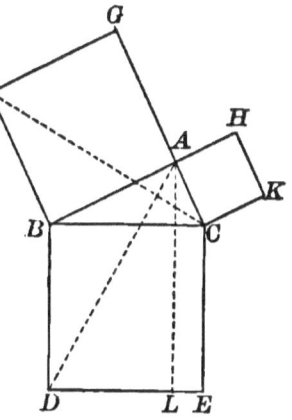

Proof. Through A draw $AL \parallel$ to CE, and draw AD and FC.

Since $\angle BAC$, BAG, and CAH are rt. $\angle$s, CAG and BAH are straight lines.

Since $BD = BC$, being sides of the same square, and $BA = BF$, for the same reason, and since $\angle ABD = \angle FBC$, each being the sum of a rt. $\angle$ and the $\angle ABC$,

$$\triangle ABD = \triangle FBC. \qquad \S\ 150$$

Now the rectangle BL is double the $\triangle ABD$,
(*having the same base BD, and the same altitude, the distance between the $\parallel$s AL and BD*),

and the square AF is double the $\triangle FBC$,
(*having the same base FB, and the same altitude, the distance between the $\parallel$s FB and GC*).

Hence the rectangle BL is equivalent to the square AF.

In like manner, by joining AE and BK, it may be proved that the rectangle CL is equivalent to the square CH.

Therefore the square BE, which is the sum of the rectangles BL and CL, is equivalent to the sum of the squares CH and AF.

Q. E. D.

380. Cor. *The square on either leg of a right triangle is equivalent to the difference of the squares on the hypotenuse and the other leg.*

Ex. 293. The square constructed upon the sum of two straight lines is equivalent to the sum of the squares constructed upon these two lines, increased by twice the rectangle of these lines.

Let AB and BC be the two straight lines, and AC their sum. Construct the squares $ACGK$ and $ABED$ upon AC and AB respectively. Prolong BE and DE until they meet KG and CG respectively. Then we have the square $EFGH$, with sides each equal to BC. Hence, the square $ACGK$ is the sum of the squares $ABED$ and $EFGH$, and the rectangles $DEHK$ and $BCFE$, the dimensions of which are equal to AB and BC.

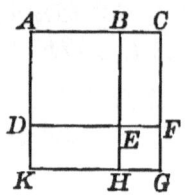

Ex. 294. The square constructed upon the difference of two straight lines is equivalent to the sum of the squares constructed upon these two lines, diminished by twice the rectangle of these lines.

Let AB and AC be the two straight lines, and BC their difference. Construct the square $ABFG$ upon AB, the square $ACKH$ upon AC, and the square $BEDC$ upon BC (as shown in the figure). Prolong ED until it meets AG in L.

The dimensions of the rectangles $LEFG$ and $HKDL$ are AB and AC, and the square $BCDE$ is evidently the difference between the whole figure and the sum of these rectangles; that is, the square constructed upon BC is equivalent to the sum of the squares constructed upon AB and AC diminished by twice the rectangle of AB and AC.

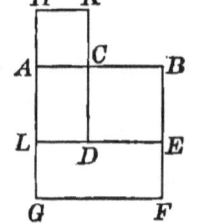

Ex. 295. The difference between the squares constructed upon two straight lines is equivalent to the rectangle of the sum and difference of these lines.

Let $ABDE$ and $BCGF$ be the squares constructed upon the two straight lines AB and BC. The difference between these squares is the polygon $ACGFDE$, which polygon, by prolonging CG to H, is seen to be composed of the rectangles $ACHE$ and $GFDH$. Prolong AE and CH to I and K respectively, making EI and HK each equal to BC, and draw IK. The rectangles $GFDH$ and $EHKI$ are equal. The difference between the squares $ABDE$ and $BCGF$ is then equivalent to the rectangle $ACKI$, which has for dimensions $AI = AB + BC$, and $EH = AB - BC$.

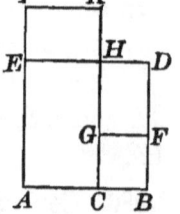

PROBLEMS OF CONSTRUCTION.

PROPOSITION XI. PROBLEM.

381. *To construct a square equivalent to the sum of two given squares.*

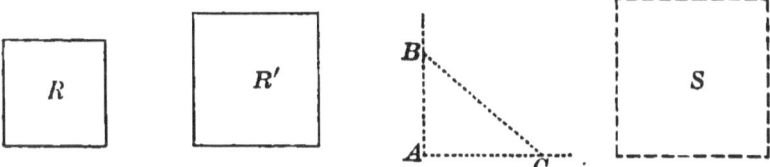

Let R and R' be two given squares.

To construct a square equivalent to $R' + R$.

Construction. Construct the rt. $\angle A$.

Take AC equal to a side of R',

AB equal to a side of R; and draw BC.

Construct the square S, having each of its sides equal to BC.

S is the square required.

Proof. $\overline{BC}^2 \Leftrightarrow \overline{AC}^2 + \overline{AB}^2,$ § 379

(*the square on the hypotenuse of a rt. $\triangle$ is equivalent to the sum of the squares on the two sides*).

$$\therefore S \Leftrightarrow R' + R.$$

Q. E. F.

Ex. 296. If the perimeter of a rectangle is 72 feet, and the length is equal to twice the width, find the area.

Ex. 297. How many tiles 9 inches long and 4 inches wide will be required to pave a path 8 feet wide surrounding a rectangular court 120 feet long and 36 feet wide?

Ex. 298. The bases of a trapezoid are 16 feet and 10 feet; each leg is equal to 5 feet. Find the area of the trapezoid.

PROBLEMS OF CONSTRUCTION.   193

Proposition XII. Problem.

382. To construct a square equivalent to the difference of two given squares.

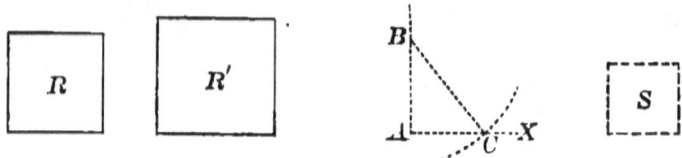

Let R be the smaller square and R' the larger.
To construct a square equivalent to $R' - R$.

Construction.   Construct the rt. $\angle A$.

Take AB equal to a side of R.

From B as a centre, with a radius equal to a side of R',
describe an arc cutting the line AX at C.

Construct the square S, having each of its sides equal to AC.

S is the square required.

Proof. $\overline{AC}^2 \doteqdot \overline{BC}^2 - \overline{AB}^2$,   § 380
(the square on either leg of a rt. $\triangle$ is equivalent to the difference of the
squares on the hypotenuse and the other leg).

$$\therefore S \doteqdot R' - R.$$

Q. E. F.

Ex. 299. Construct a square equivalent to the sum of two squares whose sides are 3 inches and 4 inches.

Ex. 300. Construct a square equivalent to the difference of two squares whose sides are $2\frac{1}{2}$ inches and 2 inches.

Ex. 301. Find the side of a square equivalent to the sum of two squares whose sides are 24 feet and 32 feet.

Ex. 302. Find the side of a square equivalent to the difference of two squares whose sides are 24 feet and 40 feet.

Ex. 303. A rhombus contains 100 square feet, and the length of one diagonal is 10 feet. Find the length of the other diagonal.

Proposition XIII. Problem.

383. *To construct a square equivalent to the sum of any number of given squares.*

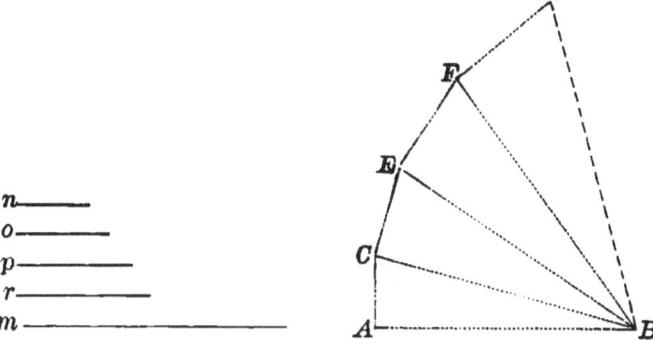

Let m, n, o, p, r be sides of the given squares.

To construct a square $\doteqdot m^2 + n^2 + o^2 + p^2 + r^2$.

Construction.   Take $AB = m$.

Draw $AC = n$ and $\perp$ to AB at A, and draw BC.
Draw $CE = o$ and $\perp$ to BC at C, and draw BE.
Draw $EF = p$ and $\perp$ to BE at E, and draw BF.
Draw $FH = r$ and $\perp$ to BF at F, and draw BH.

The square constructed on BH is the square required.

Proof. $\overline{BH}^2 \doteqdot \overline{FH}^2 + \overline{BF}^2$,
$\doteqdot \overline{FH}^2 + \overline{EF}^2 + \overline{EB}^2$,
$\doteqdot \overline{FH}^2 + \overline{EF}^2 + \overline{EC}^2 + \overline{CB}^2$,
$\doteqdot \overline{FH}^2 + \overline{EC}^2 + \overline{EF}^2 + \overline{CA}^2 + \overline{AB}^2$,   § 379

(*the sum of the squares on the two legs of a rt.* $\triangle$ *is equivalent to the square on the hypotenuse*).

That is, $\overline{BH}^2 \doteqdot m^2 + n^2 + o^2 + p^2 + r^2$.

Q. E. F.

PROBLEMS OF CONSTRUCTION. 195

PROPOSITION XIV. PROBLEM.

384. *To construct a polygon similar to two given similar polygons and equivalent to their sum.*

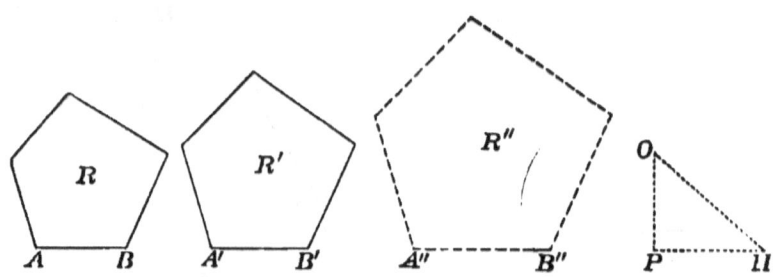

Let R and R' be two similar polygons, and AB and $A'B'$ two homologous sides.

To construct a similar polygon equivalent to $R + R'$.

Construction. Construct the rt. $\angle P$.

Take $PH = A'B'$, and $PO = AB$.

Draw OH, and take $A''B'' = OH$.

Upon $A''B''$, homologous to AB, construct R'' similar to R. Then R'' is the polygon required.

Proof. $\overline{PO}^2 + \overline{PH}^2 = \overline{OH}^2$, $\therefore \overline{AB}^2 + \overline{A'B'}^2 = \overline{A''B''}^2$.

Now $$\frac{R}{R''} = \frac{\overline{AB}^2}{\overline{A''B''}^2},$$

and $$\frac{R'}{R''} = \frac{\overline{A'B'}^2}{\overline{A''B''}^2},$$ § 376

(*similar polygons are to each other as the squares of their homologous sides*).

By addition, $$\frac{R + R'}{R''} = \frac{\overline{AB}^2 + \overline{A'B'}^2}{\overline{A''B''}^2} = 1.$$

$$\therefore R'' = R + R'.$$

Q.E.F.

PROPOSITION XV. PROBLEM.

386. *To construct a polygon similar to two given similar polygons and equivalent to their difference.*

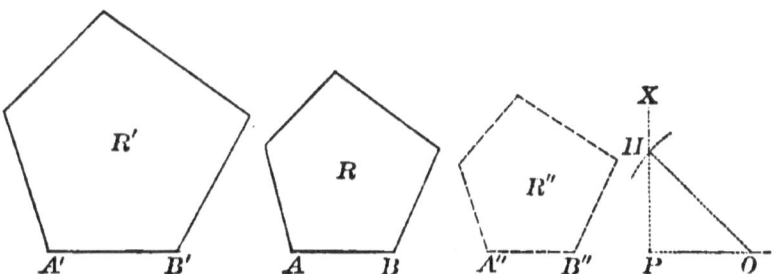

Let R and R' be two similar polygons, and AB and A'B' two homologous sides.

To construct a similar polygon equivalent to $R' - R$.

Construction. Construct the rt. $\angle P$,

and take $PO = AB$.

From O as a centre, with a radius equal to $A'B'$,

describe an arc cutting PX at H, and join OH.

Take $A''B'' = PH$, and on $A''B''$, homologous to AB,

construct R'' similar to R.

Then R'' is the polygon required.

Proof. $\overline{PH}^2 = \overline{OH}^2 - \overline{OP}^2$, $\therefore \overline{A''B''}^2 = \overline{A'B'}^2 - \overline{AB}^2$.

Now $$\frac{R'}{R''} = \frac{\overline{A'B'}^2}{\overline{A''B''}^2},$$

and $$\frac{R}{R''} = \frac{\overline{AB}^2}{\overline{A''B''}^2},\qquad\qquad \S\ 376$$

(*similar polygons are to each other as the squares of their homologous sides*).

By subtraction,
$$\frac{R' - R}{R''} = \frac{\overline{A'B'}^2 - \overline{AB}^2}{\overline{A''B''}^2} = 1.$$

$$\therefore R'' \rightleftharpoons R' - R.$$

Q. E. F.

PROPOSITION XVI. PROBLEM.

386. *To construct a triangle equivalent to a given polygon.*

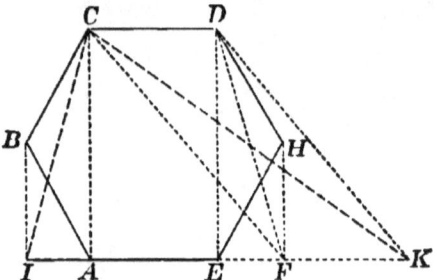

Let ABCDHE be the given polygon.
To construct a triangle equivalent to the given polygon.
Construction.   From D draw DE,
and from H draw $HF \parallel$ to DE.
Produce AE to meet HF at F, and draw DF.
Again, draw CF, and draw $DK \parallel$ to CF to meet AF produced at K, and draw CK.
In like manner continue to reduce the number of sides of the polygon until we obtain the $\triangle CIK$.

Proof. The polygon $ABCDF$ has one side less than the polygon $ABCDHE$, but the two are equivalent.
For the part $ABCDE$ is common,
and the $\triangle DEF \doteqdot \triangle DEH$,   § 369
(*for the base DE is common, and their vertices F and H are in the line $FH \parallel$ to the base*).

The polygon $ABCK$ has one side less than the polygon $ABCDF$, but the two are equivalent.
For the part $ABCF$ is common,
and the $\triangle CFK \doteqdot \triangle CFD$,   § 369
(*for the base CF is common, and their vertices K and D are in the line $KD \parallel$ to the base*).
In like manner the $\triangle CIK \doteqdot ABCK$.

Q. E. F.

Proposition XVII. Problem.

387. *To construct a square which shall have a given ratio to a given square.*

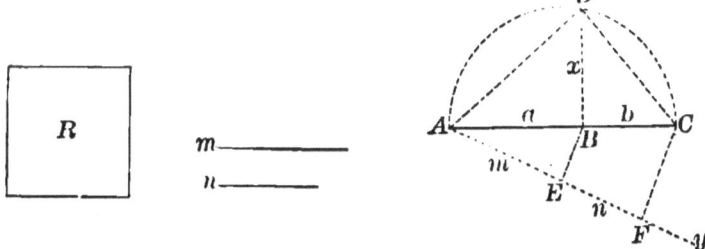

Let R be the given square, and $\frac{n}{m}$ the given ratio.

To construct a square which shall be to R as n is to m.

Construction. Take AB equal to a side of R, and draw Ay, making any acute angle with AB.

On Ay take $AE = m$, $EF = n$, and join EB.

Draw $FC \parallel$ to EB to meet AB produced at C.

On AC as a diameter describe a semicircle.

At B erect the $\perp BD$, meeting the semicircumference at D.

Then BD is a side of the square required.

Proof. Denote AB by a, BC by b, and BD by x.

Now $a : x = x : b$; that is, $x^2 = ab$. § 337

Hence, a^2 will have the same ratio to x^2 and to ab.

Therefore $a^2 : x^2 = a^2 : ab = a : b$.

But $a : b = m : n$, § 309

(*a straight line drawn through two sides of a $\triangle$, parallel to the third side, divides those sides proportionally*).

Therefore $a^2 : x^2 = m : n$.

By inversion, $x^2 : a^2 = n : m$.

Hence the square on BD will have the same ratio to R as n has to m. Q. E. F.

Proposition XVIII. Problem.

388. *To construct a polygon similar to a given polygon and having a given ratio to it.*

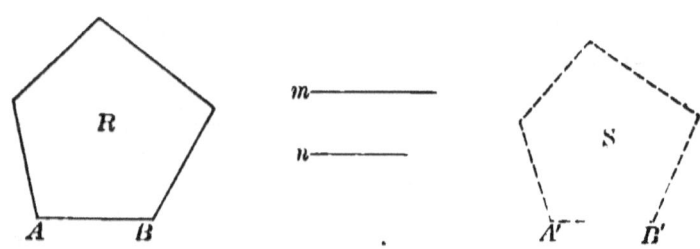

Let R be the given polygon and $\frac{n}{m}$ the given ratio.

To construct a polygon similar to R, which shall be to R as n is to m.

Construction. Find a line $A'B'$, such that the square constructed upon it shall be to the square constructed upon AB as n is to m. § 387

Upon $A'B'$ as a side homologous to AB, construct the polygon S similar to R.

Then S is the polygon required.

Proof. $S : R = \overline{A'B'}^2 : \overline{AB}^2$, § 376

(*similar polygons are to each other as the squares of their homologous sides*).

But $\overline{A'B'}^2 : \overline{AB}^2 = n : m$. Cons.

Therefore $S : R = n : m$.

Q. E. F.

Ex. 304. Find the area of a right triangle if the length of the hypotenuse is 17 feet, and the length of one leg is 8 feet.

Ex. 305. Compare the altitudes of two equivalent triangles, if the base of one is three times that of the other.

Ex. 306. The bases of a trapezoid are 8 feet and 10 feet, and the altitude is 6 feet. Find the base of an equivalent rectangle having an equal altitude.

Proposition XIX. Problem.

389. *To construct a square equivalent to a given parallelogram.*

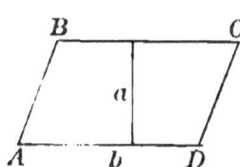
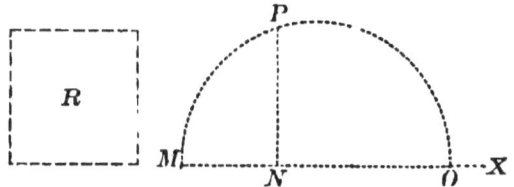

Let $ABCD$ **be a parallelogram,** b **its base, and** a **its altitude.**

To construct a square equivalent to the $\square\, ABCD$.

Construction. Upon the line MX take $MN = a$, and $NO = b$.

Upon MO as a diameter, describe a semicircle.

At N erect $NP \perp$ to MO, to meet the circumference at P.

Then the square R, constructed upon a line equal to NP, is equivalent to the $\square\, ABCD$.

Proof. $\qquad MN : NP = NP : NO, \qquad\qquad$ § 337

(*a* $\perp$ *let fall from any point of a circumference to the diameter is a mean proportional between the segments of the diameter*).

$$\therefore NP^2 = MN \times NO = a \times b.$$

That is, $\qquad\qquad R \doteq \square\, ABCD.$

Q. E. F.

390. Cor. 1. *A square may be constructed equivalent to a given triangle, by taking for its side a mean proportional between the base and one-half the altitude of the triangle.*

391. Cor. 2. *A square may be constructed equivalent to a given polygon, by first reducing the polygon to an equivalent triangle, and then constructing a square equivalent to the triangle.*

Proposition XX. Problem.

392. *To construct a parallelogram equivalent to a given square, and having the sum of its base and altitude equal to a given line.*

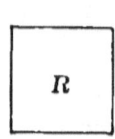
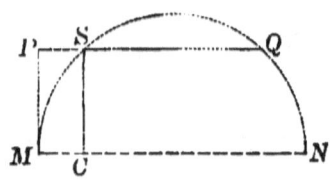

Let R be the given square, and let the sum of the base and altitude of the required parallelogram be equal to the given line MN.

To construct a □ equivalent to R, with the sum of its base and altitude equal to MN.

Construction. Upon MN as a diameter, describe a semicircle.

At M erect a ⊥ MP, equal to a side of the given square R.

Draw PQ ∥ to MN, cutting the circumference at S.

Draw SC ⊥ to MN.

Any □ having CM for its altitude and CN for its base is equivalent to R.

Proof. $\qquad SC = PM.$ §§ 100, 180

$\therefore \overline{SC}^2 = \overline{PM}^2 = R.$

But $\qquad MC : SC = SC : CN,$ § 337

(a ⊥ *let fall from any point in the circumference to the diameter is a mean proportional between the segments of the diameter*).

Then $\qquad \overline{SC}^2 = MC \times CN.$ Q.E.F.

Note. This problem may be stated: *To construct two straight lines the sum and product of which are known.*

Proposition XXI. Problem.

393. *To construct a parallelogram equivalent to a given square, and having the difference of its base and altitude equal to a given line.*

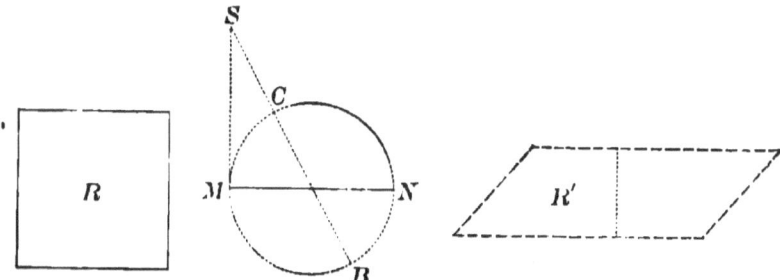

Let R be the given square, and let the difference of the base and altitude of the required parallelogram be equal to the given line MN.

To construct a $\square$ equivalent to R, with the difference of the base and altitude equal to MN.

Construction. Upon the given line MN as a diameter, describe a circle.

From M draw MS, tangent to the ⊙, and equal to a side of the given square R.

Through the centre of the ⊙ draw SB intersecting the circumference at C and B.

Then any $\square$, as R', having SB for its base and SC for its altitude, is equivalent to R.

Proof. $SB : SM = SM : SC,$ § 348

(*if from a point without a ⊙ a secant and a tangent are drawn, the tangent is a mean proportional between the whole secant and the part without the ⊙*).

Then $\overline{SM}^2 = SB \times SC,$

and the difference between SB and SC is the diameter of the ⊙, that is, MN.   Q. E. F.

Note. This problem may be stated: *To construct two straight lines the difference and product of which are known.*

PROBLEMS OF CONSTRUCTION.   203

PROPOSITION XXII. PROBLEM.

394. *To construct a polygon similar to a given polygon P, and equivalent to a given polygon Q.*

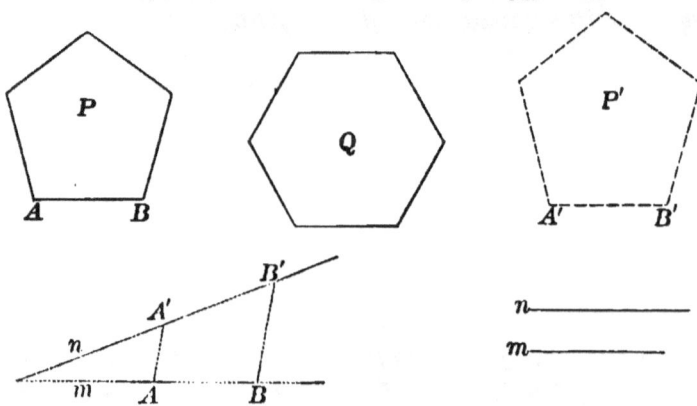

Let P and Q be two polygons, and AB a side of P.
To construct a polygon similar to P and equivalent to Q.

Construction. Find squares equivalent to P and Q, § 391
  and let m and n respectively denote their sides.

Find $A'B'$, a fourth proportional to m, n, and AB. § 351

Upon $A'B'$, homologous to AB, construct P' similar to P.

  Then P' is the polygon required.

Proof. $m : n = AB : A'B'$, Cons.

  $\therefore m^2 : n^2 = \overline{AB}^2 : \overline{A'B'}^2$.

But $P \backsimeq m^2$, and $Q \backsimeq n^2$. Cons.

  $\therefore P : Q = m^2 : n^2 = \overline{AB}^2 : \overline{A'B'}^2$.

But $P : P' = \overline{AB}^2 : \overline{A'B'}^2$, § 376

(*similar polygons are to each other as the squares of their homologous sides*).

  $\therefore P : Q = P : P'$. Ax. 1

$\therefore P'$ is equivalent to Q, and is similar to P by construction.

Q. E. F.

Problems of Computation.

Ex. 307. To find the area of an equilateral triangle in terms of its side.

Denote the side by a, the altitude by h, and the area by S.

Then
$$h^2 = a^2 - \frac{a^2}{4} = \frac{3a^2}{4}.$$

$$\therefore h = \frac{a}{2}\sqrt{3}.$$

But
$$S = \frac{a \times h}{2}.$$

$$\therefore S = \frac{a}{2} \times \frac{a\sqrt{3}}{2} = \frac{a^2\sqrt{3}}{4}.$$

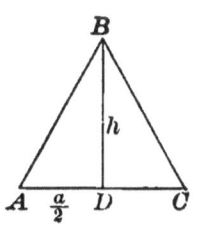

Ex. 308. To find the area of a triangle in terms of its sides.

By Ex. 219,
$$h = \frac{2}{b}\sqrt{s(s-a)(s-b)(s-c)}.$$

Hence,
$$S = \frac{b}{2} \times \frac{2}{b}\sqrt{s(s-a)(s-b)(s-c)}$$

$$= \sqrt{s(s-a)(s-b)(s-c)}.$$

Ex. 309. To find the area of a triangle in terms of the radius of the circumscribing circle.

If R denote the radius of the circumscribing circle, and h the altitude of the triangle, we have, by Ex. 222,

$$b \times c = 2R \times h.$$

Multiply by a, and we have

$$a \times b \times c = 2R \times a \times h.$$

But
$$a \times h = 2S.$$

$$\therefore a \times b \times c = 4R \times S.$$

$$\therefore S = \frac{abc}{4R}.$$

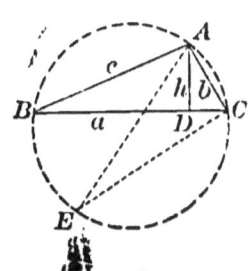

Note. The radius of the circumscribing circle is equal to $\dfrac{abc}{4S}$.

EXERCISES.

Theorems.

310. In a right triangle the product of the legs is equal to the product of the hypotenuse and the perpendicular drawn to the hypotenuse from the vertex of the right angle.

311. If ABC is a right triangle, C the vertex of the right angle, BD a line cutting AC in D, then $\overline{BD}^2 + \overline{AC}^2 = \overline{AB}^2 + \overline{DC}^2$.

312. Upon the sides of a right triangle as homologous sides three similar polygons are constructed. Prove that the polygon upon the hypotenuse is equivalent to the sum of the polygons upon the legs.

313. Two isosceles triangles are equivalent if their legs are equal each to each, and the altitude of one is equal to half the base of the other.

314. The area of a circumscribed polygon is equal to half the product of its perimeter by the radius of the inscribed circle.

315. Two parallelograms are equal if two adjacent sides of the one are equal respectively to two adjacent sides of the other, and the included angles are supplementary.

316. Every straight line drawn through the centre of a parallelogram divides it into two equal parts.

317. If the middle points of two adjacent sides of a parallelogram are joined, a triangle is formed which is equivalent to one-eighth of the entire parallelogram.

318. If any point within a parallelogram is joined to the four vertices, the sum of either pair of triangles having parallel bases is equivalent to one-half the parallelogram.

319. The line which joins the middle points of the bases of a trapezoid divides the trapezoid into two equivalent parts.

320. The area of a trapezoid is equal to the product of one of the legs and the distance from this leg to the middle point of the other leg.

321. The lines joining the middle point of the diagonal of a quadrilateral to the opposite vertices divide the quadrilateral into two equivalent parts.

322. The figure whose vertices are the middle points of the sides of any quadrilateral is equivalent to one-half of the quadrilateral.

323. ABC is a triangle, M the middle point of AB, P any point in AB between A and M. If MD is drawn parallel to PC, and meeting BC at D, the triangle BPD is equivalent to one-half the triangle ABC.

Numerical Exercises.

324. Find the area of a rhombus, if the sum of its diagonals is 12 feet, and their ratio is 3 : 5.

325. Find the area of an isosceles right triangle if the hypotenuse is 20 feet.

326. In a right triangle, the hypotenuse is 13 feet, one leg is 5 feet. Find the area.

327. Find the area of an isosceles triangle if the base $= b$, and leg $= c$.

328. Find the area of an equilateral triangle if one side $= 8$.

329. Find the area of an equilateral triangle if the altitude $= h$.

330. A house is 40 feet long, 30 feet wide, 25 feet high to the eaves, and 35 feet high to the ridge-pole. Find the number of square feet in its entire exterior surface.

331. The sides of a right triangle are as 3 : 4 : 5. The altitude upon the hypotenuse is 12 feet. Find the area.

332. Find the area of a right triangle if one leg $= a$, and the altitude upon the hypotenuse $= h$.

333. Find the area of a triangle if the lengths of the sides are 104 feet, 111 feet, and 175 feet.

334. The area of a trapezoid is 700 square feet. The bases are 30 feet and 40 feet respectively. Find the distance between the bases.

335. $ABCD$ is a trapezium; $AB = 87$ feet, $BC = 119$ feet, $CD = 41$ feet, $DA = 169$ feet, $AC = 200$ feet. Find the area.

336. What is the area of a quadrilateral circumscribed about a circle whose radius is 25 feet, if the perimeter of the quadrilateral is 400 feet? What is the area of a hexagon having an equal perimeter and circumscribed about the same circle?

337. The base of a triangle is 15 feet, and its altitude is 8 feet. Find the perimeter of an equivalent rhombus if the altitude is 6 feet.

338. Upon the diagonal of a rectangle 24 feet by 10 feet a triangle equivalent to the rectangle is constructed. What is its altitude?

339. Find the side of a square equivalent to a trapezoid whose bases are 56 feet and 44 feet, and each leg is 10 feet.

340. Through a point P in the side AB of a triangle ABC, a line is drawn parallel to BC, and so as to divide the triangle into two equivalent parts. Find the value of AP in terms of AB.

EXERCISES.

341. What part of a parallelogram is the triangle cut off by a line drawn from one vertex to the middle point of one of the opposite sides?

342. In two similar polygons, two homologous sides are 15 feet and 25 feet. The area of the first polygon is 450 square feet. Find the area of the other polygon.

343. The base of a triangle is 32 feet, its altitude 20 feet. What is the area of the triangle cut off by drawing a line parallel to the base and at a distance of 15 feet from the base?

344. The sides of two equilateral triangles are 3 feet and 4 feet. Find the side of an equilateral triangle equivalent to their sum.

345. If the side of one equilateral triangle is equal to the altitude of another, what is the ratio of their areas?

346. The sides of a triangle are 10 feet, 17 feet, and 21 feet. Find the a██ of the parts into which the triangle is divided by bisecting the angle ██ed by the first two sides.

347. In a trapezoid, one base is 10 feet, the altitude is 4 feet, the area is 32 square feet. Find the length of a line drawn between the legs parallel to the base and distant 1 foot from it.

348. If the altitude h of a triangle is increased by a length m, how much must be taken from the base a in order that the area may remain the same?

349. Find the area of a right triangle, having given the segments p, q, into which the hypotenuse is divided by a perpendicular drawn to the hypotenuse from the vertex of the right angle.

Problems.

350. To construct a triangle equivalent to a given triangle, and having one side equal to a given length l.

351. To transform a triangle into an equivalent right triangle.

352. To transform a triangle into an equivalent isosceles triangle.

353. To transform a triangle ABC into an equivalent triangle, having one side equal to a given length l, and one angle equal to angle BAC.

Hints. Upon AB (produced if necessary), take $AD = l$, draw $BE \parallel$ to CD, and meeting AC (produced if necessary) at E; $\triangle BED \backsim \triangle BEC$.

354. To transform a given triangle into an equivalent right triangle, having one leg equal to a given length.

355. To transform a given triangle into an equivalent right triangle, having the hypotenuse equal to a given length.

356. To transform a given triangle into an equivalent isosceles triangle, having the base equal to a given length.

To construct a triangle equivalent to:

357. The sum of two given triangles.

358. The difference of two given triangles.

359. To transform a given triangle into an equivalent equilateral triangle.

To transform a parallelogram into:

360. A parallelogram having one side equal to a given length.

361. A parallelogram having one angle equal to a given angle.

362. A rectangle having a given altitude.

To transform a square into:

363. An equilateral triangle.

364. A right triangle having one leg equal to a given length.

365. A rectangle having one side equal to a given length.

To construct a square equivalent to:

366. Five-eighths of a given square.

367. Three-fifths of a given pentagon.

368. To draw a line through the vertex of a given triangle so as to divide the triangle into two triangles which shall be to each other as 2 : 3.

369. To divide a given triangle into two equivalent parts by drawing a line through a given point P in one of the sides.

370. To find a point within a triangle, such that the lines joining this point to the vertices shall divide the triangle into three equivalent parts.

371. To divide a given triangle into two equivalent parts by drawing a line parallel to one of the sides.

372. To divide a given triangle into two equivalent parts by drawing a line perpendicular to one of the sides.

373. To divide a given parallelogram into two equivalent parts by drawing a line through a given point in one of the sides.

374. To divide a given trapezoid into two equivalent parts by drawing a line parallel to the bases.

375. To divide a given trapezoid into two equivalent parts by drawing a line through a given point in one of the bases.

BOOK V.

REGULAR POLYGONS AND CIRCLES.

395. A *regular polygon* is a polygon which is equilateral and equiangular; as, for example, the equilateral triangle, and the square.

PROPOSITION I. THEOREM.

396. *An equilateral polygon inscribed in a circle is a regular polygon.*

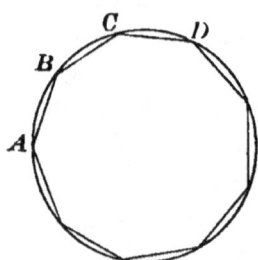

Let *ABC* etc., be an equilateral polygon inscribed in a circle.

To prove the polygon *ABC* etc., regular.

Proof. The arcs AB, BC, CD, etc., are equal, § 230
(*in the same ⊙, equal chords subtend equal arcs*).

Hence arcs ABC, BCD, etc., are equal, Ax. 6

and the ∠ A, B, C, etc., are equal,
(*being inscribed in equal segments*).

Therefore the polygon ABC, etc., is a regular polygon, being equilateral and equiangular. Q.E.D.

210 PLANE GEOMETRY. — BOOK V.

PROPOSITION II. THEOREM.

397. *A circle may be circumscribed about, and a circle may be inscribed in, any regular polygon.*

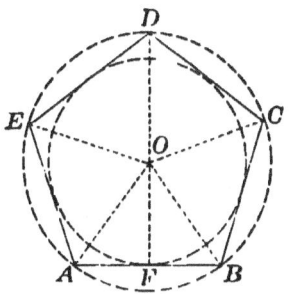

Let ABCDE be a regular polygon.

I. *To prove that a circle may be circumscribed about ABCDE.*

Proof. Let O be the centre of the circle passing through A, B, C.

Join OA, OB, OC, and OD.

Since the polygon is equiangular, and the $\triangle\,OBC$ is isosceles,

$\angle ABC = \angle BCD$,

and $\angle OBC = \angle OCB$. § 154

By subtraction, $\angle OBA = \angle OCD$.

Hence in the $\triangle\,OBA$ and OCD

the $\angle OBA = \angle OCD$,

the radius $OB =$ the radius OC,

and $AB = CD$. § 395

$\therefore \triangle OAB = \triangle OCD$, § 150

(*having two sides and the included $\angle$ of the one equal to two sides and the included $\angle$ of the other*).

$\therefore OA = OD$.

Therefore the circle passing through A, B, and C, also passes through D.

In like manner it may be proved that the circle passing through *B, C,* and *D*, also passes through *E*; and so on through all the vertices in succession.

Therefore a circle described from *O* as a centre, and with a radius *OA*, will be circumscribed about the polygon.

II. *To prove that a circle may be inscribed in ABCDE.*

Proof. Since the sides of the regular polygon are equal chords of the circumscribed circle, they are equally distant from the centre. § 236

Therefore a circle described from *O* as a centre, and with the distance from *O* to a side of the polygon as a radius, will be inscribed in the polygon. Q. E. D.

398. The radius of the circumscribed circle, *OA*, is called the *radius of the polygon.*

399. The radius of the inscribed circle, *OF*, is called the *apothem of the polygon.*

400. The common centre *O* of the circumscribed and inscribed circles is called the *centre of the polygon.*

401. The angle between radii drawn to the extremities of any side, as angle *AOB*, is called the *angle at the centre of the polygon.*

By joining the centre to the vertices of a regular polygon, the polygon can be decomposed into as many equal isosceles triangles as it has sides. Therefore,

402. Cor. 1. *The angle at the centre of a regular polygon is equal to four right angles divided by the number of sides of the polygon.*

403. Cor. 2. *The radius drawn to any vertex of a regular polygon bisects the angle at the vertex.*

404. Cor. 3. *The interior angle of a regular polygon is the supplement of the angle at the centre.*

For the $\angle ABC = 2 \angle ABO = \angle ABO + \angle BAO$. Hence the $\angle ABC$ is the supplement of the $\angle AOB$.

PROPOSITION III. THEOREM.

405. *If the circumference of a circle is divided into any number of equal parts, the chords joining the successive points of division form a regular inscribed polygon, and the tangents drawn at the points of division form a regular circumscribed polygon.*

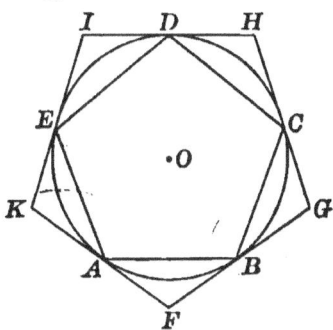

Let the circumference be divided into equal arcs, *AB, BC, CD,* etc., be chords, *FBG, GCH,* etc., be tangents.

I. To prove that *ABCDE* is a regular polygon.

Proof. The sides *AB, BC, CD,* etc., are equal, § 230
(in the same ⊙ equal arcs are subtended by equal chords).

Therefore the polygon is regular, § 396
(an equilateral polygon inscribed in a ⊙ is regular).

II. To prove that the polygon *FGHIK* is a regular polygon.

Proof. In the △ *AFB, BGC, CHD,* etc.

$AB = BC = CD$, etc. § 395

Also, $\angle BAF = \angle ABF = \angle CBG = \angle BCG$, etc., § 269
(being measured by halves of equal arcs).

Therefore the triangles are all equal isosceles triangles.

Hence $\angle F = \angle G = \angle H$, etc.

Also, $FB = BG = GC = CH$, etc.

Therefore $FG = GH$, etc.

∴ *FGHIK* is a regular polygon. § 395

Q. E. D.

406. Cor. 1. *Tangents to a circumference at the vertices of a regular inscribed polygon form a regular circumscribed polygon of the same number of sides.*

407. Cor. 2. *If a regular polygon is inscribed in a circle, the tangents drawn at the middle points of the arcs subtended by the sides of the polygon form a circumscribed regular polygon, whose sides are parallel to the sides of the inscribed polygon and whose vertices lie on the radii (prolonged) of the inscribed polygon.* For any two cor-

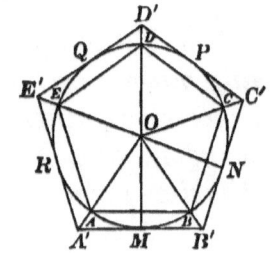

responding sides, as AB and $A'B'$, perpendicular to OM, are parallel, and the tangents MB' and NB', intersecting at a point equidistant from OM and ON (§ 246), intersect upon the bisector of the $\angle MON$ (§ 163); that is, upon the radius OB.

408. Cor. 3. *If the vertices of a regular inscribed polygon are joined to the middle points of the arcs subtended by the sides of the polygon, the joining lines form a regular inscribed polygon of double the number of sides.*

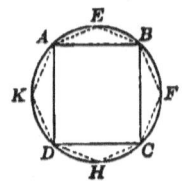

409. Cor. 4. *If tangents are drawn at the middle points of the arcs between adjacent points of contact of the sides of a regular circumscribed polygon, a regular circumscribed polygon of double the number of sides is formed.*

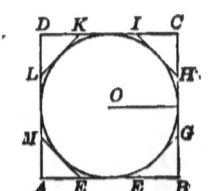

410. Scholium. The perimeter of an inscribed polygon is less than the perimeter of the inscribed polygon of double the number of sides; for each pair of sides of the second polygon is greater than the side of the first polygon which they replace (§ 137).

The perimeter of a circumscribed polygon is greater than the perimeter of the circumscribed polygon of double the number of sides; for every alternate side FG, HI, etc., of the polygon $FGHI$, etc., replaces portions of two sides of the circumscribed polygon $ABCD$, and forms with them a triangle, and one side of a triangle is less than the sum of the other two sides.

Proposition IV. Theorem.

411. *Two regular polygons of the same number of sides are similar.*

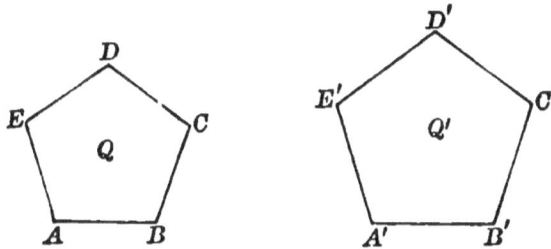

Let Q and Q' be two regular polygons, each having n sides.

To prove Q and Q' *similar polygons.*

Proof. The sum of the interior ∠s of each polygon is equal to

$$(n-2)\ 2\ \text{rt.}\ \angle\text{s},\qquad\qquad \S\ 205$$

(*the sum of the interior ∠s of a polygon is equal to 2 rt. ∠s taken as many times less 2 as the polygon has sides*).

Each angle of either polygon $=\dfrac{(n-2)\ 2\ \text{rt.}\ \angle\text{s}}{n}$, § 206

(*for the ∠s of a regular polygon are all equal, and hence each ∠ is equal to the sum of the ∠s divided by their number*).

Hence the two polygons Q and Q' are mutually equiangular.

Since $AB = BC$, etc., and $A'B' = B'C'$, etc., § 395

$$AB : A'B' = BC : B'C',\ \text{etc.}$$

Hence the two polygons have their homologous sides proportional.

Therefore the two polygons are similar. § 319

Q. E. D.

412. Cor. *The areas of two regular polygons of the same number of sides are to each other as the squares of any two homologous sides.* § 376

PROPOSITION V. THEOREM.

413. *The perimeters of two regular polygons of the same number of sides are to each other as the radii of their circumscribed circles, and also as the radii of their inscribed circles.*

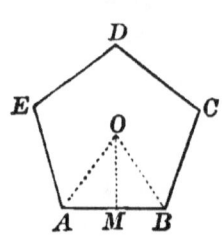 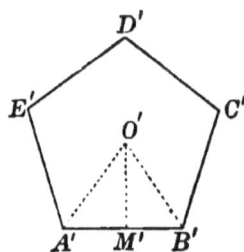

Let P and P′ denote the perimeters, O and O′ the centres, of the two regular polygons.

From O, O' draw OA, $O'A'$, OB, $O'B'$, and ⊥s OM, $O'M'$.

To prove $\quad P : P' = OA : O'A' = OM : O'M'$.

Proof. Since the polygons are similar, §411

$$P : P' = AB : A'B'. \qquad \S\,333$$

In the isosceles △ OAB and $O'A'B'$

the ∠ O = the ∠ O', §402

and $OA : OB = O'A' : O'B'$.

∴ the △ OAB and $O'A'B'$ are similar. §326

∴ $AB : A'B' = OA : O'A'$. §319

Also $\quad AB : A'B' = OM : O'M'$, §328

(*the homologous altitudes of similar △ have the same ratio as their bases*).

∴ $P : P' = OA : O'A' = OM : OM'$.

Q. E. D.

414. Cor. *The areas of two regular polygons of the same number of sides are to each other as the squares of the radii of their circumscribed circles, and also as the squares of the radii of their inscribed circles.* §376

PROPOSITION VI. THEOREM.

415. *The difference between the lengths of the perimeters of a regular inscribed polygon and of a similar circumscribed polygon is indefinitely diminished as the number of the sides of the polygons is indefinitely increased.*

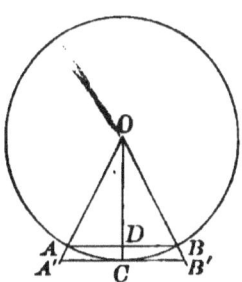

Let P and P' denote the lengths of the perimeters, AB and A'B' two corresponding sides, OA and OA' the radii, of the polygons.

To prove *that as the number of the sides of the polygons is indefinitely increased, $P' - P$ is indefinitely diminished.*

Proof. Since the polygons are similar,
$$P' : P = OA' : OA. \qquad \text{§ 333}$$
Therefore $\quad P' - P : P :: OA' - OA : OA. \qquad$ § 301
Whence $\quad OA(P' - P) = P(OA' - OA). \qquad$ § 295

Now OA is the radius of the circle, and P, though an increasing variable, *always remains less than the circumference* of the circle.

Therefore $P' - P$ is indefinitely diminished, if $OA' - OA$ is indefinitely diminished.

Draw the radius OC to the point of contact of $A'B'$.
In the $\triangle\ OA'C, \quad OA' - OC < A'C. \qquad$ § 137
Substituting OA for its equal OC, we have
$$OA' - OA < A'C.$$

REGULAR POLYGONS AND CIRCLES. 217

But as the *number* of sides of the polygon is indefinitely increased, the *length* of each side is indefinitely diminished; that is, $A'B'$, and consequently $A'C$, is indefinitely diminished.

Therefore $OA' - OA$, which is less than $A'C$, is indefinitely diminished.

Therefore $P' - P$ is indefinitely diminished.   Q. E. D.

416. Cor. *The difference between the areas of a regular inscribed polygon and of a similar circumscribed polygon is indefinitely diminished as the number of the sides of the polygons is indefinitely increased.*

For, if S and S' denote the areas of the polygons,
$$S' : S = \overline{OA'}^2 : \overline{OA}^2 = \overline{OA'}^2 : \overline{OC}^2. \qquad \S\ 414$$
By division, $S' - S : S = \overline{OA'}^2 - \overline{OC}^2 : \overline{OC}^2$.

Whence $S' - S = S \times \dfrac{\overline{OA'}^2 - \overline{OC}^2}{\overline{OC}^2} = S \times \dfrac{\overline{A'C}^2}{\overline{OC}^2}$.

Since $A'C$ can be indefinitely diminished by increasing the number of the sides, $S' - S$ can be indefinitely diminished.

417. Scholium. The perimeter P' is constantly greater than P, and the area S' is constantly greater than S; for the radius OA' is constantly greater than OA. But P' constantly decreases and P constantly increases (§ 410), and the area S' constantly decreases, and the area S constantly increases, as the number of sides of the polygons is indefinitely increased.

Since the difference between P' and P can be made as small as we please, but cannot be made absolutely zero, and since P' is decreasing while P is increasing, it is evident that P' and P tend towards a common limit. This common limit is *the length of the circumference.*   § 259

Also, since the difference between the areas S' and S can be made as small as we please, but cannot be made absolutely zero, and since S' is decreasing, while S is increasing, it is evident that S' and S tend towards a common limit. This common limit is *the area of the circle.*

PROPOSITION VII. THEOREM.

418. *Two circumferences have the same ratio as their radii.*

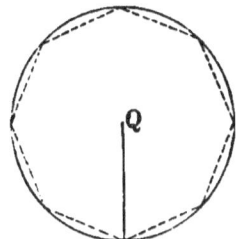 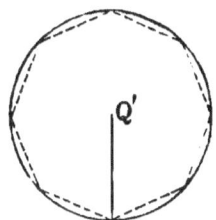

Let C and C' be the circumferences, R and R' the radii, of the two circles Q and Q'.

To prove $\quad C : C' = R : R'$.

Proof. Inscribe in the ⊙ two similar regular polygons, and denote their perimeters by P and P'.

Then $P : P' = R : R'$ (§ 413); that is, $R' \times P = R \times P'$.

Conceive the number of the sides of these similar regular polygons to be indefinitely increased, the polygons continuing to have an equal number of sides.

Then $R' \times P$ will continue equal to $R \times P'$, and P and P' will approach indefinitely C and C' as their respective limits.

$\therefore R' \times C = R \times C'$ (§ 260); that is, $C : C' = R : R'$.

Q. E. D.

419. Cor. *The ratio of the circumference of a circle to its diameter is constant.* For, in the above proportion, by doubling both terms of the ratio $R : R'$, we have

$$C : C' = 2R : 2R'.$$

By alternation, $\quad C : 2R = C' : 2R'$.

This constant ratio is denoted by π, so that for any circle whose diameter is $2R$ and circumference C, we have

$$\frac{C}{2R} = \pi, \text{ or } C = 2\pi R.$$

420. Scholium. The ratio π is incommensurable, and therefore can be expressed in figures only approximately.

Proposition VIII. Theorem.

421. *The area of a regular polygon is equal to one-half the product of its apothem by its perimeter.*

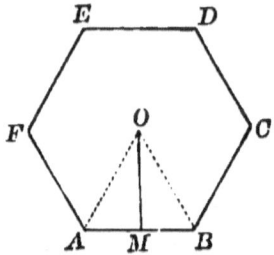

Let **P represent the perimeter, R the apothem, and S the area of the regular polygon** *ABC* **etc.**

To prove $\qquad S = \tfrac{1}{2} R \times P.$

Proof. $\qquad$ Draw *OA*, *OB*, *OC*, etc.

The polygon is divided into as many △ as it has sides.

The apothem is the common altitude of these △,

and the area of each △ is equal to $\tfrac{1}{2} R$ multiplied by the base. § 368

Hence the area of all the △ is equal to $\tfrac{1}{2} R$ multiplied by the sum of all the bases.

But the sum of the areas of all the △ is equal to the area of the polygon.

and the sum of all the bases of the △ is equal to the perimeter of the polygon.

Therefore $S = \tfrac{1}{2} R \times P.$

Q. E. D.

422. In different circles *similar arcs*, *similar sectors*, and *similar segments* are such as correspond to equal angles at the centre.

Proposition IX. Theorem.

423. *The area of a circle is equal to one-half the product of its radius by its circumference.*

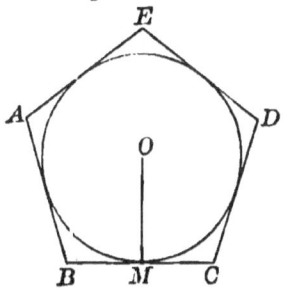

Let *R* represent the radius, *C* the circumference, and *S* the area, of the circle.

To prove $S = \tfrac{1}{2} R \times C$.

Proof. Circumscribe any regular polygon about the circle, and denote its perimeter by *P*.

Then the area of this polygon $= \tfrac{1}{2} R \times P$, § 421

Conceive the number of sides of the polygon to be indefinitely increased; then the perimeter of the polygon approaches the circumference of the circle as its limit, and the area of the polygon approaches the circle as its limit.

But the area of the polygon continues to be equal to one-half the product of the radius by the perimeter, however great the number of sides of the polygon.

Therefore $S = \tfrac{1}{2} R \times C$. § 260

Q. E. D.

424. Cor. 1. *The area of a sector equals one-half the product of its radius by its arc.* For the sector is such a part of the circle as its arc is of the circumference.

425. Cor. 2. *The area of a circle equals π times the square of its radius.*

For the area of the $\odot = \tfrac{1}{2} R \times C = \tfrac{1}{2} R \times 2\pi R = \pi R^2$.

REGULAR POLYGONS AND CIRCLES. 221

426. Cor. 3. *The areas of two circles are to each other as the squares of their radii.* For, if S and S' denote the areas, and R and R' the radii,

$$S : S' = \pi R^2 : \pi R'^2 = R^2 : R'^2.$$

427. Cor. 4. *Similar arcs, being like parts of their respective circumferences, are to each other as their radii; similar sectors, being like parts of their respective circles, are to each other as the squares of their radii.*

PROPOSITION X. THEOREM.

428. *The areas of two similar segments are to each other as the squares of their radii.*

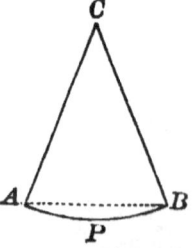 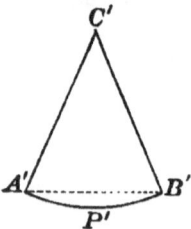

Let AC and $A'C'$ be the radii of the two similar segments ABP and $A'B'P'$.

To prove $\quad ABP : A'B'P' = \overline{AC}^2 : \overline{A'C'}^2.$

Proof. The sectors ACB and $A'C'B'$ are similar, § 422
(*having the ∠ at the centre, C and C', equal*).

In the △ ACB and $A'C'B'$

$\angle C = \angle C'$, $AC = CB$, and $A'C' = C'B'$.

Therefore the △ ACB and $A'C'B'$ are similar. § 326

Now $\quad$ sector ACB : sector $A'C'B' = \overline{AC}^2 : \overline{A'C'}^2$, § 427

and $\quad \triangle ACB : \triangle A'C'B' = \overline{AC}^2 : \overline{A'C'}^2.$ § 375

Hence $\quad \dfrac{\text{sector } ACB - \triangle ACB}{\text{sector } A'C'B' - \triangle A'C'B'} = \dfrac{\overline{AC}^2}{\overline{A'C'}^2}.$ § 301

That is, $\quad ABP : A'B'P' = \overline{AC}^2 : \overline{A'C'}^2.$

Q.E.D.

Problems of Construction.

Proposition XI. Problem.

429. *To inscribe a square in a given circle.*

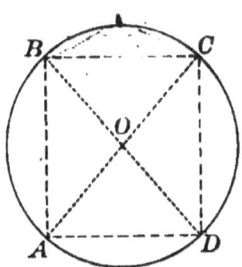

Let O be the centre of the given circle.

To inscribe a square in the circle.

Construction. Draw the two diameters AC and $BD \perp$ to each other.

Join AB, BC, CD, and DA.

Then $ABCD$ is the square required.

Proof. The $\triangle ABC$, BCD, etc., are rt. $\triangle$, § 264
(*being inscribed in a semicircle*),

and the sides AB, BC, etc., are equal, § 230
(*in the same ⊙ equal arcs are subtended by equal chords*).

Hence the figure $ABCD$ is a square. § 171

Q. E. F.

430. Cor. *By bisecting the arcs AB, BC, etc., a regular polygon of eight sides may be inscribed in the circle; and, by continuing the process, regular polygons of sixteen, thirty-two, sixty-four, etc., sides may be inscribed.*

Ex. 376. The area of a circumscribed square is equal to twice the area of the inscribed square.

Ex. 377. If the length of the side of an inscribed square is 2 inches, what is the length of the circumscribed square?

PROBLEMS OF CONSTRUCTION.   223

PROPOSITION XII. PROBLEM.

431. *To inscribe a regular hexagon in a given circle.*

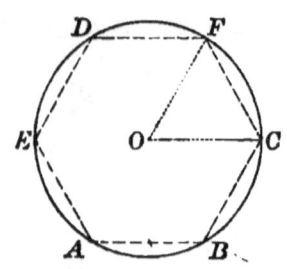

Let O be the centre of the given circle.

To inscribe in the given circle a regular hexagon.

Construction. From O draw any radius, as OC.

From C as a centre, with a radius equal to OC, describe an arc intersecting the circumference at F.

Draw OF and CF.

Then CF is a side of the regular hexagon required.

Proof. The $\triangle OFC$ is equilateral and equiangular.

Hence the $\angle FOC$ is $\tfrac{1}{3}$ of 2 rt. $\angle$s, or $\tfrac{1}{6}$ of 4 rt. $\angle$s.   § 138

And the arc FC is $\tfrac{1}{6}$ of the circumference $ABCF$.

Therefore the chord FC, which subtends the arc FC, is a side of a regular hexagon ;

and the figure CFD etc., formed by applying the radius six times as a chord, is a regular hexagon.   Q. E. F.

432. Cor. 1. *By joining the alternate vertices A, C, D, an equilateral triangle is inscribed in the circle.*

433. Cor. 2. *By bisecting the arcs AB, BC, etc., a regular polygon of twelve sides may be inscribed in the circle; and, by continuing the process, regular polygons of twenty-four, forty-eight, etc., sides may be inscribed.*

Proposition XIII. Problem.

434. *To inscribe a regular decagon in a given circle.*

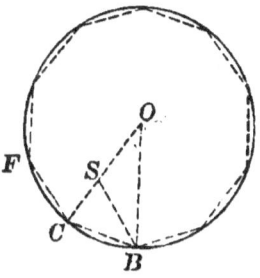

Let O be the centre of the given circle.
To inscribe a regular decagon in the given circle.
Construction.   Draw the radius OC,
and divide it in extreme and mean ratio, so that OC shall be to OS as OS is to SC.   § 356

From C as a centre, with a radius equal to OS,
describe an arc intersecting the circumference at B, and draw BC.

Then BC is a side of the regular decagon required.

Proof.   Draw BS and BO.
By construction $OC:OS = OS:SC$,
and $BC = OS$.
$$\therefore OC:BC = BC:SC.$$
Moreover, the $\angle OCB = \angle SCB$.   Iden.

Hence the $\triangle OCB$ and BCS are similar,   § 326
(having an $\angle$ of the one equal to an $\angle$ of the other, and the including sides proportional).

But the $\triangle OCB$ is isosceles,
(its sides OC and OB being radii of the same circle).

$\therefore \triangle BCS$, which is similar to the $\triangle OCB$, is isosceles,
and $CB = BS = OS$.

∴ the △ SOB is isosceles, and the ∠ O = ∠ SBO.

But the ext. ∠ CSB = ∠ O + ∠ SBO = 2 ∠ O. § 145

Hence ∠ SCB (= ∠ CSB) = 2 ∠ O, § 154

and ∠ OBC (= ∠ SCB) = 2 ∠ O. § 154

∴ the sum of the ∠s of the △ OCB = 5 ∠ O = 2 rt. ∠s,

and ∠ O = $\frac{1}{5}$ of 2 rt. ∠s, or $\frac{1}{10}$ of 4 rt. ∠s.

Therefore the arc BC is $\frac{1}{10}$ of the circumference,

and the chord BC is a side of a regular inscribed decagon.

Hence, to inscribe a regular decagon, divide the radius in extreme and mean ratio, and apply the greater segment ten times as a chord.

Q. E. F.

435. Cor. 1. *By joining the alternate vertices of a regular inscribed decagon, a regular pentagon is inscribed.*

436. Cor. 2. *By bisecting the arcs BC, CF, etc., a regular polygon of twenty sides may be inscribed; and, by continuing the process, regular polygons of forty, eighty, etc., sides may be inscribed.*

Let R denote the radius of a regular inscribed polygon, r the apothem, a one side, A an interior angle, and C the angle at the centre; show that

Ex. 378. In a regular inscribed triangle $a = R\sqrt{3}$, $r = \frac{1}{2}R$, $A = 60°$, $C = 120°$.

Ex. 379. In an inscribed square $a = R\sqrt{2}$, $r = \frac{1}{2}R\sqrt{2}$, $A = 90°$, $C = 90°$.

Ex. 380. In a regular inscribed hexagon $a = R$, $r = \frac{1}{2}R\sqrt{3}$, $A = 120°$, $C = 60°$.

Ex. 381. In a regular inscribed decagon

$$a = \frac{R(\sqrt{5}-1)}{2}, \quad r = \frac{1}{4}R\sqrt{10+2\sqrt{5}}, \quad A = 144°, \quad C = 36°.$$

Proposition XIV. Problem.

437. *To inscribe in a given circle a regular pentedecagon, or polygon of fifteen sides.*

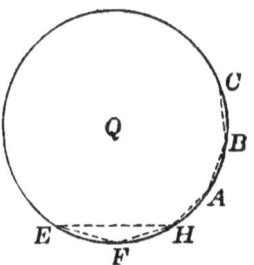

Let Q be the given circle.

To inscribe in Q a regular pentedecagon.

Construction. Draw EH equal to a side of a regular inscribed hexagon, § 431

and EF equal to a side of a regular inscribed decagon. § 434

Join FH.

Then FH will be a side of a regular inscribed pentedecagon.

Proof. The arc EH is $\frac{1}{6}$ of the circumference,

and the arc EF is $\frac{1}{10}$ of the circumference.

Hence the arc FH is $\frac{1}{6} - \frac{1}{10}$, or $\frac{1}{15}$, of the circumference,

and the chord FH is a side of a regular inscribed pentedecagon.

By applying FH fifteen times as a chord, we have the polygon required.

Q. E. F.

438. Cor. *By bisecting the arcs FH, HA, etc., a regular polygon of thirty sides may be inscribed; and, by continuing the process, regular polygons of sixty, one hundred twenty, etc., sides, may be inscribed.*

PROBLEMS OF CONSTRUCTION.   227

Proposition XV. Problem.

439. *To inscribe in a given circle a regular polygon similar to a given regular polygon.*

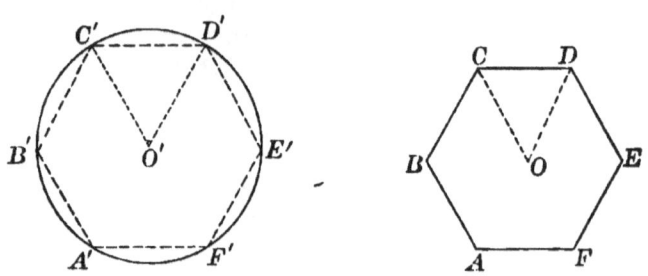

Let *ABCD* etc., be the given regular polygon, and *C'D'E'* the given circle.

To inscribe in the circle a regular polygon similar to *ABCD*, etc.

Construction. From *O*, the centre of the given polygon,

draw *OD* and *OC*.

From *O'*, the centre of the given circle,

draw *O'C'* and *O'D'*,

making the $\angle O' = \angle O$.

Draw *C'D'*.

Then *C'D'* will be a side of the regular polygon required.

Proof. Each polygon will have as many ▟▛▜ the $\angle O$ ($= \angle O'$) is contained times in 4 rt. $\angle$s.

Therefore the polygon *C'D'E'* etc., is simil▟▛ the polygon *CDE* etc.,   § 411

(*two regular polygons of the same number of sides are similar*).

Q. E. F.

PROPOSITION XVI. PROBLEM.

440. *Given the radius and the side of a regular inscribed polygon, to find the side of the regular inscribed polygon of double the number of sides.*

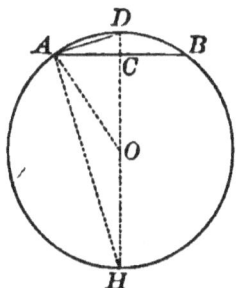

Let AB be a side of the regular inscribed polygon.

To find the value of AD, a side of a regular inscribed polygon of double the number of sides.

From D draw DH through the centre O, and draw OA, AH.

DH is $\perp$ to AB at its middle point C. § 123

In the rt. $\triangle OAC$, $\overline{OC}^2 = \overline{OA}^2 - \overline{AC}^2$. § 339

That is, $OC = \sqrt{\overline{OA}^2 - \overline{AC}^2}$.

 $AC = \tfrac{1}{2} AB$; hence $\overline{AC}^2 = \tfrac{1}{4}\overline{AB}^2$.

...ore, $OC = \sqrt{\overline{OA}^2 - \tfrac{1}{4}\overline{AB}^2}$.

In the rt. $\triangle DAH$, § 264

$\overline{AD}^2 = DH \times DC$ § 334

$= 2OA(OA - OC),$

and $AD = \sqrt{2OA(OA - OC)}.$

If we denote the radius by R, and substitute $\sqrt{R^2 - \tfrac{1}{4}\overline{AB}^2}$ for OC, then

$$AD = \sqrt{2R(R - \sqrt{R^2 - \tfrac{1}{4}\overline{AB}^2})}$$

$$= \sqrt{R(2R - \sqrt{4R^2 - \overline{AB}^2})}.$$

Q. E. F.

PROBLEMS OF COMPUTATION. 229

PROPOSITION XVII. PROBLEM.

441. *To compute the ratio of the circumference of a circle to its diameter approximately.*

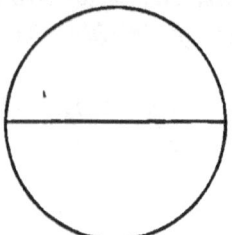

Let C be the circumference, and R the radius. To find the numerical value of π.

$$2\pi R = C. \qquad \S\,419$$

Therefore when $R = 1$, $\pi = \tfrac{1}{2} C$.

We make the following computations by the use of the formula obtained in the last proposition, when $R = 1$, and $AB = 1$ (a side of a regular hexagon).

No. Sides.	Form of Computation.	Length of Side.	Length of Perimeter.
12	$c_1 = \sqrt{2 - \sqrt{4-1^2}}$	0.51763809	6.21165708
24	$c_2 = \sqrt{2 - \sqrt{4-(0.51763809)^2}}$	0.26105238	6.25722
48	$c_3 = \sqrt{2 - \sqrt{4-(0.26105238)^2}}$	0.13080626	041
96	$c_4 = \sqrt{2 - \sqrt{4-(0.13080626)^2}}$	0.06543817	6.28206396
192	$c_5 = \sqrt{2 - \sqrt{4-(0.06543817)^2}}$	0.03272346	6.28290510
384	$c_6 = \sqrt{2 - \sqrt{4-(0.03272346)^2}}$	0.01636228	6.28311544
768	$c_7 = \sqrt{2 - \sqrt{4-(0.01636228)^2}}$	0.00818121	6.28316941

Hence we may consider 6.28317 as approximately the circumference of a ⊙ whose radius is unity.

Therefore $\pi = \tfrac{1}{2}(6.28317) = 3.14159$ nearly. Q.E.F.

442. SCHOLIUM. In practice, we generally take

$$\pi = 3.1416, \quad \frac{1}{\pi} = 0.31831.$$

230 PLANE GEOMETRY. — BOOK V.

MAXIMA AND MINIMA. — SUPPLEMENTARY.

443. Among magnitudes of the same kind, that which is greatest is the *maximum*, and that which is smallest is the *minimum*.

Thus the diameter of a circle is the maximum among all inscribed straight lines; and a perpendicular is the minimum among all straight lines drawn from a point to a given line.

444. *Isoperimetric* figures are figures which have equal perimeters.

PROPOSITION XVIII. THEOREM.

445. *Of all triangles having two given sides, that in which these sides include a right angle is the maximum.*

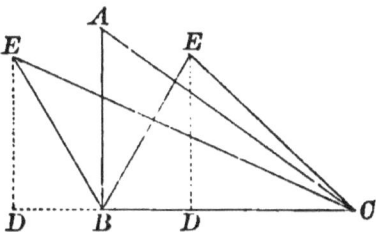

Let the triangles ABC and EBC have the sides AB and BC equal respectively to EB and BC; and let the angle ABC be a right angle.

To prove $\triangle ABC > \triangle EBC$.

Proof. From E let fall the $\perp ED$.

The $\triangle ABC$ and EBC, having the same base BC, are to each other as their altitudes AB and ED. § 370

Now $EB > ED$. § 114

By hypothesis, $EB = AB$.

∴ $AB > ED$.

∴ $\triangle ABC > \triangle EBC$.   Q.E.D.

Proposition XIX. Theorem.

446. *Of all triangles having the same base and equal perimeters, the isosceles triangle is the maximum.*

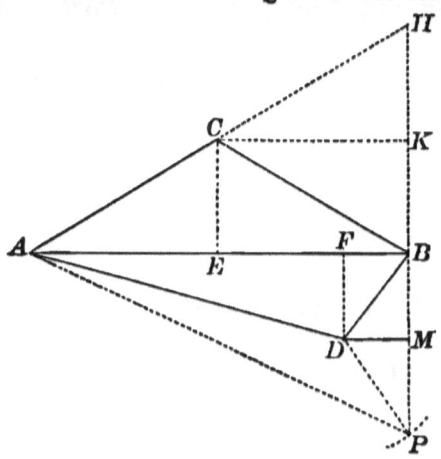

Let the △ ACB and ADB have equal perimeters, and let the △ ACB be isosceles.

To prove △ $ACB >$ △ ADB.

Proof. Produce AC to H, making $CH = AC$, and join HB.

ABH is a right angle, for it will be inscribed in the semi-circle whose centre is C, and radius CA.

Produce HB, and take $DP = DB$.

Draw CK and DM ‖ to AB, and join AP.

Now $AH = AC + CB = AD + DB = AD + DP$.

But $AD + DP > AP$, hence $AH > AP$.

Therefore $HB > BP$. § 120

But $KB = \tfrac{1}{2} HB$ and $MB = \tfrac{1}{2} BP$. § 121

Hence $KB > MB$.

By § 180, $KB = CE$ and $MB = DF$, the altitudes of the △ ACB and ADB.

Therefore △ $ABC >$ △ ADB. § 370

Q. E. D.

PROPOSITION XX. THEOREM.

447. *Of all polygons with sides all given but one, the maximum can be inscribed in a semicircle which has the undetermined side for its diameter.*

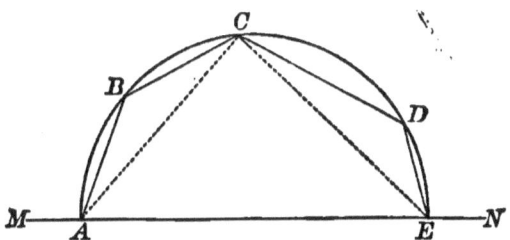

Let *ABCDE* be the maximum of polygons with sides *AB, BC, CD, DE*, and the extremities *A* and *E* on the straight line *MN*.

To prove *ABCDE* can be inscribed in a semicircle.

Proof. From *any* vertex, as *C*, draw *CA* and *CE*.

The △ *ACE* must be the maximum of all △ having the given sides *CA* and *CE*; otherwise, by increasing or diminishing the ∠ *ACE*, keeping the sides *CA* and *CE* unchanged, but sliding the extremities *A* and *E* along the line *MN*, we can increase the △ *ACE*, while the rest of the polygon will remain unchanged, and therefore increase the polygon.

But this is contrary to the hypothesis that the polygon is the maximum polygon.

Hence the △ *ACE* with the given sides *CA* and *CE* is the maximum.

Therefore the ∠ *ACE* is a right angle, § 445

(*the maximum of △ having two given sides is the △ with the two given sides including a rt. ∠*).

Therefore *C* lies on the semi-circumference. § 264

Hence *every* vertex lies on the circumference; that is, the maximum polygon can be inscribed in a semicircle having the undetermined side for a diameter.   Q.E.D.

Proposition XXI. Theorem.

448. *Of all polygons with given sides, that which can be inscribed in a circle is the maximum.*

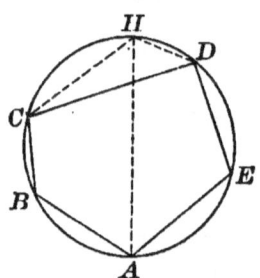
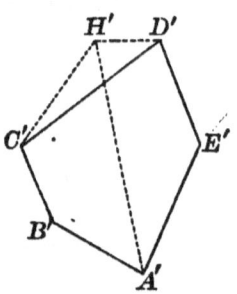

Let $ABCDE$ be a polygon inscribed in a circle, and $A'B'C'D'E'$ be a polygon, equilateral with respect to $ABCDE$, which cannot be inscribed in a circle.

To prove $ABCDE$ greater than $A'B'C'D'E'$.

Proof. Draw the diameter AH.

Join CH and DH.

Upon $C'D'$ $(= CD)$ construct the $\triangle\, C'H'D' = \triangle\, CHD$,

and draw $A'H'$.

Now $ABCH > A'B'C'H'$, § 447

and $AEDH > A'E'D'H'$,

(*of all polygons with sides all given but one, the maximum can be inscribed in a semicircle having the undetermined side for its diameter*).

Add these two inequalities, then

$ABCHDE > A'B'C'H'D'E'$.

Take away from the two figures the equal $\triangle\, CHD$ and $C'H'D'$.

Then $ABCDE > A'B'C'D'E'$.   Q.E.D.

PROPOSITION XXII. THEOREM.

449. *Of isoperimetric polygons of the same number of sides, the maximum is equilateral.*

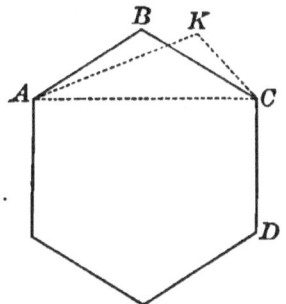

Let *ABCD* etc., be the maximum of isoperimetric polygons of any given number of sides.

To prove *AB, BC, CD*, etc., equal.

Proof. Draw *AC*.

The △ *ABC* must be the maximum of all the △ which are formed upon *AC* with a perimeter equal to that of △ *ABC*.

Otherwise, a greater △ *AKC* could be substituted for △ *ABC*, without changing the perimeter of the polygon.

But this is inconsistent with the hypothesis that the polygon *ABCD* etc., is the maximum polygon.

∴ the △ *ABC* is isosceles, § 446

(*of all △ having the same base and equal perimeters, the isosceles △ is the maximum*).

In like manner it may be proved that *BC = CD*, etc. Q.E.D.

450. Cor. *The maximum of isoperimetric polygons of the same number of sides is a regular polygon.*

For, it is equilateral, § 449

(*the maximum of isoperimetric polygons of the same number of sides is equilateral*).

Also it can be inscribed in a circle, § 448

(*the maximum of all polygons formed of given sides can be inscribed in a ⊙*).

That is, it is equilateral and equiangular,

and therefore regular. . § 395

Q. E. D.

Proposition XXIII. Theorem.

451. *Of isoperimetric regular polygons, that which has the greatest number of sides is the maximum.*

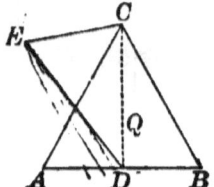

Let Q be a regular polygon of three sides, and Q' a regular polygon of four sides, and let the two polygons have equal perimeters.

To prove Q' greater than Q.

Proof. Draw CD from C to any point in AB.

Invert the $\triangle CDA$ and place it in the position DCE, letting D fall at C, C at D, and A at E.

The polygon $DBCE$ is an irregular polygon of four sides, which by construction has the same perimeter as Q', and the same area as Q.

Then the irregular polygon $DBCE$ of four sides is less than the regular isoperimetric polygon Q' of four sides. § 450

In like manner it may be shown that Q' is less than a regular isoperimetric polygon of five sides, and so on. Q.E.D.

452. Cor. *The area of a circle is greater than the area of any polygon of equal perimeter.*

---

382. Of all equivalent parallelograms having equal bases, the rectangle has the least perimeter.

383. Of all rectangles of a given area, the square has the least perimeter.

384. Of all triangles upon the same base, and having the same altitude, the isosceles has the least perimeter.

385. To divide a straight line into two parts such that their product shall be a maximum.

Proposition XXIV. Theorem.

453. *Of regular polygons having a given area, that which has the greatest number of sides has the least perimeter.*

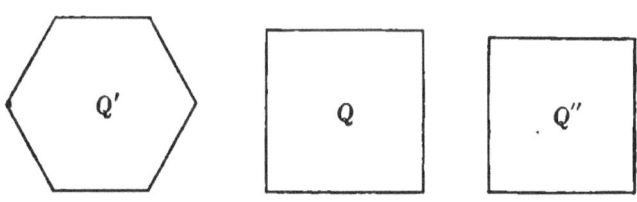

Let Q and Q' be regular polygons having the same area, and let Q' have the greater number of sides.

To prove the perimeter of Q greater than the perimeter of Q'.

Proof. Let Q'' be a regular polygon having the same perimeter as Q', and the same number of sides as Q.

Then $\qquad\qquad Q' > Q''$, $\qquad\qquad$ § 451

(*of isoperimetric regular polygons, that which has the greatest number of sides is the maximum*).

But $\qquad\qquad Q = Q'$.

$\qquad\qquad \therefore Q > Q''$.

$\therefore$ the perimeter of $Q >$ the perimeter of Q''.

But the perimeter of $Q' =$ the perimeter of Q''. $\qquad$ Cons.

$\therefore$ the perimeter of $Q >$ that of Q'.

Q. E. D.

454. Cor. *The circumference of a circle is less than the perimeter of any polygon of equal area.*

---

386. To inscribe in a semicircle a rectangle having a given area; a rectangle having the maximum area.

387. To find a point in a semi-circumference such that the sum of its distances from the extremities of the diameter shall be a maximum.

Theorems.

388. The side of a circumscribed equilateral triangle is equal to twice the side of the similar inscribed triangle. Find the ratio of their areas.

389. The apothem of an inscribed equilateral triangle is equal to half the radius of the circle.

390. The apothem of an inscribed regular hexagon is equal to half the side of the inscribed equilateral triangle.

391. The area of an inscribed regular hexagon is equal to three-fourths that of the circumscribed regular hexagon.

392. The area of an inscribed regular hexagon is a mean proportional between the areas of the inscribed and the circumscribed equilateral triangles.

393. The area of an inscribed regular octagon is equal to that of a rectangle whose sides are equal to the sides of the inscribed and the circumscribed squares.

394. The area of an inscribed regular dodecagon is equal to three times the square of the radius.

395. Every equilateral polygon circumscribed about a circle is regular if it has an *odd* number of sides.

396. Every equiangular polygon inscribed in a circle is regular if it has an *odd* number of sides.

397. Every equiangular polygon circumscribed about a circle is regular.

398. Upon the six sides of a regular hexagon squares are constructed outwardly. Prove that the exterior vertices of these squares are the vertices of a regular dodecagon.

399. The alternate vertices of a regular hexagon are joined by straight lines. Prove that another regular hexagon is thereby formed. Find the ratio of the areas of the two hexagons.

400. The radius of an inscribed regular polygon is the mean proportional between its apothem and the radius of the similar circumscribed regular polygon.

401. The area of a circular ring is equal to that of a circle whose diameter is a chord of the outer circle and a tangent to the inner circle.

402. The square of the side of an inscribed regular pentagon is equal to the sum of the squares of the radius of the circle and the side of the inscribed regular decagon.

If R denotes the radius of a circle, and a one side of a regular inscribed polygon, show that:

403. In a regular pentagon, $a = \dfrac{R}{2}\sqrt{10 - 2\sqrt{5}}$.

404. In a regular octagon, $a = R\sqrt{2 - \sqrt{2}}$.

405. In a regular dodecagon, $a = R\sqrt{2 - \sqrt{3}}$.

406. If on the legs of a right triangle, as diameters, semicircles are described external to the triangle, and from the whole figure a semicircle on the hypotenuse is subtracted, the remainder is equivalent to the given triangle.

Numerical Exercises.

407. The radius of a circle $= r$. Find one side of the circumscribed equilateral triangle.

408. The radius of a circle $= r$. Find one side of the circumscribed regular hexagon.

409. If the radius of a circle is r, and the side of an inscribed regular polygon is a, show that the side of the similar circumscribed regular polygon is equal to $\dfrac{2ar}{\sqrt{4r^2 - a^2}}$

410. The radius of a circle $= r$. Prove that the area of the inscribed regular octagon is equal to $2r^2\sqrt{2}$.

411. The sides of three regular octagons are 3 feet, 4 feet, and 5 feet, respectively. Find the side of a regular octagon equal in area to the sum of the areas of the three given octagons.

412. What is the width of the ring between two concentric circumferences whose lengths are 440 feet and 330 feet?

413. Find the angle subtended at the centre by an arc 6 feet 5 inches long, if the radius of the circle is 8 feet 2 inches.

414. Find the angle subtended at the centre of a circle by an arc whose length is equal to the radius of the circle.

415. What is the length of the arc subtended by one side of a regular dodecagon inscribed in a circle whose radius is 14 feet?

416. Find the side of a square equivalent to a circle whose radius is 56 feet.

EXERCISES.

417. Find the area of a circle inscribed in a square containing 196 square feet.

418. The diameter of a circular grass plot is 28 feet. Find the diameter of a circular plot just twice as large.

419. Find the side of the largest square that can be cut out of a circular piece of wood whose radius is 1 foot 8 inches.

420. The radius of a circle is 3 feet. What is the radius of a circle 25 times as large? $\frac{1}{2}$ as large? $\frac{1}{10}$ as large?

421. The radius of a circle is 9 feet. What are the radii of the concentric circumferences that will divide the circle into three equivalent parts?

422. The chord of half an arc is 12 feet, and the radius of the circle is 15 feet. Find the height of the arc.

423. The chord of an arc is 24 inches, and the height of the arc is 9 inches. Find the diameter of the circle.

424. Find the area of a sector, if the radius of the circle is 28 feet, and the angle at the centre $22\frac{1}{2}°$.

425. The radius of a circle $= r$. Find the area of the segment subtended by one side of the inscribed regular hexagon.

426. Three equal circles are described, each touching the other two. If the common radius is r, find the area contained between the circles.

PROBLEMS.

To circumscribe about a given circle:

427. An equilateral triangle. **429.** A regular hexagon.

428. A square. **430.** A regular octagon.

431. To draw through a given point a line so that it shall divide a given circumference into two parts having the ratio 3 : 7.

432. To construct a circumference equal to the sum of two given circumferences.

433. To construct a circle equivalent to the sum of two given circles.

434. To construct a circle equivalent to three times a given circle.

435. To construct a circle equivalent to three-fourths of a given circle.

To divide a given circle by a concentric circumference:

436. Into two equivalent parts. **437.** Into five equivalent parts.

Miscellaneous Exercises.

Theorems.

438. The line joining the feet of the perpendiculars dropped from the extremities of the base of an isosceles triangle to the opposite sides is parallel to the base.

439. If AD bisect the angle A of a triangle ABC, and BD bisect the exterior angle CBF, then angle ADB equals one-half angle ACB.

440. The sum of the acute angles at the vertices of a pentagram (five-pointed star) is equal to two right angles.

441. The bisectors of the angles of a parallelogram form a rectangle.

442. The altitudes AD, BE, CF of the triangle ABC bisect the angles of the triangle DEF.

Hint. Circles with AB, BC, AC as diameters will pass through E and D, E and F, D and F, respectively.

443. The portions of any straight line intercepted between the circumferences of two concentric circles are equal.

444. Two circles are tangent internally at P, and a chord AB of the larger circle touches the smaller circle at C. Prove that PC bisects the angle APB.

Hint. Draw a common tangent at P, and apply §§ 263, 269, 145.

445. The diagonals of a trapezoid divide each other into segments which are proportional.

446. The perpendiculars from two vertices of a triangle upon the opposite sides divide each other into segments reciprocally proportional.

447. If through a point P in the circumference of a circle two chords are drawn, the chords and the segments between P and a chord parallel to the tangent at P are reciprocally proportional.

448. The perpendicular from any point of a circumference upon a chord is a mean proportional between the perpendiculars from the same point upon the tangents drawn at the extremities of the chord.

449. In an isosceles right triangle either leg is a mean proportional between the hypotenuse and the perpendicular upon it from the vertex of the right angle.

450. The area of a triangle is equal to half the product of its perimeter by the radius of the inscribed circle.

MISCELLANEOUS EXERCISES.

451. The perimeter of a triangle is to one side as the perpendicular from the opposite vertex is to the radius of the inscribed circle.

452. The sum of the perpendiculars from any point within a convex equilateral polygon upon the sides is constant.

453. A diameter of a circle is divided into any two parts, and upon these parts as diameters semi-circumferences are described on opposite sides of the given diameter. Prove that the sum of their lengths is equal to the semi-circumference of the given circle, and that they divide the circle into two parts whose areas have the same ratio as the two parts into which the diameter is divided.

454. Lines drawn from one vertex of a parallelogram to the middle points of the opposite sides trisect one of the diagonals.

455. If two circles intersect in the points A and B, and through A any secant CAD is drawn limited by the circumferences at C and D, the straight lines BC, BD, are to each other as the diameters of the circles.

456. If three straight lines AA', BB', CC', drawn from the vertices of a triangle ABC to the opposite sides, pass through a common point O within the triangle, then

$$\frac{OA'}{AA'} + \frac{OB'}{BB'} + \frac{OC'}{CC'} = 1.$$

457. Two diagonals of a regular pentagon, not drawn from a common vertex, divide each other in extreme and mean ratio.

Loci.

458. Find the locus of a point P whose distances from two given points A and B are in a given ratio $(m:n)$.

459. OP is any straight line drawn from a fixed point O to the circumference of a fixed circle; in OP a point Q is taken such that $OQ:OP$ is constant. Find the locus of Q.

460. From a fixed point A a straight line AB is drawn to any point in a given straight line CD, and then divided at P in a given ratio $(m:n)$. Find the locus of the point P.

461. Find the locus of a point whose distances from two given straight lines are in a given ratio. (The locus consists of two straight lines.)

462. Find the locus of a point the sum of whose distances from two given straight lines is equal to a given length k. (See Ex. 73.)

Problems.

463. Given the perimeters of a regular inscribed and a similar circumscribed polygon, to compute the perimeters of the regular inscribed and circumscribed polygons of double the number of sides.

464. To draw a tangent to a given circle such that the segment intercepted between the point of contact and a given straight line shall have a given length.

465. To draw a straight line equidistant from three given points.

466. To inscribe a straight line of given length between two given circumferences and parallel to a given straight line. (See Ex. 137.)

467. To draw through a given point a straight line so that its distances from two other given points shall be in a given ratio ($m:n$).

HINT. Divide the line joining the two other points in the given ratio.

468. Construct a square equivalent to the sum of a given triangle and a given parallelogram.

469. Construct a rectangle having the difference of its base and altitude equal to a given line, and its area equivalent to the sum of a given triangle and a given pentagon.

470. Construct a pentagon similar to a given pentagon and equivalent to a given trapezoid.

471. To find a point whose distances from three given straight lines shall be as the numbers m, n, and p. (See Ex. 461.)

472. Given two circles intersecting at the point A. To draw through A a secant BAC such that AB shall be to AC in a given ratio ($m:n$).

HINT. Divide the line of centres in the given ratio.

473. To construct a triangle, given its angles and its area.

474. To construct an equilateral triangle having a given area.

475. To divide a given triangle into two equal parts by a line drawn parallel to one of the sides.

476. Given three points A, B, C. To find a fourth point P such that the areas of the triangles APB, APC, BPC, shall be equal.

477. To construct a triangle, given its base, the ratio of the other sides, and the angle included by them.

478. To divide a given circle into any number of equivalent parts by concentric circumferences.

479. In a given equilateral triangle, to inscribe three equal circles tangent to each other and to the sides of the triangle.

www.ingramcontent.com/pod-product-compliance
Lightning Source LLC
Chambersburg PA
CBHW020756230426
43666CB00007B/721